ROAD BIKING™

New Mexico

Help Us Keep This Guide Up to Date

Every effort has been made by the author and editors to make this guide as accurate and useful as possible. However, many things can change after a guide is published—roads are rerouted, regulations change, techniques evolve, facilities come under new management, etc.

We would love to hear from you concerning your experiences with this guide and how you feel it could be improved and kept up to date. While we may not be able to respond to all comments and suggestions, we'll take them to heart and we'll also make certain to share them with the author. Please send your comments and suggestions to the following address:

The Globe Pequot Press
Reader Response/Editorial Department
P.O. Box 480
Guilford, CT 06437

Or you may e-mail us at:

editorial@GlobePequot.com

Thanks for your input, and happy travels!

A **FALCON** GUIDE®

Road Biking™ Series

ROAD BIKING™
New Mexico

Nicole Blouin

FALCON GUIDES®

GUILFORD, CONNECTICUT
HELENA, MONTANA

AN IMPRINT OF THE GLOBE PEQUOT PRESS

A FALCON GUIDE ®

Copyright © 2002 Morris Book Publishing, LLC

Road Biking is a trademark and Falcon and FalconGuides are registered trademarks of Morris Book Publishing, LLC.

All photos by Nicole Blouin unless otherwise noted.
Text design by Lesley Weissman-Cook
Maps by Trailhead Graphics © Morris Book Publishing, LLC

Library of Congress Cataloging-in-Publication Data
Blouin, Nicole, 1966–
    Road biking New Mexico / Nicole Blouin.—1st ed.
        p. cm. — (A FalconGuide)
    ISBN 978-0-7627-1190-1
        1. Bicycle touring—New Mexico—Guidebooks. 2. New Mexico—Guidebooks. I. Title. II. Falcon guide.

GV1045.5.N6 B56 2002
796.6'3'09789—dc21

                                                        2002069348

Manufactured in the United States of America
First Edition/Second Printing

Contents

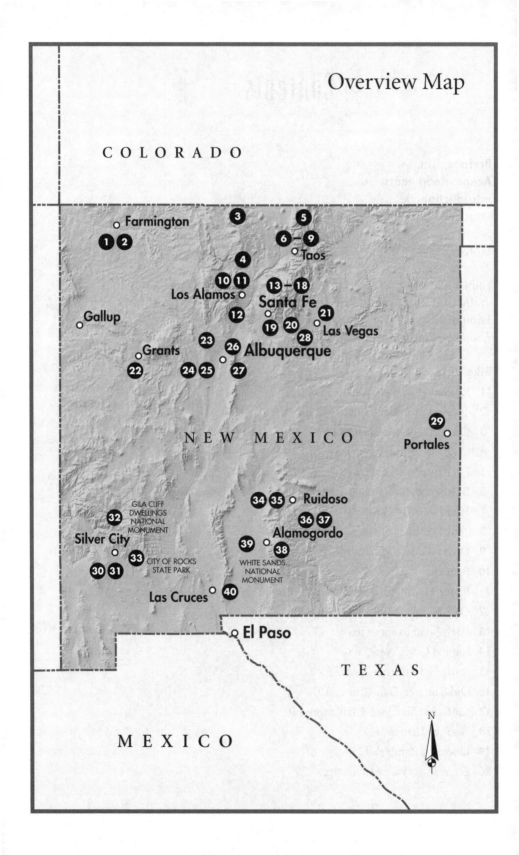

Overview Map

Preface

I spent a year researching and writing this book about road bicycling in New Mexico—the Land of Enchantment. Not only did it give me the opportunity to cycle a lot, it was a wonderful excuse to experience more of this great state. I've lived here for several years, and before the project, I had primarily cycled in and around Santa Fe. I had never seen the dunes at White Sands National Monument, the lava flow near Grants, the Gila (our country's first designated wilderness area), or the mountain ranges to the south. I loved being on the bike, traveling around New Mexico, and enjoying the state's plentiful sunshine and great weather. I hope you do too!

Selecting the rides was easy. Bike shops, cycling clubs, and racing groups around the state pointed me in the right direction and shared their local rides. I made sure to check out many of New Mexico's state and national scenic byways, and occasionally I discovered a ride after looking at maps and driving some back roads. I've included as many scenic, historic, and cultural areas as possible. Three rides were sent in at crunch time by cyclists in Farmington and Portales-Clovis (thanks, David and Ted!).

In this guidebook, you will find rides from easy to challenging with lengths ranging from 15 miles to more than 100 miles. The end result—40 rides—turned out to be a good mix, which happened, for the most part, by accident (or with some luck). New Mexico doesn't have an extensive road network, so the rides represent a good sampling of what the state has to offer. I did try to find as many weekend warrior rides as possible—moderate loops around 50 miles—what many cyclists are looking for on their longer Saturday and Sunday rides. Don't miss the loops out of Abiquiu, Las Vegas, and Ruidoso.

Acknowledgments

I have written several guidebooks, and I am always amazed at the amount of help it takes to make it happen and the willingness of people to lend a hand. I had cyclists across the state sharing their favorite rides, answering questions, reading rough drafts, and even acting as a tour guide (thanks, Chisom!).

First, I'd like to thank everyone at the New Mexico Touring Society (NMTS). They helped me get rolling. Their Web site provided a wealth of information, including cue sheets on rides around the state; and their members assisted on the project in a variety of ways. We are lucky here in New Mexico to have an organization like this. Special thanks to the president in 2001, Tom Sullivan, especially for the help with the Albuquerque Perimeter Loop.

A lot of critical information about riding in New Mexico came from local bike shops. Many are listed under the specific rides near their shops. Please give them your support. They are a great place to find out about more rides in a particular area. Also, state and national agencies, as well as local chambers of commerce, were there to help me as I traveled. They are too numerous to list, but I continually came in contact with people who were psyched about promoting the state.

Three of the rides in the book came from cyclists other than myself. This help came at a time when I needed it most. Thanks to David Ortiz in Farmington for La Plata–Animas Cruise and Tour de San Juan Cruise and to Ted Glasscock in Clovis for the Portales–Clovis Cruise. I also had some help with getting photos together. Thanks to Enchanted Lands Enterprise, Inc. for letting me use some of their material; and thanks to Peter Stirbis, who leads the NMTS event on the Gila Inner Loop, for slides of that area.

My cycling buddy and best friend, Rob Edwards, was beside me (usually in front of me) as we explored many of the rides in this book. We had some great times on the road, especially the car camping trip down south—memories I'll cherish for a lifetime. Thanks for everything!

And finally, thanks to the folks at The Globe Pequot Press. I appreciate your taking me along when you purchased Falcon Publishing. Best of everything to you. Happy cycling!

Introduction

Where do I begin describing to you what I discovered when I moved to New Mexico, the Land of Enchantment? In addition to the blue sky, sunshine, and solitude, one thing that I repeat often is the fact that living (or traveling) here is as close as you can get to a foreign country without leaving the United States. And what I mean by that is a flavor, a culture, a feeling of enchantment—whatever you want to call it—that you don't often find in other places. You see it in the architecture, the food, the language, the people, and the festivals.

I don't think I'll ever consider myself a local. I still feel as if I'm on an extended vacation visiting an exciting, foreign land. Everything is colorful and different, and you can experience it all from your bicycle. The highways and back roads of the Land of Enchantment offer some of the best cycling in the Southwest.

With the help of this book, you can choose from some of the well-known favorites—popular scenic drives like the High Road to Taos, the Enchanted Circle, and the Gila Inner Loop—or the undiscovered gems that will take you through rural countryside, along river valleys, and to little-visited state parks. Some of the routes follow historic paths like the Santa Fe Trail. And there is no shortage of Indian ruins in New Mexico. Rides incorporate these well-preserved sites at several national monuments—Bandelier, Aztec, El Morro, and Gila Cliff Dwellings.

If you are ready for a challenge, you can climb up the roads that lead to the ski areas in Taos, Santa Fe, Albuquerque, and Ruidoso. You'll cycle to altitudes between 9,000 and 10,600 feet. Some of the best views from the bike are on these hill climbs. If you'd rather go around, there are several perimeter loops in the book—one accepted by the Perimeter Bicycle Association of America. You can do loops around Taos, Santa Fe, Albuquerque, Alamogordo, and Las Cruces.

As for century (100-mile) events, the state has two every year—the Santa Fe Century in May and the Enchanted Circle Century (near Taos) in September. Races are held throughout the state; one in particular is described under the Bandelier Cruise. And there's also the Tour of the Gila, New Mexico's premier road race and one of the toughest in the country. The rides around Silver City use several stretches of this five-day stage race. New Mexico Cycling has a Web site that caters to racers and includes a list of cycling clubs, a calendar of events, and race results. Check it out at www.swcp.com/nmcycling.

The book offers some unusual cycling ideas as well. A beautiful forested ride takes you from Chama, New Mexico, to Antonito, Colorado, where you can return on a scenic narrow-gauge train. In the Sacramento Mountains you can ride from bike shop to bike shop (Cloudcroft to Ruidoso), arranging a shuttle with High Altitude, or climb to the National Solar Observatory along the Sunspot Scenic Byway. And several times a year you can cycle under a full moon in the largest gypsum dune field in the world—white sand dunes as far as you can see.

You could write volumes about what to do and where to eat along your rides in this part of the Southwest. For information about a specific area, contact the bike shops or chamber of commerce listed under the ride description. For general information contact the New Mexico Department of Tourism (www.newmexico.org), 491 Old Santa Fe Trail, Santa Fe, NM 87501; (800) 733–6396. You can get the free publication, *New Mexico Vacation Guide,* sent to you in the mail.

SCENERY

New Mexico's 121,600 square miles include a landscape from high desert grasslands, mesas, and canyons to dramatic mountain ranges. There are red sandstone cliffs and deep canyons, juniper-pinon woodlands, hillsides covered with ponderosa pine, and stands of aspen, spruce, and fir. You won't be bored by the views you'll have from the bike. Rarely will you cycle a forested road for long before coming to a beautiful overlook, and most of the routes provide continuous wide open views.

The state's scenery is enchanting, and it has been inspiring artists and writers for centuries. Thanks to Georgia O'Keeffe, much of that magic comes to life in her images. She loved the Southwest, and you can cycle through some of the landscape that fascinated this world-famous artist—colorful mesas, towering cliffs, quiet river valleys, and unusual rock formations.

New Mexico boasts twenty-four scenic byways, six with national designations. Half of these routes are incorporated into rides in this book, which take you through some of the state's most beautiful landscapes. If you can only pick one ride, choose one of the state's scenic byways. They are given the designation for their history, culture, recreation, and outstanding scenery.

You can't talk about New Mexico without commenting on the quality of the light—clear and radiant, untouched by major industry and pollution. Watching the sky illuminate the horizon or come alive on the earth-toned adobe walls is almost a pastime in itself. I have never seen sunsets like I have seen here in New Mexico. Some of my favorite New Mexico scenes from the bike include herds of antelope, hillsides covered with golden patches of aspen in the fall, centuries-old adobe buildings, colorful hot air balloons against a blue sky, snowcapped peaks in the summertime, the cholla and yucca in bloom, and bright red strings of chiles hanging out to dry.

You can't help but be touched by the fascinating history of New Mexico, from the relics of Clovis man and Sandia man—evidence of human habitation more than 11,000 years ago—to the development of the first atomic bomb in the 1940s in the Secret City of Los Alamos. Even if you never get off the bike, you can get a taste of the state's unique and diverse history as you ride through Indian reservations, cycle past seventeenth-century Spanish mission churches, negotiate the narrow roads around historic plazas, and travel down the main streets of old mining towns. Many rides follow the legendary roads of the past—the ancient trade routes of the Anasazi, the paths taken by the Spanish conquistadors, and the Western trails established by the American pioneers.

The state's cultural heritage is among the oldest in the United States (Santa Fe is the oldest state capital). It is really three stories—that of the Native Americans, the Hispanics, and the Anglos—that blend together to create a unique and festive charm influencing all corners of the state. Traditions live on in the religions, languages, legends, food, dress, art, and architecture of New Mexico. You'll find numerous opportunities to experience history—watch practicing artisans, tour ancient cliff dwellings, and visit museums and monuments. A history buff may never want to leave the state.

The way of life of the Native Americans is deeply rooted in the state. New Mexico comprises nineteen pueblos, two Apache reservations, and a portion of the Navajo Nation. Particularly interesting are the Indian ruins and artifacts of the Pueblos' ancestors—the Mogollon in the south and the Anasazi in the north. Visiting a reservation and seeing one of the largest multistoried pueblos in the country or climbing down into a ceremonial *kiva* are experiences not to miss, especially during dances and feast days. Please respect their traditions and obey their regulations. And try the Indian fry bread, a cyclist's dream and local favorite, which can be found at roadside stands in reservations throughout the state.

Participating in the Trek for Trash, a state program to keep New Mexico's roads litter free.

You can experience some of the Spanish-colonial atmosphere of Old Mexico in many of the state's rural villages. Beautiful mission churches stand much as they did hundreds of years ago. The Spanish exploration and colonization of the area provides a colorful history, and it all began in the early 1500s with the search for the reported "seven cities of gold." The first official European colony was established north of Espanola in 1598, and the Palace of the Governors on Santa Fe's Plaza was built in 1610 and remained the seat of government for almost three centuries.

The new frontier developed out of a rush for land, gold, timber, and goods. In 1821 when Mexico won its independence from Spain and New Mexico became part of Mexico, a trader from Missouri, William Becknell, "opened" the Santa Fe Trail. For the next sixty years, the trail was an important trade route, and merchants, pioneers, and adventurers flocked to the area, which became a U.S. territory in 1848. In 1880 the railroad gradually replaced the trail. Rides in this book will take you through old mining towns and historic districts where you can relive some of that spirit of the Old West.

TERRAIN

The state's terrain is as diverse as its culture. New Mexico encompasses six of the planet's seven life zones—from Lower Sonoran (elevations below 4,500 feet) to Alpine (elevations above 12,000 feet). Most of the rides in the book are between 5,000 and 7,000 feet, and there are seven rides that climb above 9,000 feet. You'll reach 10,678 feet if you climb up to the Sandia Crest outside of Albuquerque, and you can cycle miles of flat at about 3,800 feet when you ride around Las Cruces, just north of El Paso.

Most of the rides are easy to moderate with mixed terrain—stretches of flat, rolling foothills, and gentle climbs and descents. You'll also find easy spins where any elevation gain is barely noticeable, a few areas with awesome rollers, and ski hills that provide a continuous workout followed by a screaming descent. There are several rides through mountainous terrain that include steep grades, mountain passes, and more than 5,000 feet of climbing in 80 miles. There are major mountain ranges throughout the state, including the southern end of the Rockies. This is the highest range, the Sangre de Cristo Mountains, which run between Taos and Santa Fe. The state's highest mountain is near Taos—Wheeler Peak (elevation 13,161 feet), and Sierra Blanco, outside Ruidoso in the southern part of the state, reaches 12,003 feet. Almost every ride in the book includes views of rugged mountains.

The Rio Grande, the state's agricultural lifeline, flows north-south creating a large ribbon of green on the desert landscape. It has been important to the people of the Southwest since prehistoric days. The river is wild near the state's northern border, and the Taos Box, a steep-walled canyon, is enjoyed by whitewater enthusiasts. The Rio Grande Gorge Bridge, the second highest suspension bridge in the country, provides views 650 feet down to the mighty river. As the river mellows, it travels through the largest continuous cottonwood forest in the country, called a *bosque,* Spanish for "woods." This beautiful floodplain is dominated by cottonwood trees but also includes coyote willow, Russian olive, salt cedar, and tamarisk.

New Mexico's terrain is full of other interesting features. Volcanic activity created the Jemez Mountains millions of years ago, and there you'll find the Valle Grande, one of the largest calderas in the world. South of Grants you'll travel through a badlands of sorts—a massive lava flow now protected as El Malpais National Monument. Outside of Silver City there are millions of acres of wild lands, the Gila Wilderness Area, our country's first designated wilderness; and there are 230 square miles of white sand dunes in the Tularosa Basin, the northern end of the Chihuahuan Desert. The eastern part of the state includes the Llano Estacado or "staked plains," which the Spanish named because of the numerous yuccas that looked like stakes on a prairie. This large expanse of land is an extension of the Great Plains.

And while the terrain isn't as rugged and steep as that of the Rocky Mountain states, New Mexico's lowest elevation is higher than any other state's low point and the average elevation is 5,700 feet. The magic line for noticing the effects of altitude seems to be at about a mile above sea level (5,000 feet), and all but three rides in the book are above that elevation. The altitude will sap your energy at a minimum, and you may feel dizzy and nauseous or get a headache, but more serious problems can develop. Before taking on any major rides, limit your activity for a day or two. Hydrate, pace yourself, and keep alcohol consumption to a minimum.

CLIMATE/SEASONS

The state's mild climate and four distinct seasons make the road cycling routes in New Mexico some of the best in the Southwest. The sun shines almost every day of the year. Cities throughout the state boast an average number of sunny days per year at around 300. The summers are relatively dry, the winters are mild, and you can cycle just about anywhere in the state year-round. This book covers a range of elevations, which is good news because there are rides for every season—get farther into the mountains or head for the high desert.

While the climate varies from region to region, characteristically you'll find warm days and cool nights. Don't equate New Mexico with unbearable heat. Maximum highs are usually in the 70s and 80s in most areas, not 100 degrees! The overall elevation keeps it from being as extreme as other states in the Southwest. And because this is high desert, you get a large fluctuation in highs and lows, sometimes as much as 35 degrees, which means cool summer mornings.

For the most part New Mexico is a dry state with enough precipitation to keep summer temperatures moderate. Surprisingly, the state has a rainy period, even called the "monsoon season" in some areas, which can produce intense lightning and flash floods. In July and August you have to deal with thunderstorms. A little more than 2 inches of rain falls during each of these months in wetter areas like Santa Fe, and the drier areas like Albuquerque average a little more than an inch in July and August. The rain is amazingly predictable though. Clear mornings give way to clouds and thunder in the afternoon. If you take off in the afternoon in northern New Mexico during July and August, it's very likely that you'll get wet. Watch for thunderheads and ride early.

The farther south you go, the warmer and drier it gets, and you can count on summer temperatures in the nineties. Many people perceive the southern half of the state as hot and barren, but there are many mountain ranges, and you can find rides over 7,000 feet. It is rare to find a day too hot to ride, but I wouldn't want to be in the Tularosa Basin or at the City of Rocks during the dog days of summer. On the other hand, southern New Mexico has several ideal winter cycling destinations to choose from.

The temperature chart gives you an idea of the average highs and lows of the cities throughout the state. With the information provided for each ride, it's easy to match a ride with a city. The exceptions may be the O'Keeffe Country Tour (Espanola) and the City of Rocks Cruise (Deming).

AVERAGE TEMPERATURES

	January	April	July	October
Alamogordo	57/28	78/44	95/65	78/46
Albuquerque	46/28	69/42	91/66	71/45
Chama	33/3	51/20	73/37	57/23
Cloudcroft	41/19	57/31	73/48	60/35
Deming	55/26	77/42	95/66	78/46
Espanola	45/13	68/43	90/55	72/33
Farmington	43/17	69/34	92/57	71/36
Grants	45/11	67/27	87/52	69/29
Las Cruces	56/25	77/41	94/65	78/44
Las Vegas	46/18	62/31	83/54	66/36
Los Alamos	40/19	58/34	80/56	62/39
Portales	53/21	75/40	93/63	75/43
Red River	36/3	53/22	76/40	59/25
Ruidoso	50/17	65/28	82/48	68/31
Santa Fe	42/18	62/33	85/56	65/38
Silver City	49/24	67/37	87/59	70/41
Taos	40/10	64/29	87/50	67/32

September and October are my favorite months to cycle here in New Mexico. The fall starts with warm, sunny days and little wind or rain. Crisp, cool temperatures bring a dramatic change in the scenery—brilliant colors on the hillsides. Crowds thin out in the tourist areas, the spicy smell of pinon smoke fills the air, and green chiles are roasting at roadside stands.

Between November and March, snow covers the higher elevations and climbing the roads to ski areas is out, but the rideable winter days far outnumber the snowy ones, especially below 5,000 feet. Because of the high elevation and low humidity, a sunny New Mexico day with no wind feels warmer than what the weatherman forecasts. You can get out on a sunny, windless winter day when it's about forty-five degrees and enjoy a fairly pleasant ride. The southern half of the state has days with temperatures in the sixties throughout the winter.

Spring tends to be unpredictable. Days of beautiful cycling weather will be interrupted by storm fronts moving across the state. This is the windiest season, and usually it's mild, dry, and gusty.

Summer brings warm temperatures, but the humidity is low. On the hottest days you can climb into the mountains or find a riverside ride, and a couple of the routes start near recreational lakes. Cycle in the morning and enjoy cool temperatures and no worry of thunderstorms. The tourist areas see more visitors in July and August. Many Native American and Spanish ceremonies, festivals, and events attract crowds during the summer. Be sure to make lodging reservations ahead of time.

TRAFFIC AND ROAD SAFETY

New Mexico is sparsely populated (a million and a half people), and it's the fifth biggest state (in size) in the country. The largest city, and the only real metro area, is Albuquerque, and a third of the population lives there. That leaves a lot of open space and rural areas. You'll encounter busy sections on some of the rides, but in general, traffic is light. You won't find yourself pedaling alongside lines of cars and trucks. And while there are few official bike paths in the state, in Albuquerque you can ride traffic-free for miles on one of the city's urban trails.

The streets are narrow and winding around the historic plazas. You'll find short, one-way sections and confusing intersections. Be aware of pedestrians, parked cars, and general chaos around the plazas, especially in July and August. Gawking tourists are a problem in some areas, and a few of the rides follow routes that are considered scenic drives or lead to popular recreation areas. You'll have to share these roads with other outdoor enthusiasts. Watch for pickups, RVs, horse trailers, and leaf-lookers. The heaviest use is on summer weekends and holidays.

Pavement quality varies from region to region, as does the width of the shoulders. Many rides have sections without shoulders, but this is usually in quiet, rural areas. On a few rides, you'll encounter some sections of "chip and seal" pavement, which is a bit rougher. And we have our fair share of bumps, humps, rumble strips, patched pavement, and open potholes, but in general, the roads in New Mexico are in good condition. Particularly bad or dangerous stretches of road are mentioned under the ride's description. (Note: New Mexico is usually one of the top five states for alcohol-related crashes and fatalities. This results in glass on some shoulders and makes you wonder about the potential danger of some drivers.)

Interstate riding always comes with some risks because of the high-speed traffic. Few rides in the book use any stretches of interstate. "Where not otherwise prohibited, bicyclists are permitted to use the interstate highways in New Mexico provided that they ride on the shoulder." This pertains to most of the state. The only exceptions are interstates within the boundaries of a city with a population of 50,000 or more. For example, you can't ride on Interstate 25 through Albuquerque.

Like any sport, cycling comes with its own inherent risks. Vehicles are our most serious threat—riding when and where there is little traffic is always the

challenge, and it differs from ride to ride and from season to season. But most accidents happen because we take curves too fast, slip on gravel, drift off the road, or run into each other. Be particularly cautious on the fast descents on the ski area roads. Other people—walkers and runners—and dogs should always make you alert.

The latest story I heard was about a group of cyclists out doing time trials on a stretch of the Capital City Cruise. A man with his dog on one of those retractable leashes was walking on the wrong side of the road. It was ugly and involved several bikers hitting the pavement. They were lucky—another bike crash with an "always wear your helmet" conclusion.

The Greater Albuquerque Spokes Persons (GASP) has the best Web site for advocacy issues in New Mexico. Log on to www.abq.spokes.org. You can get information on their statewide organization, Bicycle

Car camping with bicycles in southern New Mexico.

Advocacy Coalition of New Mexico, which now has members in Santa Fe, Los Alamos, Albuquerque, Corrales, Las Cruces, and Silver City. Another source of information about cycling issues in New Mexico is Ronald Montoya, Bicycle/Pedestrian/Equestrian Coordinator, New Mexico State Highway Department, P.O. Box 1149, Santa Fe, NM 87504; (505) 827–5248. Also, you can see a copy of the state's bicycle codes on the NMTS Web site at www.swcp.com/~russells/nmts. Click on "Advocacy."

EQUIPMENT

"Where-to" is one thing, but "how-to," that's another book. It takes most cyclists a season or two to figure out what equipment is necessary to enjoy being in the saddle mile after mile. You'll need your cycling shorts, gloves, and a helmet—often a windproof or waterproof jacket—and the rest is about comfort and safety.

Consider a couple of things that are relevant to cycling in New Mexico. The low humidity and high desert sun make sunburn and dehydration a problem, which in turn can lead to more serious conditions. Many cyclists don't use sunscreen or take enough water. I put on sunscreen year-round, on just about every ride. You need to apply it frequently; every hour or so is best. Sunglasses are also a must, and a wet bandana can do wonders in the heat.

Services can be few and far between on some rides, so you need to bring a lot of water. Large gaps between rest stops are noted under the ride's description. Take as much as you can carry to start with—a minimum of two water bottles for most rides and a hydration system is ideal for many others. I drink about a quart per hour, taking in some about every 5 miles. In addition, use sports drinks to replenish electrolytes, and refuel often with energy bars, fruit, and snacks. Douse yourself with water when you can, take advantage of the shade when you find it, and consider trying one of those lightweight, long-sleeve shirts made for sun protection.

Here in New Mexico we have goatheads, tiny thorns the size of your pinky nail that have stickers that look like horns. These things will attack your tubes, more likely below 7,000 feet and near urban areas. Many road cyclists never go without some sort of flat protection—slime, tire liners, etc. I only use slime for my mountain bike, but locals in Albuquerque told me I was taking a big risk when I cycled in and around the city. Knock on wood, and of course, always carry what you need to repair several tubes.

ABOUT THE ROUTES

The routes are divided into four categories according to their degree of difficulty. These classifications are subjective, taking into account the combination of distance, road grade, and bike-handling skills necessary to negotiate the full tour. Each route's name indicates its relative degree of difficulty.

♦ *Rambles* are the easiest and shortest rides in the book, accessible to almost all riders, and should be easily completed in one day. They are less than 35 miles long and are generally on flat to slightly rolling terrain.

♦ *Cruises* are intermediate in difficulty and distance. They are generally 25 to 50 miles long and may include some moderate climbs. Cruises will generally be completed easily by an experienced rider in one day, but inexperienced or out-of-shape riders may want to take two days with an overnight stop.

♦ *Challenges* are difficult, designed especially for experienced riders in good condition. They are usually 40 to 60 miles long and may include some steep climbs. They should be a challenge even for fairly fit riders attempting to complete them in one day. Less experienced or less fit riders should expect to take two days.

♦ *Classics* are long and hard. They are more than 60 miles and may be more than 100. They can include steep climbs and high-speed downhills. Even fit and experienced riders will want to take two days. These rides are not recommended for less fit and experienced riders unless they are done in shorter stages.

Don't let the distance of a longer tour dissuade you from trying a ride in an attractive area. Out-and-back rides along portions of a route provide options that may be well suited to your schedule and other commitments. Likewise, don't automatically dismiss a shorter ride in an interesting area.

Directions in the route narrative for each ride include the cumulative mileage to each turn and to significant landmarks along the way. It's possible that your mileage may differ slightly. Over enough miles, differences in odometer calibration, tire pressure, and the line you follow can have a significant effect on the measurement of distance. Use the cumulative mileage in connection with your route descriptions and maps.

Each route has been designed with specific criteria in mind, although not all of them could be addressed in every instance. Starting points are normally easy to find, with convenient parking and reasonable access to provisions. Roads should be moderately traveled, be in good repair, and have adequate shoulders where traffic volume requires. I've also made an effort to guide the reader to interesting places along the way.

To fashion the most useful routes, some worthwhile features were bypassed for practical considerations. As a result you might find it appropriate to use these routes as starting points or suggestions in designing your own routes. Rides can begin at any point along the course described in the route directions. You can always leave the route to explore interesting side roads and create your own routes.

Construction, development, improvements, and other changes are commonplace on New Mexico roadways. As a result the route descriptions and maps in this book can only be records of conditions as they once were; they may not always describe conditions as you find them. Comments, updates, and corrections from interested and critical readers are always appreciated and can be sent to the author in care of the publisher.

La Plata–Animas Cruise

Credit for the contribution of this loop in New Mexico's Four Corners Region goes to David Ortiz, a local cyclist and outdoor enthusiast. This loop travels through the La Plata and Animas river valleys, which were occupied by the Anasazi, or Ancient Ones, until around 1300. Remnants of their culture are left in this corner of the state in the form of ruins—some buried underneath New Mexico Route 170, the first leg of the ride, and others visible at the Aztec Ruins National Monument, a side trip of about a mile. You'll enjoy rolling through high-desert mesas and green farmland with distant views of Colorado's rugged San Juan Mountains along the route. The terrain includes flat straightaways and short inclines, and you'll encounter moderate uphill pulls as you approach Aztec.

This ride is located in the desert highlands of the Four Corners and begins at San Juan College. You'll head west through the Glade Canyon before reaching New Mexico Route 170, locally known as La Plata Highway. The highway meanders through La Plata River valley with good views north of La Plata Mountains, the southwestern end of the San Juans. This range is the source of the creek in the valley bottom. La Plata River has good brown trout fishing in the spring.

After cycling a few miles north, you'll pass Jackson Lake on the left and a wildlife refuge on the right. There is absolutely no access to the wildlife refuge, but you can walk up over the dam to view the lake. This 840-acre area is managed by New Mexico Game and Fish, and there is a large gravel parking lot at the north end of the lake—no facilities, only a trash can.

Turning east from the community of La Plata, New Mexico Route 574 climbs

Start: San Juan College in Farmington.

Length: 43.1-mile loop.

Terrain: Flat to rolling with two hill climbs around Farmington Glade.

Traffic and hazards: Most of the ride is rural, and traffic is generally light, especially between La Plata and Aztec. Some shoulders exist but are narrow in places.

Getting there: From U.S. Highway 64, which travels through Farmington, get onto East Main Street. Drive about 6 miles, passing the Animas Valley Mall on the right, and turn left on Pinon Hills Boulevard. (Pinon Hills Boulevard is 0.6 mile past the mall.) Travel 1.8 miles to College Boulevard, where you have two parking options. Turn left to reach San Juan College. After 0.3 mile turn right on Sunrise Parkway. There is a large parking lot on the left at the first four-way stop. For the second option turn right on College Boulevard to reach Lions Wilderness Park. After about a mile park in the large lot at the amphitheater, where the gate is locked at sunset. This area also provides access to the Road Apple Trail (great mountain biking). There are rest rooms available to the public at both locations. (*Note:* Lions Wilderness Park is a natural sandstone amphitheater that hosts outdoor drama productions throughout the summer. The rest rooms are locked in the winter.)

a gentle grade into the clay and sandstone hills of the Farmington Glade, a drainage from Colorado with an extensive mountain bike trail system on both sides of the valley. The Road Apple Rally, in existence for more than twenty years, is held here every year in early October.

Your route drops into Aztec, the county seat and location of the Aztec Ruins National Monument, where you can tour the excavated ruins of the Anasazi. The UFO Information Center contains information relating to the alleged crash of an unidentified flying object (UFO) in 1948 that supposedly occurred several miles northeast of town. The UFO Information Center is on Main Avenue.

The Aztec Ruins, a side trip of about a mile, preserves a 450-room pueblo, one of the best restored ruins of the Anasazi. The Great Kiva, a ceremonial structure 48 feet in diameter, is one of the largest reconstructed kivas in the country. The mystery behind the disappearance of the Anasazi around 1300 is often explained by the fact that they might be the ancestors to the Pueblo Indians. To visit the monument, turn left (instead of right) at mile 32.2 onto New Mexico Route 516. At the next light, turn left again on Ruins Road (County Road 2900) and reach the monument in about a half mile. There is a bike rack to the left along the wall.

A mile south of Aztec on New Mexico Route 516, you'll follow several county roads through the Animas River valley. The Durango Narrow Gauge Railroad passed through this valley until the late 1960s, when modern freight hauling made the railroad unprofitable. A few relics can still be found scattered along the old railroad bed. Enjoy a mellow farmland greenbelt for several miles before rejoining New Mexico Route 516 and arriving back at the parking lot of your choice.

LOCAL INFORMATION

♦ Farmington Convention and Visitors Bureau (www.farmingtonnm.org), 3041 East Main Street, Farmington, NM 87402; (800) 448–1240.
♦ Aztec Welcome Center (www.aztecnm.com), 110 North Ash, Aztec, NM 87410; (888) 838–9551.

EVENTS/ATTRACTIONS

♦ Aztec Ruins National Monument, 84 County Road 2900, Aztec, NM 87410; (505) 334–6174 (open daily 8:00 A.M. to 6:00 P.M. in the summer; cost $4.00).

RESTAURANTS

Here are some suggested Farmington restaurants in or near the Animas Mall:
♦ Applebee's Neighborhood Grill, 4601 East Main Street, Farmington, NM 87402; (505) 599–0998 (in the mall; visible from street).
♦ Chelsea's London Pub, 4601 East Main Street, Farmington, NM 87402; (505) 327–9644 (backside of the mall).
♦ Dad's Diner, 4395 Largo Street, Farmington, NM 87402; (505) 564–2516 (south and across the street from the mall).

ACCOMMODATIONS

♦ The Web site for the Road Apple Rally has an extensive list of accommodation choices. Go to www.roadapplerally.com and click on "Lodging."

BIKE SHOPS

♦ Cottonwood Cycles, 4370 East Main Street, Farmington, NM 87401; (505) 326–0429.
♦ Havens Bikes & Boards Inc., 500 East Main Street, Farmington, NM 87401; (505) 327–1727.

REST ROOMS

♦ Mile 0.0: San Juan College or Lions Wilderness Park.
♦ Mile 5.2: Circle S convenience store.
♦ Mile 16.0: Sundial Conoco.
♦ Mile 32.2: Another Sundial Conoco.
♦ Mile 40.8: 7-Eleven (stop in and say "hi" to the manager, Tim).

MAPS

♦ USGS 7.5-minute quads Farmington North, La Plata, Adobe Downs Ranch, Flora Vista, and Aztec.
♦ Delorme *New Mexico Atlas & Gazetteer,* map 13.

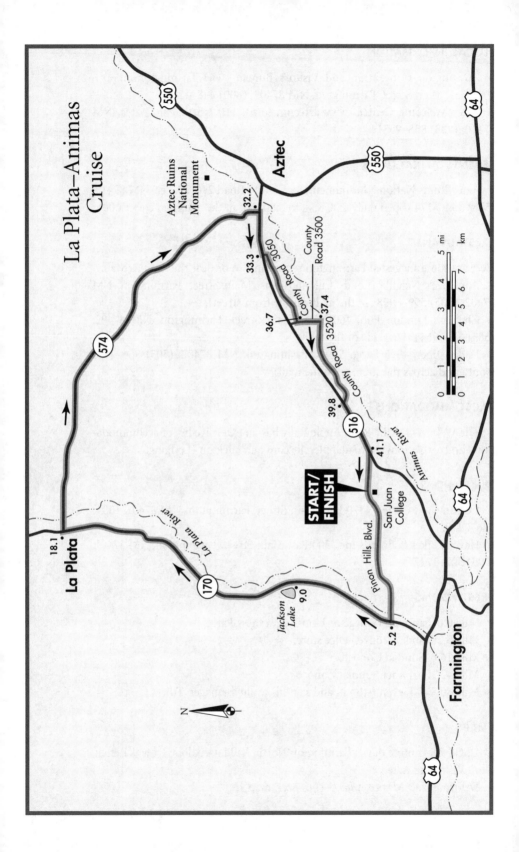

MILES AND DIRECTIONS

0.0 From the parking lot at San Juan College, head north on College Boulevard.

0.3 Turn left on Pinon Hills Boulevard, which heads west and drops into the Glade Canyon. (*Note:* Add about a half mile if you parked at Lions Wilderness Park.)

4.0 Cycle up a small hill past Thirtieth Street.

5.2 Turn right on La Plata Highway (New Mexico Route 170); Circle S convenience store on the left.

9.0 Pass the parking lot for Jackson Lake on the left and tackle a half-mile hill climb.

16.0 Sundial Conoco on the left.

18.1 Enter the community of La Plata and turn right on New Mexico Route 574. A sign directs you toward Aztec.

24.1 A long grade takes you to the top of the hill, where the Road Apple Trail emerges on the right. Drop into the Glade Valley, and climb up to the top of the east side, the high point of the trip at 6,280 feet. The Road Apple Trail continues on the right as the highway descends toward Aztec.

28.0 Ride past a community of trailers.

31.5 Enter the city limits of Aztec, and pass Koogler Junior High School.

32.2 Reach the junction with New Mexico Route 516; Sundial Conoco on the left. Turn right onto New Mexico Route 516 to continue on the loop; turn left to do a side trip to Aztec Ruins.

33.3 Leave the city limits of Aztec, and turn left onto County Road 3050. Enjoy this road's brand new pavement!

36.7 Reach the junction with County Road 3500, and turn left.

37.4 Turn right on County Road 3520.

39.8 At the stop sign, turn left on New Mexico Route 516 toward Farmington.

40.8 At the 7-Eleven on the right, Tim, the manager, is a strong cyclist and triathlete.

41.1 At the traffic light, turn right onto Pinon Hills Boulevard.

41.8 Continue straight through the traffic light at English Drive.

42.8 Turn left on College Boulevard.

43.1 Return to San Juan College.

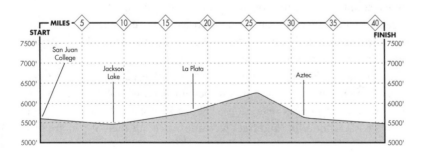

Tour de San Juan Cruise

C redit for the contribution of this loop in New Mexico's Four Corners Region goes to David Ortiz, a local cyclist and outdoor enthusiast. This 50-mile loop, east and south of Farmington, takes you through two river valleys—the Animas and the San Juan. Most of the ride follows rural county roads through farm and ranch country, wide open spaces, high-desert mesas, and colorful badlands. Part of the route crosses into the Navajo Indian Reservation; this Indian nation is the largest in the country. Ride highlights include lush river bottoms and distant mountain views—even high peaks in Colorado. Services are limited on this rural loop, but there is a spa at the start/end and a Mennonite bakery a quarter of the way into the trip.

The loop starts at the Royal Spa & Court Club, a health club facility with hot tub, sauna, and pool located on U.S. Highway 64. As you head out of Farmington, you will begin cycling northeast up the Animas River Valley for several miles on a rural county road lined with sandstone outcroppings. Another county road takes you up onto Crouch Mesa, where you descend through a Mennonite community and eventually arrive in the San Juan River valley. The route south of the river travels through farm and ranch country and includes more sandstone outcroppings.

U.S. Highway 550 heads south into an area of badlands, a multicolored landscape of eroding hills and unusual rock formations. You'll see the prominent landmark Angel Peak (elevation 6,988 feet) rising from the eastern horizon. There is a wonderful (and free) recreation area out there if you are lucky enough to locate the graded dirt road that seems to lead to nowhere. (It is about 20 miles south of Bloomfield.) Managed by the U.S. Bureau of Land Management (BLM), the Angel Peak Recreation Area offers a hiking trail, overlooks, sheltered picnic tables, and campsites (pit toilets and no water) in a beautiful setting among the eroding remains of an ancient sea bed.

Next it's west across the Navajo Agricultural Project Industries (NAPI), the Navajo's farming and agribusiness enterprise. Here, you'll be at the highest point (elevation 6,310 feet) on the loop. The dark green fields contrast with the yellow, red, and brown of the New Mexico high desert. A fast descent into the Gallegos Canyon quickly turns into a 4-mile hill climb out through more badlands.

You'll head back into town on New Mexico Route 371 through open prairie along the east edge of the Navajo Indian Reservation, which stretches for 200 miles west across into Arizona. As you approach the city limits of Farmington, enjoy (but be careful) on the fast downhill. The road descends 400 feet in three-quarters of a mile. Cyclists can generate speeds up to 50 miles per hour, if they dare. You'll cross both rivers—the San Juan and the Animas—before arriving back at the spa for a relaxing soak.

THE BASICS

Start: Royal Spa & Court Club on U.S. Highway 64 in Farmington.

Length: 50.5-mile loop.

Terrain: Easy to moderate hill climbs and a fast descent (several hundred feet) near the end of the trip.

Traffic and hazards: Mostly rural two-lane with light traffic except some heavy truck traffic on a section of County Road 3500. These county roads are narrow at times with a small or nonexistent shoulder. U.S. Highway 550 has a large shoulder with rumble strips, and New Mexico Route 371 also has a large shoulder. Watch your speed on the descent into Farmington; there's a 1-inch fissure in the shoulder on the steep downhill that could (and has) been dangerous.

Getting there: U.S. Highway 64 travels east-west through Farmington, turning into Broadway Street in town. The Royal Spa & Court Club is in the east part of Farmington just past the traffic light at Camina Flora, which is where the road changes back to U.S. Highway 64 (also known as Bloomfield Highway). The parking lot is 200 feet east of the traffic light at Camina Flora. Or you can turn onto Camina Flora and make a hard left into the parking lot.

LOCAL INFORMATION

♦ Farmington Convention and Visitors Bureau (www.farmingtonnm.org), 3041 East Main Street, Farmington, NM 87402; (800) 448–1240.

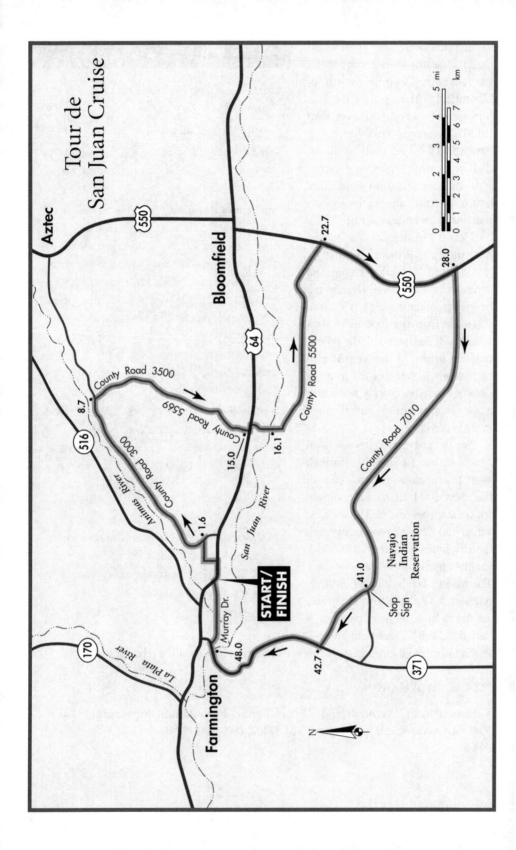

0.0 Leave the parking lot at the Royal Spa & Court Club, and turn right (east) onto U.S. Highway 64.

0.3 As you pass the day care center, Kid's Korner, on the right, immediately enter the left turning lane and turn left onto South Dustin Road; the Villager Lodge is on the right.

0.8 Reach a stop sign at Southside River Road and turn right. This road heads toward Browning Parkway.

1.6 Reach the intersection with Browning Parkway and turn left.

1.8 At the traffic light, turn right onto Morningstar Drive; 7-Eleven is on the corner. Begin a small uphill climb in 0.3 mile.

3.1 Hilltop affords great views of north Farmington and the Animas River valley as well as the distant peaks in Colorado. Enjoy a downhill toward the Animas River. Morningstar Drive veers off to the right, and your route changes to County Road 3000 here. Continue straight.

3.7 Start of a short and fast downhill on switchbacks. You will lose about 180 feet in elevation on your way to river level.

4.8 The road straightens out and meanders through the river bottoms and farmlands of the Animas River valley. Interesting sandstone outcroppings line the road to the right; road is narrow in spots.

7.1 The sandstone outcroppings on the right have natural springs oozing water and creating large icicles in winter.

8.1 Short hill climb; Anasazi residential subdivision on both sides of the road.

8.7 Reach a four-way stop and turn right onto County Road 3500. Pedal a moderate climb to the top of Crouch Mesa.

9.9 Top of Crouch Mesa; follow the road straight ahead (south). *Note:* High traffic area due to mobile home and oil industry businesses.

10.9 Descend toward the San Juan River valley. The road changes numbers two times after the descent-briefly to County Road 5570, then to County Road 5569 at the S curve.

(continued)

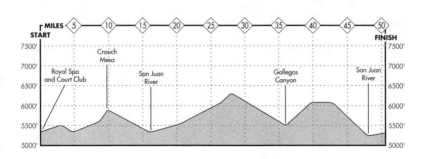

12.5 S curve where road changes to County Road 5569. Mennonite community on both sides of the road.

12.9 Mennonite bakery (the Little Barn Bake Shop) on the left; great pastries! El Paso gas plant is just past the community on the right.

15.0 Traffic light at U.S. Highway 64; turn left and travel a short distance east on U.S. Highway 64. Entrance to Sunray Casino immediately on the right.

15.1 Reach the next traffic light and turn right (south) onto County Road 5500; Mustang convenience store visible to the right. Pass the Lee Acres subdivision and fire station.

16.1 Cross the San Juan River.

16.4 As County Road 5500 curves toward the east, see more sandstone outcroppings to the right.

17.8 County Road 5500 straightens out and passes through rural farmland and ranches.

20.1 County Road 5500 curves to the right as you climb an easy half mile.

21.6 Pass by the now-defunct Thriftway Refinery on the left—a monument to its better days before environmental issues and aging equipment forced its closure.

22.7 Reach a stop sign at U.S. Highway 550 and turn right (south). Moderate uphill climb on brand new pavement through badlands country. View Angel Peak on the left horizon.

26.0 Highway crosses the Main Canal of the NAPI.

28.0 Intersection with County Road 7010 on the right. This turn is not well marked, however, there is a hand-painted sign that indicates NAPI in multicolors on the southwest corner of the intersection. Turn right (west) onto County Road 7010. This is the highest point on the trip-elevation 6,310 feet.

28.1 A sign directs travelers to several NAPI divisions; continue straight toward the headquarters.

31.0 Pass the NAPI feedlot and descend toward Gallegos Canyon.

32.9 Cross the Main Canal of the NAPI.

36.0 Bridge over Gallegos Canyon followed by moderate climb (4 miles). The route continues through sandstone/badland formations as you ascend.

41.0 Reach a four-way stop; advertisement across the road for the convenience store "Farm-n Go." There are no road signs here. Turn right (northwest), heading toward the NAPI headquarters. (*Note:* If you continue straight, no problem. After a mile, the road intersects with New Mexico Route 371, where you can turn right, heading north to Farmington.)

42.5 NAPI headquarters on the left.

(continued)

42.7 Reach a stop sign at Bisti Highway (New Mexico Route 371) and turn right (north) toward Farmington.

45.4 Pass through a television/microwave antenna farm.

45.8 Asphalt ends and concrete pavement begins; steep downhill with S curves.

46.5 Concrete ends, back to asphalt, and the steep descent mellows out as you near the San Juan River at Bisti.

48.0 Cross the San Juan River at Bisti Bridge; Mustang convenience store on the left.

48.1 Reach the traffic light at Murray Drive and turn right (east).

48.9 Cross the Animas River.

49.3 Continue straight at Miller Avenue.

49.9 Continue straight at McCormick School Road; the Mexican restaurant Taco Y Mas on the right.

50.3 7-Eleven Store on the left.

50.5 Continue straight at Camina Flora, where Murray Drive merges with U.S. Highway 64. Return to the Royal Spa & Court Club about 200 feet after the traffic light on the right.

EVENTS/ATTRACTIONS

♦ Royal Spa & Court Club, 2101 Bloomfield Highway, Farmington, NM 87401; (505) 326–2211 (day passes available for $10).

♦ Angel Peak Recreation Area, BLM Farmington Field Office, 1235 La Plata Highway, Farmington, NM 87401; (505) 599–8900 (free!).

RESTAURANTS

♦ Little Barn Bake Shop, 206A County Road 5569, Farmington, NM 87401; (505) 632–0387.

♦ Taco Y Mas, 1101 East Murray Drive, Farmington, NM 87401; (505) 326–6499.

♦ Sonya's Cookin' USA, 2001 Bloomfield Highway, Farmington, NM 87401; (505) 327–3526 (family-style).

ACCOMMODATIONS

♦ Villager Lodge, 2530 Bloomington Highway, Farmington, NM 87401; (505) 327–4433 (on-route; loud on weekends if there's a Mexican dance at the reception hall).

♦ The Web site for the Road Apple Rally has an extensive list of accommodation choices. Go to www.roadapplerally.com and click on "Lodging."

BIKE SHOPS

♦ Cottonwood Cycles, 4370 East Main Street, Farmington, NM 87401; (505) 326–0429.

♦ Havens Bikes & Boards Inc., 500 East Main Street, Farmington, NM 87401; (505) 327–1727.

REST ROOMS

♦ Mile 1.8: 7-Eleven Store on Browning Parkway.

♦ Mile 15.1: Mustang convenience store on U.S. Highway 64.

♦ Mile 48.0: Mustang convenience store on New Mexico Route 371.

♦ Mile 50.3: 7-Eleven Store on Murray Drive.

♦ There are rest rooms and showers at the Royal Spa & Court Club, which are accessible with the purchase of a day pass.

MAPS

♦ USGS 7.5-minute quads Farmington South, Farmington North, Flora Vista, Horn Canyon, Bloomfield, and Gallegos Trading Post.

♦ Delorme *New Mexico Atlas & Gazetteer,* map 13.

Cumbres-Toltec Challenge

*C*ome chase the narrow-gauge train of the Cumbres-Toltec
Scenic Railroad (C&TSR) in the mountains of north-central
New Mexico and southern Colorado. Stay overnight at the end of your
cycling day and return by train through the Toltec Gorge, alongside the
spires of Phantom Curve, and up and over Cumbres Pass (elevation
10,022 feet), crossing the state line eleven times. Chama, New Mexico,
and Antonito, Colorado, are small towns at either end of the scenic rail
line. These towns are also connected by New Mexico/Colorado Route 17,
a beautiful forested road through the Rio Grande National Forest that
climbs two mountain passes and follows the Conejos River. The train
ride and the cycling route travel through large aspen groves; this part of
the high country is amazing in the fall.

This high country tour on New Mexico/Colorado Route 17 climbs through
the southern San Juan Mountains along the New Mexico/Colorado border
where you are surrounded by the Rio Grande National Forest for most of the
ride. You'll enjoy forested slopes, ponderosa pine and aspen, towering peaks, and
rushing streams along the way. The high altitude will be one of the challenges—
two mountain passes that surpass 10,000 feet. The total elevation gain is more
than 3,500 feet.

The two-lane state road follows the railroad closely for the first 18 miles (to
Los Pinos), crossing into Colorado and up and over Cumbres Pass along the way.
You may see one of the trains, with its black coal smoke chugging along beside
you, or just hear the train's whistle off in the distance. After climbing the second
pass, La Manga Pass (elevation 10,230 feet), the road travels through the Conejos

Start: New Mexico Visitor Center in Chama at the junction of U.S. Highway 64/84 and New Mexico Route 17.

Length: 48.5 miles one-way (train ride back).

Terrain: Mountainous terrain, difficult climbs, and high elevation.

Traffic and hazards: Light traffic with a shoulder and good road surface.

Getting there: You can reach Chama heading east from Farmington (U.S. Highway 64, 110 miles), heading west from Taos (U.S. Highway 64, 95 miles), or heading north from Santa Fe (U.S. Highway 84, 100 miles). At the intersection of U.S. Highway 64/84 and New Mexico Route 17, you'll find the New Mexico Visitor Center (northwest corner) and the Chama Supermarket (southwest corner). There is ample parking at either location. The Donut Depot is on the east side of the highway. (For overnight parking, continue on to the C&TSR, 1.5 miles on the right, and be sure to ask permission.)

River valley. Your destination is Antonito, Colorado, on U.S. Highway 285 south of Alamosa and just north of the New Mexico state line.

When gold and silver mineral deposits were discovered, the Denver and Rio Grande Railway built an extension (1880) to reach the mining camps in the San Juans. A narrow gauge was needed to negotiate the rugged mountains. Eventually the line was abandoned, and the two states bought the historic track, jointly running it as a tourist attraction, which is now a National Historic Site. Many people visit the area to ride the authentic steam railroad, and there are special events that include moonlight rides, chamber music, and theme days.

The C&TSR derives its name from the fact that it runs over Cumbres Pass and through the Toltec Gorge. The track covers 64 miles between Chama and Antonito, and train rides are available from late May to mid-October. The trip takes most of a day, with trains leaving from both locations every morning, making it impossible to bike the road and ride the train without an overnight stop. Of course, you can ride this as an out-and-back and do the train another time.

Be sure to call ahead and mention that you'll have a bike with you. Sometimes the train is full with inventory or passengers, especially in the fall, and can't accommodate a bicycle. It is good to make reservations at least two weeks in advance. There are a number of train trips scheduled, but one of the best options is No. 5, which will get you from Antonito (10:00 A.M.) back to Chama (4:05 P.M.) for $50. Snacks are available on the train, and you can bring a picnic or pay for a meal at the lunch stop—the old stagecoach town of Osier.

Chama and Antonito, both established in the late 1800s, prospered as railroad towns. Today their local economies include ranching, lumber, and tourism, and they each have a train depot on the C&TSR. In Chama you can take a historic walking tour of the yards, buildings, and equipment. There are motels near both depots, but the area's wonderful B&Bs and rustic lodges are

Chase the narrow gauge train of the Cumbres-Toltec Scenic Railroad on New Mexico Route 17. (Photo courtesy of Enchanted Lands Enterprise)

not to be missed. You could also camp at one of several forest service camp-grounds along the river (water and vault toilets; $12). There is a great hostel at Browles Bridge, also along the river, and a homemade breakfast is included.

LOCAL INFORMATION

♦ Chama Valley Chamber of Commerce (www.chamavalley.com), Box 306, Chama, NM 87520; (800) 477–0149.
♦ Antonito Chamber of Commerce, P.O. Box 427, Antonito, CO 81120; (719) 376–2277.

EVENTS/ATTRACTIONS

♦ Cumbres & Toltec Scenic Railroad (www.cumbrestoltec.com), Box 789, Chama, NM 87520; (888) 286–2737.
♦ Rio Grande National Forest (Conejos Ranger District), 15571 County Road T-5, La Jara, CO 81140; (719) 274–8971.

RESTAURANTS

♦ Donut Depot, Highway 17, Chama, NM 87520; (505) 756–1060 (breakfast and box lunches in addition to pastries).
♦ Viva Vera's Mexican Kitchen, 2202 Highway 17, Chama, NM 87520; (505) 756–2557 (flavorful New Mexican food).

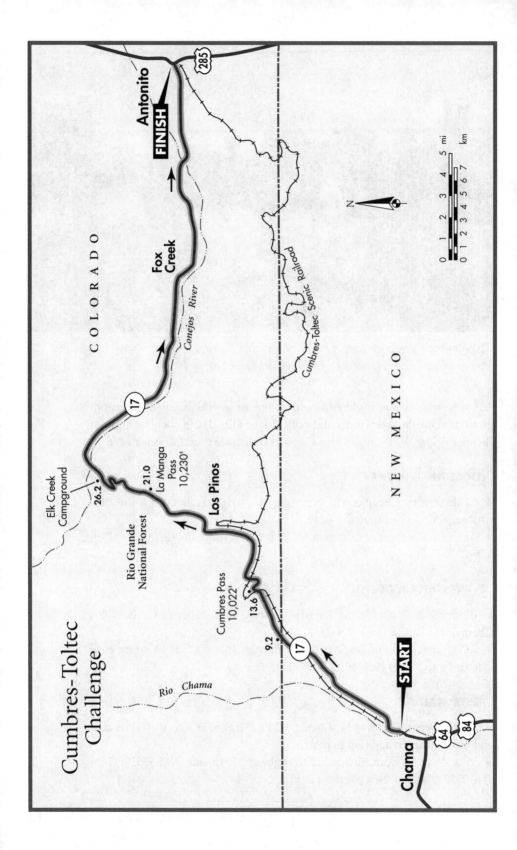

0.0 Leave the New Mexico Visitor Center and head north on New Mexico Route 17, the main drag through Chama.

0.2 Pass Viva Vera's Mexican Kitchen (local favorite) on the right. Back porch has great views.

1.5 C&TSR on the right and Parlor Car B&B on the left.

9.2 Reach the Colorado border; the highway changes to Colorado Route 17. Steady climbing continues to the first pass.

13.6 Cumbres Pass (no access to historic buildings). Descend for several miles, and prepare for the climb to the second pass.

16.0 Rendezvous Steakhouse on the right. Vandalized at the beginning of 2002, its reopening is uncertain.

21.0 La Manga Pass. Mostly downhill from here with some rolling hills.

26.2 Elk Creek Campground on the left, just before the intersection with Federal Road 250. Two seasonal restaurants and a motel near the junction with Federal Road 250.

33.3 Aspen Glade Campground on the right.

36.8 Mogote Campground on the right; locals call it Smokies because of the Smokey Bear sign.

38.5 Browles Bridge crosses the Conejos River to the right. The hostel is about 100 yards after the bridge.

44.0 Small community of Mogote.

48.5 Reach the junction with U.S. Highway 285. Turn right (south) to reach the train depot, which is just down on the left. (To go into Antonito, continue on Colorado Route 17, which becomes U.S. Highway 285 heading north.)

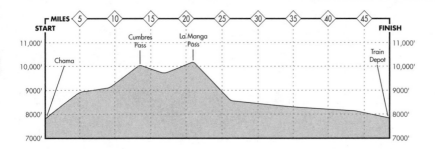

◆ Stefan's Restaurant, 101 Rail Lane, Antonito, CO 81120; (505) 376–5292 (near the train depot and Narrow Gauge Railroad Inn).

ACCOMMODATIONS

◆ A good source for lodging is the C&TSR Web site. Click on "Our local partners."

♦ Parlor Car B&B, 311 Terrace Avenue, Chama, NM 87520; (888) 849–7800 (across from the C&TSR depot).

♦ Narrow Gauge Railroad Inn, 5200 State Highway 285, Antonito, CO 81120; (800) 323–9469 (walking distance from the C&TSR depot).

♦ Conejos River AYH-Hostel, 3591 County Road D-5, Antonito, CO 81120; (719) 376–2518 ($9–$12).

♦ Conejos Ranch, 25390 Highway 17, Antonito, CO 81120; (719) 376–2464.

♦ Twin Ranch Guest Ranch, 34044 Highway 17, Antonito, CO 81120; (888) 689–6787.

BIKE SHOPS

There are no bike shops nearby. You'll have to travel to Taos, Farmington, Los Alamos, or Santa Fe for sales and service.

REST ROOMS

♦ Mile 0.0: New Mexico Visitor Center.

♦ Mile 1.5: C&TSR.

♦ Mile 48.5: Train depot in Antonito.

♦ There are vault toilets at several forest service campgrounds along the way.

MAPS

♦ USGS 7.5-minute quads Chama and West Fork Rio Brazos; Cumbres (CO), La Jara Canyon (CO), Osier (CO), Fox Creek (CO), and Antonito (CO).

♦ Delorme *New Mexico Atlas & Gazetteer*, map 15; *Colorado Atlas & Gazetteer*, maps 89 and 90.

O'Keeffe Country Challenge

G eorgia O'Keeffe loved the Southwest. On this loop you will see some of the landscape that captivated this world-famous artist—colorful mesas, towering cliffs, and unusual rock formations. In addition you can plan your trip to include a visit to Ojo Caliente Mineral Springs, one of the oldest health resorts in the country. Most of this loop travels quiet roads through rural countryside where the sagebrush of the high desert transitions to pine forest.

The ride starts in the Rio Chama valley at the Abiquiu Inn, where you need to ask permission in order to park. Next door, tours depart to O'Keeffe's home and studio. At the inn you can get a room, *casita* (cottage), or suite with fireplace and tiled bath, and the specialties at the cafe include Middle Eastern, Mediterranean, and New Mexican cuisine—or get a boxed lunch for the road.

For the tours (April to November), you need to call the Georgia O'Keeffe Foundation, but be sure to make your reservations months in advance. O'Keeffe, the best-known painter in New Mexico, moved from New York to her home in Abiquiu in 1949. Her eighteenth-century hacienda with its famed "black door" and the views from her property inspired some of her greatest works.

From Abiquiu you will begin the loop along the Rio Chama, and you will be cycling near or alongside a river for the entire ride—first the Rio Chama, then El Rito and Rio Ojo Caliente, and finally the Rio Chama again. The lush corridor of cottonwoods in these river valleys in contrast to the high desert plateau is part of what makes this such a magical place, especially in the fall. A rural back road takes you through a piece of Carson National Forest, into the village of El Rito, and along Main Street, where you can sample award-winning

Start: The Abiquiu Inn in Abiquiu.

Length: 60.2-mile loop.

Terrain: Gentle climbs and descents through high desert terrain; the biggest challenge is a couple miles of gradual climbing to the ride's high point on New Mexico Route 554.

Traffic and hazards: Moderate traffic on U.S. Highway 84 and U.S. Highway 285 but wide shoulders. New Mexico Route 554 has little traffic, especially after passing through El Rito. You'll encounter a section of narrow, tight curves on the descent to New Mexico Route 111.

Getting there: Take U.S. Highway 285/84 north out of Espanola for about 20 miles. Stay on the main road, U.S. Highway 84 toward Chama. The Abiquiu Inn is on the right about 3 miles past the junction with New Mexico Route 554. If you reach Bode's General Store and the post office in Abiquiu, you've gone about 0.5 mile too far.

green chili at El Farolito. Continuing through juniper-pinon woodlands, you won't see anything of civilization until you near Ojo Caliente. You'll ride along the base of Black Mesa, with unusual rock formations in the foreground and distant views of the Jemez Moutains, before reaching the Rio Chama again.

One of the ride's highlights, Ojo Caliente Mineral Springs, is on the National Register of Historic Places. The springs have been used for bathing for centuries—by prehistoric pueblo Indians, then Spanish and Anglos. Spanish explorer Cabeza de Vaca named the area during a visit in 1535. Ojo Caliente means "hot springs," and these springs have five different types of geothermal mineral water and range from 98 to 113 degrees.

The "quick soak" starts at $10 (90 minutes), but stay a little longer in this beautiful setting. The original bathhouse was built in 1860 as a sanatorium, and today the facility offers a variety of tubs, a full-service restaurant, and a long list of spa treatments including massage, mud baths, and herbal wraps. A hiking trail leads up the sandstone cliffs to petroglyphs and the ancient ruins of Posi Pueblo. A bike rack is located in front of the lodge.

It might be hard to get back on the bike after a visit to the hot springs, so consider spending the night. The resort offers simple rooms in their historic lodge, comfortable cottages, and tent camping. Other options? Suellen Bowersock with Enchanted Lands Bicycle Tours recommends the Inn and Mercantile at Ojo, and the least expensive room in town is along U.S. Highway 285 at Lomita Motel.

LOCAL INFORMATION:

♦ Espanola Valley Chamber of Commerce, 417 Big Rock Center, Espanola, NM 87532; (505) 753–2831.

EVENTS/ATTRACTIONS

♦ Georgia O'Keeffe Foundation, P.O. Box 40, Abiquiu, NM 87510; (505) 685–4369.
♦ Ojo Caliente Mineral Springs (www.ojocalientespa.com), P.O. Box 68, Ojo Caliente, NM 87549; (505) 583–2233.

RESTAURANTS

♦ El Farolito, 1212 Main Street, El Rito, NM 87530; (505) 581–9509 (open 11:00 A.M. to around 7:00 P.M.; closed Mondays and weekdays from around 3:30 P.M. to 4:30 P.M.).

ACCOMMODATIONS

♦ Abiquiu Inn (www.abiquiuinn. com), P.O. Box 120, Abiquiu, NM 87510; (505) 685–4378.
♦ Inn and Mercantile at Ojo, P.O. Box 214, Ojo Caliente, NM 87549; (505) 583–9131.
♦ Lomita Motel, 35305 U.S. Highway 285, Ojo Caliente, NM 87549; (505) 583–2109.

BIKE SHOPS

The closest bike shops are in Los Alamos, Santa Fe, and Taos; these towns are each about an hour away by car.

Catch interesting views of the Sangre de Cristo Mountains in O'Keeffe Country.

REST ROOMS

♦ Mile 0.0: Abiquiu Inn (or Bode's General Store, just 0.5 mile north on the right).
♦ Mile 15.4: Martins General Store.
♦ Mile 30.3: Olivers Store.
♦ Mile 45.8: Chevron, just off-route to the left.

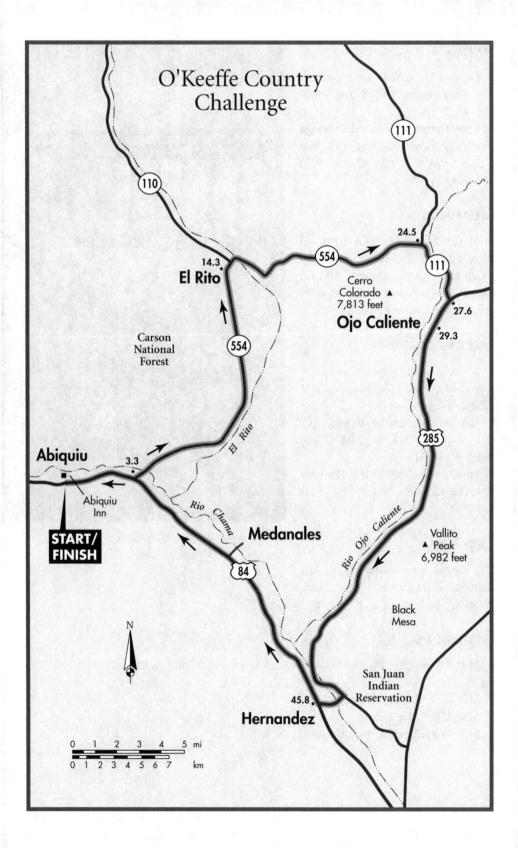

0.0 From the Abiquiu Inn head south on U.S. Highway 84, which has a wide shoulder.

1.1 First good view of the Rio Chama on the left. Also, notice the roadside ruins of a church, the original site of the town of Abiquiu.

1.8 Los Trujillos Country Store on the right; open daily with rest rooms for paying customers only.

3.3 Junction with New Mexico Route 554; turn left after catching a glimpse of the Truchas Peaks to the east. Ride along a small shoulder with loose gravel.

3.8 Cross the Rio Chama, lose the shoulder, and start a gentle climb.

7.9 Enter the Carson National Forest; soon the road is straight as an arrow for miles.

14.3 Ride along the narrow main street through the tiny town of El Rito.

14.4 Pass Northern New Mexico Community College on the left.

15.4 Martins General Store (rest rooms) on the left, and El Farolito Restaurant (don't miss the blue-ribbon green chili) on the right.

15.5 Pass the El Rito Ranger Station (open weekdays; rest rooms) on the left. The road makes a sharp turn to the east as you leave town and begin climbing.

19.2 Reach the high point of the ride at 7,200 feet and begin a fun descent. A section of the road looks like a snake, with several continuous curves.

24.5 T intersection with New Mexico Route 111; turn right.

25.4 Enter a small, rocky river gorge and cross a bridge over the Rio Ojo Caliente.

27.6 T intersection with U.S. Highway 285; turn right and ride on a large shoulder while you enjoy views of the Jemez Mountains.

29.1 A cluster of roadside eateries (Mesa Vista Cafe, Wild Iris Vegetarian Cafe, and Gordo's Cafe) provide a variety of choices including New Mexican and vegan.

29.3 Look for signs advertising Ojo Caliente Mineral Springs; detour by turning right. Cycle 0.5 mile to reach the resort, passing the Inn and Mercantile at Ojo on the right on the way in. The loop continues straight.

(continued)

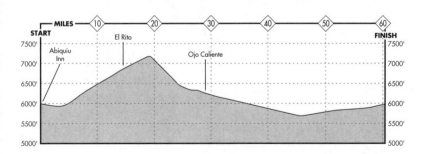

30.3 Olivers Store on the right (open daily; rest rooms).

44.3 A roadside overlook with picnic tables on the left along the base of Black Mesa. A good place to stop and enjoy the view.

45.5 Cross the Rio Chama again.

45.8 At the junction with U.S. Highway 84, turn right and ride on a good shoulder. (For rest rooms, turn left and stop in at the Chevron.)

48.7 Shoulder widens to 6 feet.

49.2 Pass the small town of Rio Chama.

51.7 Road on the right leads to Medanales, known as a center for wood carving and weaving.

56.9 Pass the turn off for New Mexico Route 554, where you started the loop.

60.2 Return to the Abiquiu Inn.

MAPS

♦ USGS 7.5-minute quads Abiquiu, Medanales, El Rito, Ojo Caliente, Lyden, San Juan Pueblo, and Chili.

♦ Delorme *New Mexico Atlas & Gazetteer,* map 15.

5

Enchanted Circle Classic

For a quarter century the Red River Chamber of Commerce held the twenty-fourth annual Enchanted Circle Century. Each September about 600 cyclists start at 8:00 A.M. on Main Street in front of Red River's town hall to ride one of the most scenic loops in the Southwest. The Enchanted Circle Scenic Byway is an 80-mile loop (the century adds an out-and-back leg to get to 100) that connects several mountain resort towns in north-central New Mexico, travels through two separate districts of Carson National Forest, and encircles the state's highest mountains, including Wheeler Peak, the highest at 13,161 feet. Many bicycle tour companies that visit the Land of Enchantment incorporate this loop in the trips they offer. Come and see why this is a favorite for visitors and locals alike!

The Enchanted Circle Scenic Byway has a lot to offer whether you are a long-distance rider or a cycle tourist. The scenery includes some of the state's best-rugged peaks, rushing streams, aspen-fir forest, and mountain meadows, lakes, and valleys. The loop uses New Mexico Route 38, U.S. Highway 64, and New Mexico Route 522 to connect five charming northern New Mexico towns-Red River, Eagle Nest, Angel Fire, Taos, and Questa. You'll pass many points of interest and climb two passes of more than 9,000 feet. The cool summer temperatures are a bonus (Red River's summer average is seventy-five degrees!).

The loop begins in the frontier town of Red River, complete with Western-style store fronts, shoot-outs and square dancing, and lots of steak and BBQ. This old mining town boomed nearly a century ago with the discovery of gold in the mountains. You'll ride along the mile-long Main Street, which is lined

Start: Red River Town Hall.

Length: 80.5-mile loop.

Terrain: Challenging and mountainous with more than 5,000 feet of climbing and some awesome downhill.

Traffic and hazards: A wide variety of conditions exists from busy highways with large shoulders to rural two-lane without shoulders. Usually light to moderate traffic; car tourists circle the loop in the summer and fall. For the most part the road surface is good throughout the ride. Taos is the only town where you'll encounter congestion, traffic lights, and some craziness.

Getting there: Red River is easy to find. It's about 35 miles northeast of Taos. Take New Mexico Route 522 north and be sure to turn right in Questa onto New Mexico Route 38. You can also come in from the east on New Mexico Route 38, 16 miles from Eagle Nest. New Mexico Route 38 becomes Main Street through Red River. The town hall is right in the center of town on the north side of the road, across the street from a city park and Texas Reds Steakhouse. You'll find a phone, water, and rest rooms. There is parking directly in front of the town hall, but it is better to use the new public lot behind Texas Reds. Turn onto the side street between the restaurant and the park. You will see the parking lot on your left.

with a variety of specialty shops, restaurants, and lodging. The ski hill rises straight up from town (summer chairlift rides!). This rustic ski and summer resort is a bit touristy but is still a fun place to visit and makes a great starting point or overnight spot for a tour.

Everything is within walking distance, or you can use the free trolley for transportation. You'll find all types of accommodations here except large hotel chains. The town offers cabins, B&Bs, inns, lodges, and small motels. At Texas Reds Steakhouse, one of the favorite eateries on Main Street, you are served dry-roasted peanuts instead of the usual chips and salsa. It is customary to throw your shells on the floor while you wait for your meal.

Enjoy your time in Red River because your first few miles east out of town involve climbing to Bobcat Pass (elevation 9,820 feet), an ascent of 1,100 feet in 4 miles. This workout is followed by a thrilling descent into the beautiful Moreno Valley and through the lakeside resort village of Eagle Nest. The lake is popular with fishermen, sailors, and windsurfers; and the tiny main street is a good place for a leg-stretcher with several shops and restaurants.

The New Mexico Touring Society, which starts its annual two-day trip in Taos, recommends the reasonably priced Moore Rest Inn, on the east end of Eagle Nest's Main Street. The DAV (Disabled American Veterans) Vietnam Veterans National Memorial, located south of Eagle Nest, was the very first monument of its kind. It was originally built as a tribute to one man's son killed in 1968, and today honors all the men and women of the Vietnam War. Definitely worth a stop!

The Western-style town of Red River, the start of the Enchanted Circle Classic.

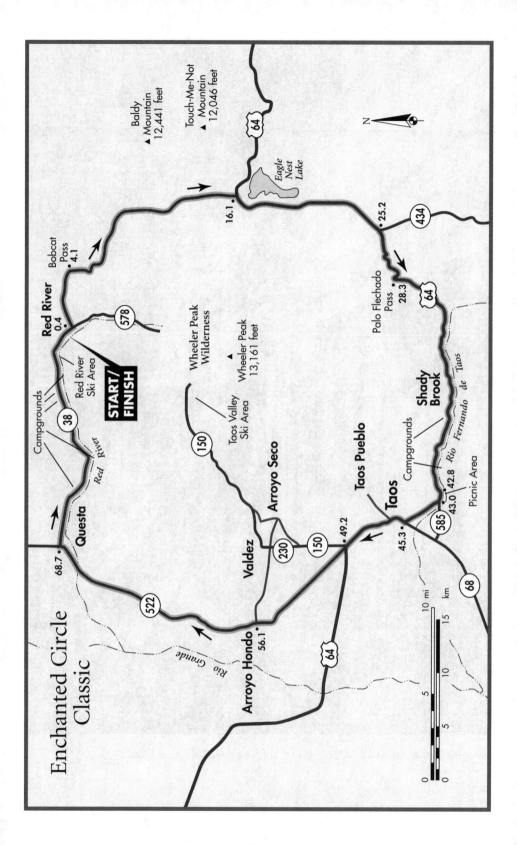

Enchanted Circle Classic

Baldy Mountain
▲ 12,441 feet

Touch-Me-Not Mountain
▲ 12,046 feet

N

64

Eagle Nest Lake

16.1

434

25.2

Bobcat Pass
• 4.1

Red River
0.4

578

Palo Flechado Pass
• 28.3

64

Campgrounds

38

Red River Ski Area

START/FINISH

Wheeler Peak Wilderness

Wheeler Peak
▲ 13,161 feet

Shady Brook

Red River

Taos Valley Ski Area

150

Rio Fernando de Taos

Arroyo Seco

Campgrounds

42.8

Questa

68.7 •

Taos Pueblo

43.0 •

Picnic Area

522

Valdez

230

150

• 49.2

Taos

585

45.3 •

68

Rio Grande

Arroyo Hondo
56.1 •

64

10 mi

km

0   5   10   5

0   5   10   15

0.0 Leaving the Red River town hall, head east down Main Street (New Mexico Route 38).

0.4 The road splits at the edge of town. Head left (small shoulder), and begin climbing to the first of two passes on the loop.

3.5 Pass the Enchanted Forest Cross-Country Ski Area (30 kilometers of groomed trails in the winter).

4.1 Reach Bobcat Pass; sign indicates the elevation at 9,820 feet. Descend!

6.9 The shoulder disappears for the most part.

9.5 The terrain opens up and levels out as you enter the Moreno Valley.

13.4 First views of Eagle Nest Lake.

16.1 Junction with New Mexico Route 64; Diamond Shamrock on the left. (Turn left to visit downtown Eagle Nest.) Gain a wide shoulder that soon narrows to a foot wide.

19.5 Historic marker on the right and good place to stop and view Wheeler Peak.

24.4 Entrance to the DAV Vietnam Veterans National Memorial on the right.

25.2 Junction with New Mexico Route 434, which goes through Angel Fire and on to Mora.

25.4 A gas station called the Barn on the left.

26.2 Enter Carson National Forest. A sign indicates a steep climb for the next 2 miles; tight turns, no shoulder.

28.3 Reach Palo Flechado Pass; no sign but the elevation is about 9,100 feet.

33.3 Enchanted Moon Campground (see big covered wagon) and Shady Brook Village (inn, cafe, and gift shop).

38.3 La Sombra Campground on the left.

38.8 Capulin Campground on the left.

40.4 Sierra Village Vacation Park on the left (snacks and convenience store).

41.4 Las Petacas Campground (primitive) on the left.

42.8 El Nogal Picnic Area (no water) on the left; trailhead for the South Boundary Trail (great mountain biking).

(continued)

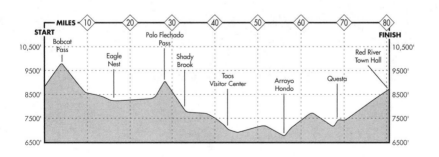

43.0 Junction with New Mexico Route 585 on the left, which leads to the Taos Visitor Center. Continue straight on Kit Carson Road (U.S. Highway 64).

45.3 Traffic light and junction with New Mexico Route 68. Turn right onto Paseo Del Pueblo Norte (U.S. Highway 64), a busy wide street with a parking lane. Pass Kit Carson Park on right in a block and a half. You'll pick up a shoulder as you head out of town. A section is chewed up through El Prado.

45.8 Camino Del Pueblo, the road to the Taos Pueblo veers off to the right at Allsup's. Slight upgrade out of town.

49.2 Major four-way intersection with several gas stations. Continue straight, which is now New Mexico Route 522. U.S. Highway 64 goes left to the Rio Grande Gorge Bridge, and New Mexico Route 150 goes right to the Taos Ski Valley. High-speed traffic on New Mexico Route 522 but large shoulder to Questa.

51.4 Reach a high point on the sage-covered Taos Plateau, and enjoy a few flat miles.

56.1 Pass through the tiny village of Arroyo Hondo and cross the Rio Hondo. Herb's Lounge on the left has snacks, water, and a public rest rooms. Rolling terrain as you climb to Questa.

68.1 Chevron on the left.

68.7 Traffic light at the Village Stop and Go in Questa. Turn right onto New Mexico Route 38.

69.1 Artesanos de Questa, a community arts and crafts center, and the Questa Visitor Center on the left.

70.0 Eagle Rock Lake on the right. This small pond is stocked with rainbow trout and makes a great ice skating spot in the winter.

70.3 Questa Ranger Station on the right; begin riding alongside the Red River, gently climbing for the next 10 miles.

72.1 Goat Hill Campground (primitive).

73.5 Columbine Campground.

75.1 Pass the Questa Molybdenum Mine, and see the scarred hillside.

77.5 Fawn Lakes Campground.

77.9 Elephant Rock Campground.

78.5 Junebug Campground.

78.9 Reach the town limit of Red River; a sign indicates the elevation at 8,650 feet.

80.5 Return to Red River Town Hall and BBQ at Texas Reds.

Before leaving the Moreno Valley, you can take a detour into Angel Fire, a four-season resort that caters to skiers, golfers, and fishermen. Then it's another mountain pass, climbing two steep miles on switchbacks to Palo Flechado Pass (elevation 9,100 feet), followed by an incredible descent through Taos Canyon along the Rio Fernando de Taos. You are in the national forest again as you follow the river past picnic areas and campgrounds. Shady Brook Village, a great place for a break or overnight stop, offers an inn, a cafe, a gift shop, and hummingbird watching.

Taos is steeped in history and famed for its art, its studios and galleries, and its famous figures like Georgia O'Keeffe, D. H. Lawrence, and Thomas Wolfe. The town sits in a large valley up against the base of the highest mountains in the state, while the Rio Grande cuts a deep gorge through the mesa to the west. If you have time take a stroll through the historic plaza (mile 45.3). Heading west out of town onto the Taos Plateau, you have the option of an out-and-back to the Rio Grande Gorge Bridge, the second highest suspension bridge in the country. This 14-mile out-and-back is fairly flat and provides views 650 feet down to the mighty river.

As you tackle the rolling hills toward Questa, the last town on the loop, you'll gain 2,000 feet in 20 miles. This rural community is home to several businesses, including El Seville Restaurant, known for great sopapillas. When you turn right onto New Mexico Route 38, you'll pass Eagle Rock Lake and the Questa Ranger Station. On New Mexico Route 38, the last leg, the traffic is lighter and you'll have a small shoulder as you gradually climb 1,000 feet along the Red River back to the start of the loop. You'll pass Molycorp, Inc., where they've been mining molybdenum in this canyon since 1921. Molybdenum is a steel-hardening agent and lubricant. There are several forest service campgrounds along this beautifully wooded stretch of road. Back in Red River, BBQ anyone?

In addition to Red River's century, many touring companies, charitable organizations, and cycling clubs use the Enchanted Circle. The New Mexico–based Enchanted Lands Enterprise (see sidebar in High Road to Taos Classic) offers a two-day trip starting in Taos with an overnight in Red River. The Rio Grande Division of the National Multiple Sclerosis Society includes the Enchanted Circle in their Tour De Taos MS-150 (see sidebar in Ski Apache Challenge).

You can plan this tour a number of ways, but nothing beats riverside camping. Most of the national forest campgrounds on the route are open from May to October and provide water and outhouse facilities for a small fee. The primitive sites are free but don't have water. For the campgrounds on the northern half of the loop, which are along the Red River, contact the Questa Ranger District; and for the campgrounds on the southern half of the loop, which are along the Rio Fernando de Taos, contact the Camino Real Ranger District.

(*Note:* Go into the town hall in Red River and see someone in the marshal's office about overnight parking. A few times during the year, like Memorial Day and Fourth of July, they won't be able to help you. The local number is (505) 754–6166.)

LOCAL INFORMATION

♦ River Chamber of Commerce (www.redrivernewmex.com), Box 870, Red River, NM 87558; (800) 348–6444.
♦ Eagle Nest Chamber of Commerce (www.eaglenest.org), Box 322, Eagle Nest, NM 87718; (800) 494–9117.
♦ Angel Fire Chamber of Commerce (www.angelfirechamber.org), P.O. Box 547, Angel Fire, NM 87710; (800) 446–8117.
♦ Questa Visitor Center (Artesanos de Questa), 41 Highway 38, Questa, NM 87556; (505) 586–9302.
♦ Taos County Chamber of Commerce (www.taoschamber.com), P.O. Drawer 1, Taos, NM 87571; (800) 732–8267.
♦ Questa Ranger District, P.O. Box 110, Questa, NM 87556; (505) 586–0520.
♦ Camino Real Ranger District, P.O. Box 68, Penasco, NM 87553; (505) 587–2255.

EVENTS/ATTRACTIONS

♦ DAV Vietnam Veterans National Memorial, P.O. Box 68, Angel Fire, NM 87710; (505) 377–6900 (visitor center open year-round—summer from 9:00 A.M. to 7:00 P.M.—and the chapel is always open).
♦ For information on the Enchanted Circle Century, contact the Red River Chamber of Commerce.

RESTAURANTS

♦ Texas Reds Steakhouse, Main Street, Red River, NM 87558; (505) 754–2922 (across from the start, and the end, of the ride).
♦ Orlando's New Mexican Cafe, 1114 Don Juan Valdez Lane, Taos, NM 87571; (505) 751–1450 (on-route; one of my favorites in Taos, but there are many more great restaurants).
♦ El Seville Restaurant, Highway 522, Questa, NM 87556; (505) 586–0300 (famed for their sopapillas).

ACCOMMODATIONS

♦ Moore Rest Inn (www.moorerestinn.ohgolly.com), 715 U.S. Highway Highway 64 East, Eagle Nest, NM 87718; (505) 377–6813.
♦ Shady Brook Village, Route 1, Box 5, Highway 64, Taos, NM 87571; (505) 751–1315.

♦ Sierra Village Vacation Park, HC 71, Box 12, Highway 64, Taos, NM 87571; (505) 758–3660.

♦ Enchanted Moon RV Park and Campground, #7 Valle Escondido Road, Valle Escondido, NM 87571; (505) 758–3338.

♦ Taos Reservation Central, P.O. Box 1713, Taos, NM 87571; (800) 821–2437.

♦ Budget Host Inn, 1798 Paseo Del Pueblo Sur, Taos, NM 87557; (800) 323–6009 (inexpensive option in Taos; off-route by a few miles).

BIKE SHOPS

♦ Gearing Up Bicycle Shop, 129 Paseo Del Pueblo Sur, Taos, NM 87571; (505) 751–0365 (off-route from mile 45.3; down a block or two to the left, on the left).

REST ROOMS

♦ Mile 0.0: Red River Town Hall (inside to the left across from the chamber of commerce office).

♦ Mile 16.1: Diamond Shamrock.

♦ Mile 25.4: The Barn.

♦ Mile 38.3–42.8: Several forest service campgrounds and picnic areas with outhouses (some with water).

♦ Mile 45.3: Kit Carson Park.

♦ Mile 56.1: Herb's Lounge.

♦ Mile 68.1: Chevron.

♦ Mile 70.3: Questa Ranger Station.

♦ Mile 72.1–78.5: Several forest service campgrounds with outhouses (some with water).

MAPS

♦ USGS 7.5-minute quads Red River, Red River Pass, Eagle Nest, Palo Flechado Pass, Pueblo Peak, Shady Brook, Taos, Los Cordavas, Arroyo Hondo, Guadalupe Mountain, and Questa.

♦ Delorme *New Mexico Atlas & Gazetteer,* maps 16 and 17.

Blueberry Hill Ramble

*T*aos is steeped in history and famed for its art, its studios and galleries, and its famous figures like Georgia O'Keeffe, D. H. Lawrence, and Thomas Wolfe. The town sits in a large valley up against the base of the highest mountains in the state, while the Rio Grande cuts a deep gorge through the mesa to the west. This easy loop around the city is suitable for any level of rider. You can make it a brisk cruise, or take some time off the bike to visit one of the best museums in Taos and one of the most painted and photographed adobe churches in the Southwest. The Taos Plaza, just a block and a half away from the start, is worth a walking tour, and side roads off the loop lead to the Taos Pueblo and the Rio Grande Gorge Bridge for an additional 20 miles on the bike.

This short loop and two other tours in the book that start near the Plaza were suggested in part by the folks at Gearing Up Bicycle Shop as some of the popular day rides in and around Taos. The Blueberry Hill Ramble, the Hondo-Seco Cruise, and the Taos Ski Valley Challenge can be combined and modified in several ways. They all start at Kit Carson Park and share the first 3.9 miles.

The twenty-five-acre Kit Carson Park provides free parking and a grassy picnic spot. The first leg has you cycling along the beautiful pastoral lands of the Taos Pueblo, nestled at the base of the Taos Mountains. A 6-mile round trip will take you to this World Heritage Site, the largest existing multistoried pueblo in the country. You will find artwork and traditional foods offered in the village. These Native Americans are known for their mica-flecked pottery.

At the major four-way intersection north of town, New Mexico Route 522 (straight ahead) heads for Arroyo Hondo and New Mexico Route 150 (turn right) heads for the Taos Ski Valley. Take U.S. Highway 64 (turn left) to ride out to the Rio Grande Gorge Bridge, the second highest suspension bridge in the country. When the "Bridge to Nowhere" was being built in 1965, there weren't enough funds to continue the road on the other side. This 14-mile out-and-back is fairly flat and provides views 650 feet down to the mighty river. Today, U.S. Highway 64 continues west to Tres Piedras.

Blueberry Hill Road is quiet and rural, a stretch favored by locals as a way to get around town with little traffic and great views. Gazing across the Taos Valley, you'll see the Truchas Peaks to the south and the Jemez Mountains to the southwest. Two-thirds of the way around the loop, you'll reach Rancho de Taos where you can visit San Francisco de Asis Mission Church, depicted in works by Georgia O'Keeffe and Ansel Adams. The church stands much as it did in the 1800s with its thick adobe walls and enormous buttresses. Toward the end of the ride, as you circle back toward the center of town, you'll ride along Kit Carson Road, lined with mature cottonwoods, studios and galleries, and impressive adobe architecture.

THE BASICS

Start: Kit Carson Park in downtown Taos.

Length: 17.3-mile loop.

Terrain: Relatively little elevation gain; any ascent is gradual.

Traffic and hazards: Summer tourist traffic, congestion around the Plaza, and a stretch on Paseo Del Pueblo Norte with a chewed-up shoulder. Blueberry Hill Road is lightly traveled.

Getting there: Travel to the intersection of U.S. Highway 64 and New Mexico Route 68, near the Plaza in downtown Taos. North of this junction, New Mexico Route 68 is called Paseo Del Pueblo Norte. It's the main street through town. Go one block north of the Plaza on Paseo Del Pueblo Norte through the traffic light at Civic Plaza Drive. Go another half block and turn right into Kit Carson Park.

LOCAL INFORMATION

♦ Taos County Chamber of Commerce (www.taoschamber.com), P.O. Drawer 1, Taos, NM 87571; (800) 732–8267.

EVENTS/ATTRACTIONS

♦ Taos Pueblo Tourism Office, P.O. Box 1846, Taos, NM 87571; (505) 758–1028 (8:00 A.M. to 4:30 P.M. Monday through Saturday and 8:30 A.M. to 4:00 P.M. on Sunday, but call ahead; cost $10).
♦ Millicent Rogers Museum, 1504 Millicent Rogers Road, Taos, NM 87571; (505) 758–2462 (10:00 A.M. to 5:00 P.M. daily and closed on Mondays in the winter and on major holidays; cost $6.00).

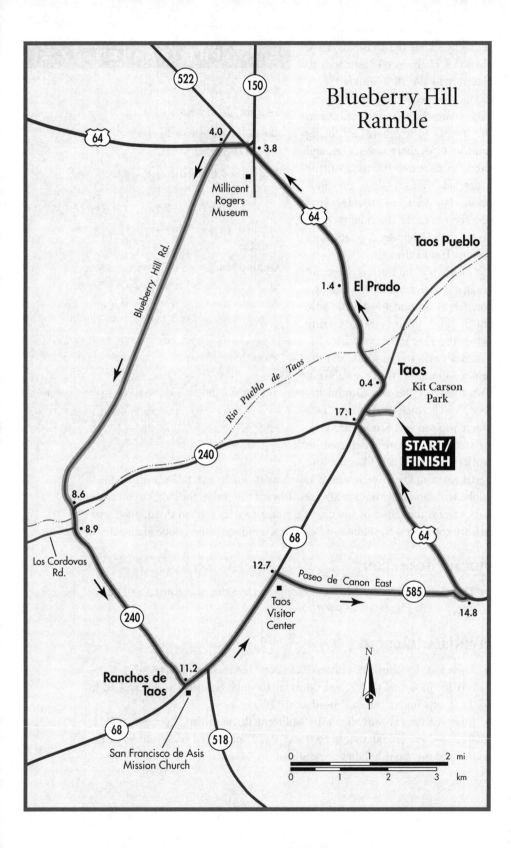

0.0 Head out of Kit Carson Park and turn right on Paseo Del Pueblo Norte, a busy, wide street with a parking lane.

0.4 Camino Del Pueblo, the road to the Taos Pueblo, veers off to the right at the Allsup's Convenience Store.

0.5 Traffic light at Camino De La Placita marks the beginning of a good shoulder.

1.4 Small community of El Prado.

1.6 Look for Orlando's on the left; patio dining and great shrimp burritos. This popular eatery opens at 5:00 P.M. for dinner. *Note:* Be there when the doors open, especially on the weekend.

2.3 Overland Sheepskin Company on the right; the cluster of shops includes a cafe with home cooking. Most of the shoulder is chewed up from here to the next traffic light.

3.5 Millicent Rogers Museum, excellent exhibits of Native American and Hispanic art. Features Rogers's collections of weavings and silver and turquoise jewelry. Turn left on Millicent Rogers Road; the museum is down on the right. Straight on U.S. Highway 64 to continue on the loop.

3.8 Major four-way intersection; several gas stations. Turn left to stay on U.S. Highway 64. New Mexico Route 522 continues straight ahead, and New Mexico Route 150 goes right to Taos Ski Valley.

4.0 Here you have the option to ride out to the Rio Grande Gorge Bridge. To stay on the route, turn left on Blueberry Hill Road (BIA 007); gradual descent, lose the shoulder. Good views of the Taos Valley.

7.4 Pass Blueberry Hill B&B.

8.2 Short (0.4 mile), steep descent to T intersection.

8.6 At the stop sign, turn right on New Mexico Route 240 (Ranchitos Road).

8.9 Cross the Rio Pueblo de Taos and reach another T intersection. This time turn left, staying on New Mexico Route 240 (Lower Ranchitos Road). Los Cordovas Road goes right.

11.2 At the stop sign, junction with New Mexico Route 68 in Rancho de Taos, turn left. The mission church is just across the street from the stop sign.

(continued)

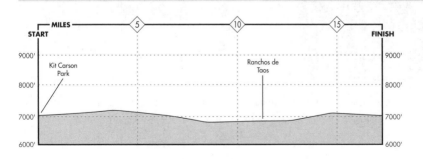

San Francisco de Asis, one of the most painted and photographed churches in the Southwest. You'll pass by it on several of the rides in Taos. (Courtesy of Enchanted Lands Enterprise)

11.5 Gain a good shoulder as New Mexico Route 518 comes in from the right.

12.7 Reach the Taos Visitor Center on the right. Turn right on Paseo De Canon East (New Mexico Route 585) and enjoy a large shoulder.

14.8 Stop sign and junction with U.S. Highway 64 (Kit Carson Road). Turn left; the shoulder disappears.

17.1 Traffic light and junction with New Mexico Route 68. Turn right and go through the light at Civic Plaza Drive.

17.3 Return to Kit Carson Park.

♦ San Francisco de Asis Mission Church, 60 Ranchos Plaza Road, Rancho de Taos, NM 87557; (505) 758–2754 (Monday through Saturday from 9:00 A.M. to 4:00 P.M.).

RESTAURANTS

♦ Orlando's New Mexican Cafe, 1114 Don Juan Valdez Lane, Taos, NM 87571; (505) 751–1450 (on-route).

ACCOMMODATIONS

♦ Taos Reservation Central, P.O. Box 1713, Taos, NM 87571; (800) 821–2437.
♦ Blueberry Hill B&B (www.taosbbhill.com), P.O. Box 881, Taos, NM 87571; (888) 587–0824 (on-route).

BIKE SHOPS

♦ Gearing Up Bicycle Shop, 129 Paseo Del Pueblo Sur, Taos, NM 87571; (505) 751–0365.

REST ROOMS

♦ Mile 0.0: Kit Carson Park (vault toilets).
♦ Mile 3.9: Junction of U.S. Highway 64, New Mexico Route 522, and New Mexico Route 150 (gas stations).
♦ Mile 12.7: Taos Visitor Center.

MAPS

♦ USGS 7.5-minute quads Taos, Los Cordovas, and Rancho de Taos.
♦ Delorme *New Mexico Atlas & Gazetteer,* map 16.

Hondo–Seco Cruise

I f you just arrived in Taos to do the Enchanted Circle (5) or the High Road (13), this moderate loop, which takes you through the countryside outside of Taos, is a good warm-up for those bigger adventures. The north end of this high mountain valley is still very rural and will give you an idea of what the area looked like years ago. You'll pass through two small villages—Arroyo Hondo and Arroyo Seco, hence the ride's name. The small arts community of Arroyo Seco, which is enroute to the Taos Ski Valley, offers shops and galleries, a few places to get something to eat, and a hostel called the Abominable Snowmansion.

This local favorite starts at Kit Carson Park, which provides free parking and a grassy picnic spot shaded by old cottonwoods. The ride first takes you along the beautiful pastoral lands of the Taos Pueblo, nestled at the base of the Taos Mountains, then out toward the Rio Grande and up on a plateau where you can see the top of the 650-foot deep gorge that cuts through the mesa. There are excellent views west of the rounded, isolated dome of San Antonio Mountain.

You'll descend into Arroyo Hondo, known in part for its primitive hot springs along the banks of the Rio Grande. You can get directions from the folks at Herb's Lounge. (You'll have to come back in your vehicle because the road out to the hot springs is dirt.) The road begins to climb toward Arroyo Seco; and while you push the pedals, you can gaze at the Sangre de Cristo Mountains, which include the highest peaks in the state.

You may want to spend some time in the village of Arroyo Seco. The "main street" runs from the Abominable Snowmansion (a hostel) north about a block or so to Abe's Cantina Y Cocina (good breakfast burritos). The tiny downtown

Start: Kit Carson Park in downtown Taos.

Length: 25.1-mile loop.

Terrain: Moderate grades have you gently climbing or descending for most of the ride; one steep 0.5-mile ascent.

Traffic and hazards: Congestion and traffic around the Plaza. The first 10 miles have a good shoulder but highway traffic. (There is a section of shoulder coming out of town that is chewed up but great coming back on the other side.) The back roads to and out of Arroyo Seco have little or no shoulder but light traffic.

Getting there: Travel to the intersection of U.S. Highway 64 and New Mexico Route 68, near the Plaza in downtown Taos. North of this junction, New Mexico Route 68 is called Paseo Del Pueblo Norte. It's the main street through town. Go one block north of the Plaza on Paseo Del Pueblo Norte through the traffic light at Civic Plaza Drive. Go another half block and turn right into Kit Carson Park.

contains galleries like Annabell's and Claire Works, as well as a post office and mercantile. The village is a popular stop on the way to the Taos Ski Valley—in the summer with hikers and bikers and in the winter with skiers. At Casa Vaca and the Taos Cow, you can get ice cream, bagel sandwiches, and fresh baked goods.

There is an unusual place to stay in Arroyo Seco that caters to adventure travelers. The historic Abominable Snowmansion, a hostel located in the old mercantile building, offers an affordable alternative to area accommodations—$16 to $36 with breakfast. In the two-story adobe lodge, you can choose from bunks in a dorm room or get a private room. The three-acre compound also includes tipis, cabins, and tent sites.

The loop through Arroyo Hondo and Arroyo Seco can be connected

A leg of the Hondo–Seco Cruise with the Taos Mountains as a backdrop.

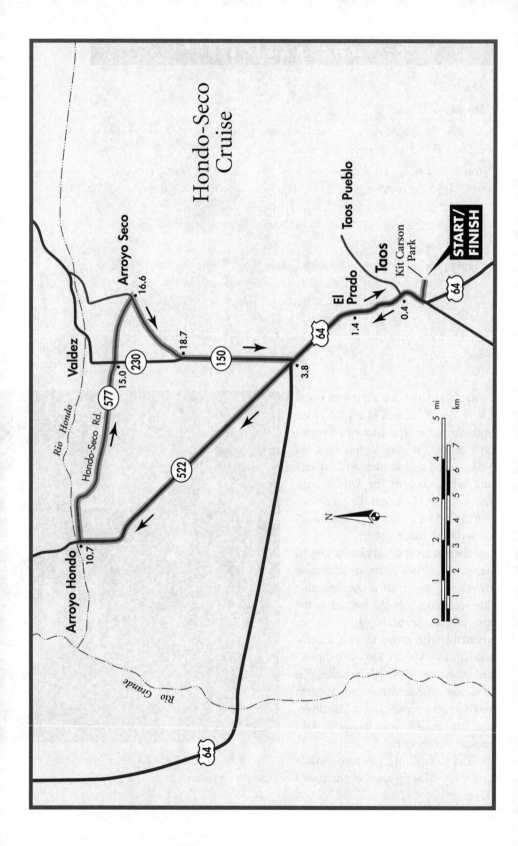

Hondo-Seco Cruise

0.0 Head out of Kit Carson Park, and turn right onto Paseo Del Pueblo Norte, a busy wide street with a parking lane.

0.4 Camino Del Pueblo, the road to the Taos Pueblo, veers off to the right at the Allsup's convenience store.

0.5 Traffic light at Camino De La Placita marks the beginning of a good shoulder.

1.4 Small community of El Prado. Ride alongside the beautiful pastoral lands of the Taos Pueblo.

3.8 Major four-way intersection, several gas stations. Continue straight, which is now New Mexico Route 522 and enjoy a large shoulder. U.S. Highway 64 goes left to the Rio Grande Gorge Bridge, and New Mexico Route 150 goes right to the Taos Ski Valley, your return route.

6.0 Reach a plateau, one of the high points of the loop. Ride a few flat miles before descending to Arroyo Hondo.

10.7 Herb's Lounge on the left in Arroyo Hondo, which includes a convenience store with public rest rooms. Turn right, before crossing the Rio Hondo, onto Hondo-Seco Road (New Mexico Route 577). The street sign reads B-143. This quiet back road has almost no traffic.

11.8 Take a sharp curve to the right and pass a church before beginning the steepest climb on the ride. The road turns to smooth blacktop with no center line.

12.3 The top of the climb and great views of the Sangre de Cristo Mountains.

15.0 At the four-way stop, continue straight ahead, crossing New Mexico Route 230.

16.6 Reach Arroyo Seco and the junction with New Mexico Route 150. The Abominable Snowmansion is on the corner on the right. Turn left to visit the village, and turn right to continue back to Taos.

18.7 New Mexico Route 230 heads off to the right. You may encounter moderate traffic for the next 2 miles (little or no shoulder).

21.3 Return to the major four-way intersection, the end of New Mexico Route 150. Turn left and retrace your route into town. The shoulder is better in this direction.

25.1 Return to Kit Carson Park.

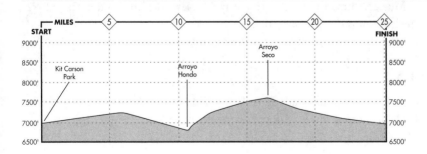

with two other tours in the book that start near the Plaza—Blueberry Hill Ramble (6) and Taos Ski Valley Challenge (8), which were suggested in part by the folks at Gearing Up Bicycle Shop as some of the popular day rides in and around Taos. There are several possible combinations; all three rides start at Kit Carson Park and share the first 3.9 miles.

LOCAL INFORMATION

♦ Taos County Chamber of Commerce (www.taoschamber.com), P.O. Drawer 1, Taos, NM 87571; (800) 732–8267.

EVENTS/ATTRACTIONS

You pass the Taos Pueblo and Millicent Rogers Museum in the first few miles of the ride. For information, see the Blueberry Hill Ramble. Also, for the hot springs in Arroyo Hondo, ask at Herb's for directions.

RESTAURANTS

♦ Abe's Cantina Y Cocina, Highway 150, Arroyo Seco, NM 87515; (505) 776–8643.
♦ Casa Vaca and the Taos Cow, P.O. 1124, El Prado, NM 87529; (505) 776–5640 (7:00 A.M. to 6:00 P.M. daily).

ACCOMMODATIONS

♦ Taos Reservation Central, P.O. Box 1713, Taos, NM 87571; (800) 821–2437.
♦ Abominable Snowmansion (www.taoswebb.com/hotel/snowmansion), 476 State Road 150, Arroyo Seco, NM 87515; (505) 776–8298.

BIKE SHOPS

♦ Gearing Up Bicycle Shop, 129 Paseo Del Pueblo Sur, Taos, NM 87571; 505-751-0365.

REST ROOMS

♦ Mile 0.0: Kit Carson Park (vault toilets).
♦ Mile 3.9: Junction of U.S. Highway 64, New Mexico Route 522, and New Mexico Route 150 (gas stations).
♦ Mile 10.7: Herb's Lounge (rest rooms in convenience store).

MAPS

♦ USGS 7.5-minute quads Taos, Arroyo Hondo, and Arroyo Seco.
♦ Delorme *New Mexico Atlas & Gazetteer*, map 16.

Taos Ski Valley Challenge

I f you love hill climbing and creekside cycling in beautiful wooded scenery, then head up the road that leads to the Taos Ski Valley. It isn't quite as steep as the ascents to the ski areas in Santa Fe or at Sandia Peak but should satisfy even the strongest cyclist. The end of the road, and the turnaround point for the ride, brings you to the Taos Ski Valley, a European-style village that is bustling with activity year-round. This hill climb is a good workout, despite the moderate length; and after the huffing and puffing, you get to fly back down, stopping for ice cream at the well-known Taos Cow in Arroyo Seco.

In the winter Taos Ski Valley has a famous ski school and a reputation with ski lovers for challenging terrain. The rest of the year, other outdoor enthusiasts, including horseback riders, mountain bikers, hikers, and, of course, road cyclists, come out to play in this alpine forest. On a hot summer day it may reach seventy-five degrees! This is definitely a retreat from the heat.

The first few miles offer a good warmup on straight roads with a gentle grade. Then the route curves through the quaint village of Arroyo Seco and travels the edge of Valdez Valley. The climbing begins as you enter Carson National Forest. In Hondo Canyon, the road parallels the Rio Hondo, and rocky outcroppings dot the steep, forested hillsides. Several recreation pullouts along the rushing mountain stream give you a chance to take a break. The facilities include picnic tables, campsites, and pit toilets (no water).

A hundred years ago this road led to what was then called Twinning Valley, where a gold and copper mining camp was located. It took a full day along the rough, rutted road to get into town. In the 1950s Ernie Blake discovered the

Start: Kit Carson Park in downtown Taos.

Length: 35.2 miles round-trip.

Terrain: Slight upgrade at the start that turns into continual, moderate climbing with more than 2,000 feet of climbing and miles of downhill on the way back.

Traffic and hazards: Some congestion for the first mile. The shoulder coming out of town is chewed up but is great coming back on the other side. Scarcely any shoulder on the road to the ski area where there is some recreational traffic.

Getting there: Travel to the intersection of U.S. Highway 64 and New Mexico Route 68, near the Plaza in downtown Taos. North of this junction, New Mexico Route 68 is called Paseo Del Pueblo Norte. It's the main street through town. Go one block north of the Plaza on Paseo Del Pueblo Norte through the traffic light at Civic Plaza Drive. Go another half block and turn right into Kit Carson Park.

valley and began construction on what has become Taos Ski Valley. Today more than a hundred people live in the village, which boasts dozens of restaurants, lodges, and shops. Trails from the village lead to the highest peaks in the state, including the highest, Wheeler Peak (elevation 13,161 feet).

The list of summer events in the village is long. The ski area offers scenic chairlift rides above Al's Run from late June through early September (10:00 A.M. to 4:00 P.M. on Thursday through Sunday). The students at the Taos School of Music perform informal concerts while rehearsing every day at Hotel St. Bernard. There are barn dances, star-watching parties, wine tastings, and guided nature walks on the schedule. Big celebrations on Labor Day and Oktoberfest in mid-September may not be the best times to ride up the ski road.

I recommend lunch at Tim's Stray Dog Cantina at the base of the ski area. You'll find casual dining and an outdoor deck. They have a reputation for great New Mexican fare, in addition to burgers, sandwiches, and soups. Try the green chile cheeseburger or shrimp quesadillas. Another idea is to get your exercise out of the way and stop for a break on the way back through Arroyo Seco, home of the Taos Cow. This local company makes all-natural ice cream in a variety of yummy flavors like Pinon Carmel. You may have already tried some in one of the 50 locations around the state where it's sold and served. At the ice cream shop, you can get scoops, pints, sundaes, floats, the works (7:00 A.M. to 6:00 P.M. daily)!

The Taos Ski Valley Road can be connected with two other loops in the book that start near the Plaza—Blueberry Hill Ramble (6) and Hondo-Seco Cruise (7). These short tours were suggested in part by the folks at Gearing Up Bicycle Shop as some of the popular day rides in and around Taos. There are several possible combinations; all three rides start at Kit Carson Park and share the first 3.9 miles.

LOCAL INFORMATION

♦ Ski Valley Visitor & Convention Bureau (www.TaosSkiValley.com), P.O. Box 91, Taos Ski Valley, NM 87525; (800) 992–7669.

♦ Carson National Forest, Questa Ranger District, P.O. Box 110, Questa, NM 87556; (505) 586–0520.

EVENTS/ATTRACTIONS

♦ Taos Ski & Boot, P.O. Box, Taos Ski Valley, NM 87525; (505) 776–2291 (for chairlift tickets; cost $6.00).

RESTAURANTS

♦ Tim's Stray Dog Cantina, 105 Sutton Place, Taos Ski Valley, NM 87525; (505) 776–8806 (11:00 A.M. to 9:00 P.M. daily in the summer; closed mid-April through May).

ACCOMMODATIONS

Taos Ski Valley has just about every type of accommodation—lodges, inns, B&Bs, condos, and vacation rentals. Go to www.taosskivalley.com and click on "Lodging/Travel."

Cyclists on the Taos Plateau. (Photo courtesy of Enchanted Lands Enterprise)

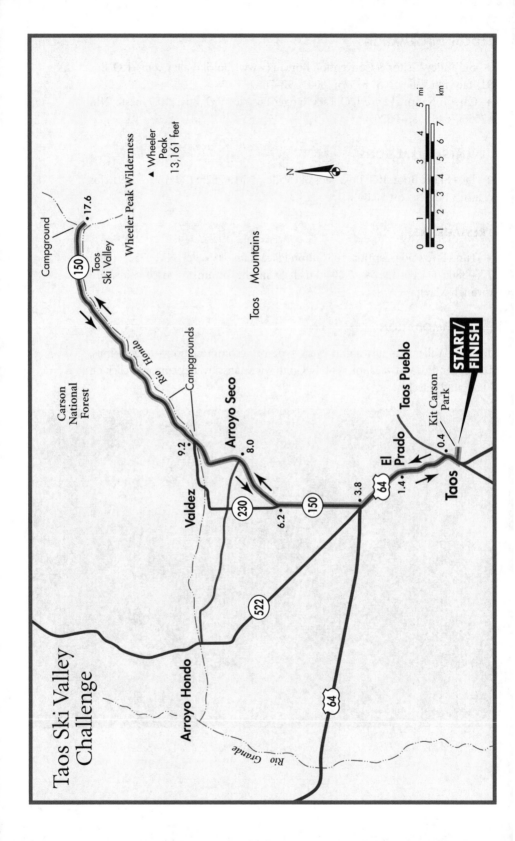

Taos Ski Valley
Challenge

0.0 Head out of Kit Carson Park and turn right onto Paseo Del Pueblo Norte, a busy wide street with a parking lane.

0.4 Camino Del Pueblo, the road to the Taos Pueblo, veers off to the right at the Allsup's convenience store.

0.5 Traffic light at Camino De La Placita marks the beginning of a good shoulder.

1.4 Small community of El Prado. Ride alongside the beautiful pastoral lands of the Taos Pueblo.

3.8 Major four-way intersection, several gas stations. Turn right on New Mexico Route 150, Taos Valley Ski Road. New Mexico Route 522 continues straight ahead, and New Mexico Route 64 goes left to the Rio Grande Gorge Bridge.

6.2 New Mexico Route 230 branches off to the left; continue on New Mexico Route 150 as the road begins to twist and turn.

8.0 Enter Arroyo Seco; Abominable Snowmansion Hostel on the left. The short strip through the village is lined with shops and galleries. You'll leave Arroyo Seco as the road takes a sharp left curve.

9.2 First good glimpse of the mouth of Hondo Canyon. New Mexico Route 150 takes a sharp right; Rim Road heads left. Stay with New Mexico Route 150.

10.1 Junction with the other end of New Mexico Route 230 on the left; continue straight. Enter Carson National Forest, and begin cycling alongside the Rio Hondo.

11.0 Lower Hondo Campground on the right.

11.6 Cuchillo del Medio Campground on the right.

12.0 Cuchillo Campground on the right.

14.0 Reach a string of lodging accommodations along the road.

15.9 A sign marks the elevation at 9,200 feet.

17.0 A sign welcomes you to Taos Ski Valley!

17.6 Reach the top of the ski area parking lot and the center of the village. (Twinning Campground is near the trailhead for Wheeler Peak.)

35.2 Retrace your route down the mountain to Kit Carson Park.

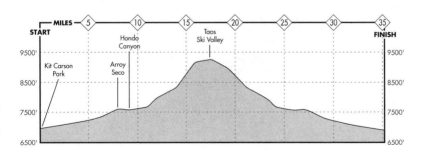

BIKE SHOPS

◆ Gearing Up Bicycle Shop, 129 Paseo Del Pueblo Sur, Taos, NM 87571; (505) 751–0365.

REST ROOMS

◆ Mile 0.0: Kit Carson Park.
◆ Mile 3.8: Junction of U.S. Highway 64, NM 522, and NM 150 (gas stations).
◆ Mile 11.0: Lower Hondo Campground with outhouses. (In the next mile, there are two other recreation sites with outhouses.)
◆ Mile 17.6: Taos Ski Valley.

MAPS

◆ USGS 7.5-minute quads Taos, Arroyo Seco, and Wheeler Peak.
◆ Delorme *New Mexico Atlas & Gazetteer,* map 16.

Dixon–Penasco Challenge

T he credit for this ride goes to the Santa Fe Road Riders. It's one of their favorites. The loop typifies northern New Mexico—old Spanish villages, fertile valleys, and little development. Cottonwoods line the riverbeds, and apple orchards dot the landscape. You'll descend along the Rio Grande and climb into the Sangre de Cristo Mountains. There's nothing like riverside riding and long forested climbs. Some off-the-bike highlights include the Rio Grande Gorge Visitor Center, Casa de Piedra Gallery, and Picuris Pueblo.

I didn't consider including this loop until I got an e-mail about an upcoming ride from the Santa Fe Road Riders. I had heard the traffic was no fun on New Mexico Route 68, but Tom Berg said, "The traffic is no problem, especially early on a Sunday morning." That's all I needed to hear because I knew the road between Dixon and Penasco had all the elements of a great ride. (*Note:* You can sign up to get weekly e-mail announcements about the club's rides by going to www.clubs.yahoo.com/clubs/sfroadriders; regular rides on Tuesday evenings and Sunday mornings.)

You'll begin heading southwest out of Taos along a sagebrush-covered mesa. To the west the Rio Grande cuts a 650-foot deep gorge through the plateau, and two rest stops on the route provide picnic tables and incredible views. In Pilar, stop and visit the Rio Grande Gorge Visitor Center, which is open daily in the summer and has a great book selection. Across the street you can get burritos, sandwiches, baked goods, and snacks at the Pilar Yacht Club. The paved New Mexico Route 570 (turn right in Pilar; off-route) follows the Rio Grande upstream and leads to Orilla Verde Recreation Area. There are five

Start: Taos Visitor Center, 2 miles south of downtown.

Length: 57-mile loop.

Terrain: Several long climbs, but long descents too. The biggest challenges are Dixon to Penasco and U.S. Hill.

Traffic and hazards: Some truck traffic on New Mexico Route 68 and a short stretch with a rough shoulder. Otherwise back roads with little shoulder but light traffic.

Getting there: Travel to the intersection of U.S. Highway 64 and New Mexico Route 68 near the Plaza in downtown Taos. The Taos Visitor Center is about 2 miles south at the junction with New Mexico Route 585 (Paseo De Canon East). If you are coming into town from the south on New Mexico Route 68, the Taos Visitor Center will be on your right at the first traffic light.

campgrounds along the river, as well as day-use areas for picnicking.

The loop continues on New Mexico Route 68 south through a narrow canyon and parallels the stretch of river called the Race Course, a popular entry-level run offered by area whitewater rafting companies. The season is from mid-April through mid-October, and several pullouts provide an opportunity to watch the action.

The small village of Dixon, located in the Embudo Valley just east of where the Rio Embudo flows into the Rio Grande, is home to a large variety of artisans and known for its studio tour held every fall, which would be a great time to do this ride. The whole town gets involved in the weekend event. Casa de Piedra Gallery is a cooperative where you can learn more about the artists in northern New Mexico. The facility includes a store selling gifts, antiques, and gourmet food products.

After the climb out of Dixon, you'll pass through the Picuris Indian Reservation. Picuris is the smallest of the pueblo tribes in New Mexico. It is also the most physically isolated. A beautiful 200-year-old church stands in the center of the pueblo, and the tribe operates a restaurant and museum.

The rest of the ride is the northern "third" of the High Road to Taos Classic, one of the most popular scenic drives in the state. Don't worry; the traffic is usually light as you climb into Carson National Forest and tackle the locally known U.S. Hill (elevation 8,540 feet). You will have earned the 13-mile descent back into Taos.

New Mexico Touring Society

NMTS, a recreational cycling club based in Albuquerque and affiliated with the League of American Bicyclists, encourages cyclists of all ages and abilities, road and mountain bikers alike. The group has monthly meetings and produces a newsletter called *The Freewheel*. Members lead a variety of weekly rides around Albuquerque. You can find out what is scheduled by logging on to their Web site. You can also participate in multiday trips around the state like the club's Gila Inner Loop Bike Tour or Taos Enchanted Circle Tour. These weekend events follow some of the most scenic byways in New Mexico. For more information, contact MNTS (www.swcp.com/~russells/nmts), P.O. Box 1261, Albuquerque, NM 87128; (505) 237–9700.

LOCAL INFORMATION

◆ Taos County Chamber of Commerce (www.taoschamber.com), P.O. Drawer 1, Taos, NM 87571; (800) 732–8267.

EVENTS/ATTRACTIONS

◆ Casa de Piedra Gallery, P.O. Box 432, Dixon, NM 87527; (505) 579–4111 (10:00 A.M. to 5:00 P.M.; closed Mondays).
◆ Picuris Pueblo, P.O. Box 127, Penasco, NM 87553; (505) 587–2519 (8:00 A.M. to 5:00 P.M. daily).

RESTAURANTS

◆ Pilar Yacht Club & Cafe, Highways 68 and 570, Embudo, NM 87531; (505) 758–9072.

ACCOMMODATIONS

◆ Taos Reservation Central, P.O. Box 1713, Taos, NM 87571; (800) 821–2437.
◆ Budget Host Inn, 1798 Paseo Del Pueblo Sur, Taos, NM 87557; (800) 323–6009 (reasonably priced and near the Taos Visitor Center).
◆ Orilla Verde Recreation Area, BLM/Taos Field Office, 226 Cruz Alta Road, Taos, NM 87571; (505) 758–8851.

BIKE SHOPS

◆ Gearing Up Bicycle Shop, 129 Paseo Del Pueblo Sur, Taos, NM 87571; (505) 751–0365.

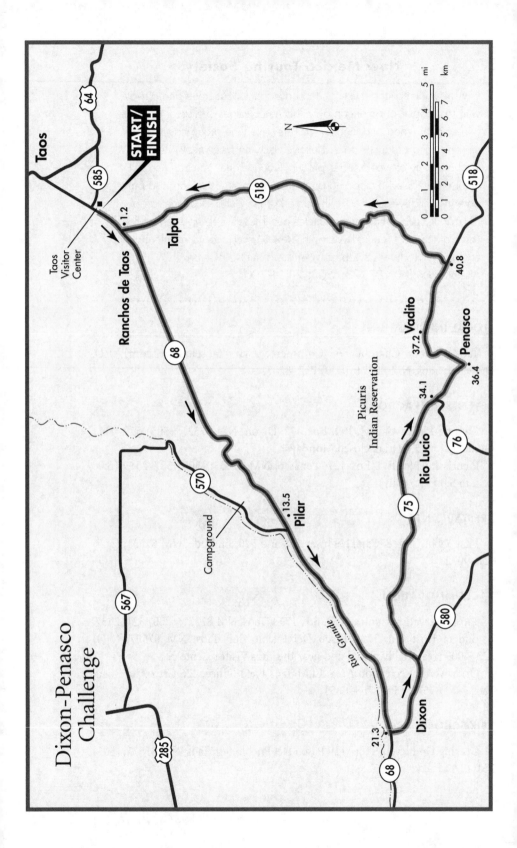

0.0 Leave the Taos Visitor Center and head south on New Mexico Route 68. Start with a good shoulder.

1.2 New Mexico Route 518 on the left-your return route; continue straight.

1.6 Look on the left for the San Francisco de Asis Mission, the most painted and photographed adobe church in the Southwest. For the next few miles, the shoulder is tiny or nonexistent.

3.2 Larger shoulder but very rough surface.

9.0 Sheltered picnic tables on the left; good views back across the Taos Valley and of the Rio Grande Gorge.

10.2 Another area with picnic tables; lose the shoulder for a while.

13.5 Rio Grande Gorge Visitor Center on the left and junction with New Mexico Route 570 in Pilar on the right. As you ride alongside the river, you'll have a small shoulder. Several river access points provide a place to pull over and get a better look.

14.4 Rim Overlook has picnic tables on the right.

19.0 Ride through the small community of Rinconado, where you may find a roadside fruit stand.

21.3 Turn left on New Mexico Route 75, cross the Rio Embudo, and head for Dixon.

22.5 Pass the library, Atencio's (small grocery), and Casa de Piedra Gallery on the left as you ride through Dixon. Begin climbing as you leave town. Watch for a glimpse of the Truchas Peaks.

24.3 Pass La Chiripada Winery on the left.

30.5 High point on this stretch—descend.

32.1 Turn for Picuris Pueblo on the left. Cross the Rio Pueblo and ride through the town of Rio Lucio, where a good shoulder exists.

32.8 Conoco station on the left.

34.1 New Mexico Route 76, the High Road, comes in on the right; continue straight and cycle through Penasco. Enjoy an incredibly smooth section of road for 6.5 miles.

(continued)

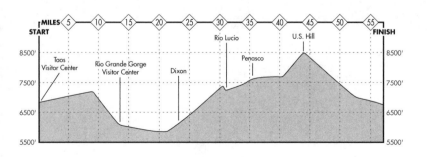

34.9 A-1 Auto on the right (sodas and rest room).

35.4 Penasco Valley Food Store, ice cream and coffee, on the right.

35.9 Camino Real Ranger Station (weekdays 8:00 a.m. to 4:30 p.m.) on the left.

37.2 Vadito, where the road levels out for a few miles along the Rio Del Pueblo.

40.8 T intersection with New Mexico Route 518; turn left and begin climbing U.S. Hill.

44.0 The top! Pass a forest service outhouse on the right, then an overlook with views north and east. Descend!

52.7 Leave Carson National Forest and the ponderosas; view the Taos Valley as you head into Talpa.

55.8 T intersection with New Mexico Route 68 at Rancho de Taos; turn right.

57.0 Return to the Taos Visitor Center.

REST ROOMS

- Mile 0.0: Taos Visitor Center.
- Mile 13.5: Rio Grande Gorge Visitor Center.
- Mile 34.9: A-1 Auto, one of several gas stations in Penasco.
- Mile 44.0: Forest service outhouse atop U.S. Hill.

MAPS

- USGS 7.5-minute quads Taos, Ranchos De Taos, Taos SW, Carson, Trampas, Velarde, Penasco, and Tres Ritos.
- Delorme *New Mexico Atlas & Gazetteer,* map 16.

Bandelier Cruise

*L*os Alamos County sits atop fingerlike mesas cut by steep canyons—above the Rio Grande and at the base of the Jemez Mountains. While there are few roads up on the mesas and limited riding, the county boasts one of the best loops in the state, which circles around the Los Alamos National Laboratory (LANL). On any given summer weekend, you'll see a dozen-plus people out riding the roads around LANL. For many cyclists on their lunch break, the question is whether to do the Big Loop or use Pajarito Road and ride one of the two smaller loops. Bruce Letellier, member of the club that organizes a race on the loop, believes this is "one of the most unique and scenic places you can ever choose to ride." For much of the loop, you will be traveling in or alongside Santa Fe National Forest. The route has remote feel with incredible views.

The Roadrunners Cycling Club in Los Alamos organizes one of New Mexico's premier road races every summer—the Tour de Los Alamos, which uses the Bandelier Cruise as well as part of the Jemez Mountain Trail. The event, which has been ongoing for thirty years, is one of the oldest continuously running races in the country. It is sanctioned by the American Cycling Association and is run as two separate races—not a stage race.

There is a citizens' ride on Sunday that uses the loop. The start is in Los Alamos. Top finishers' times for one lap usually range between 1:21 and 1:40. The Roadrunners Cycling Club, which started as an informal group interested in promoting cycling in the area, now exists mainly to organize this race. (Velo

Ancho Canyon on the Bandelier Cruise.

del Norte out of Santa Fe has co-sponsored the event for the last few years.)

The Bandelier Cruise (not the race) starts at Overlook Park in White Rock. This sports complex has water, rest rooms, and a shaded picnic table. Before starting on the loop, ride 0.3 mile farther out Overlook Road to the amazing vista overlooking the Rio Grande. In White Rock on New Mexico Route 4, you will find a couple gas stations, a grocery store, a visitor center, and a shopping center with McDonalds and Pizza Hut.

The climbing starts on East Jemez Road, or the Truck Route, as you make your way up to Los Alamos. You can turn right on Diamond Drive, then right on Trinity Drive, for a side trip to downtown Los Alamos. Continuing on the loop takes you away from town where you can do another side trip to Pajarito Mountain Ski Area. Back on New Mexico Route 501, the road is lined with charred ponderosa pine, a reminder of the Cerro Grande fire in 2000. After passing Bandelier National Monument, you'll reach Ancho Canyon. Letellier's favorite part of the ride is descending into the canyon before the hairpin turn.

To do a shorter loop, you can use Pajarito Road, which cuts through LANL and is open to the public. You pick it up on the west end, just west of Diamond Drive, or on the east end, just west of White Rock (see map). There are two options. If you use Pajarito Road with the Truck Route, the loop will be about 20 miles; with the Bandelier section of New Mexico Route 4, the loop will be about 25 miles. If you have paid the vehicle entrance fee to Bandelier (good for seven days), you can park/start your ride at Tsankawi Ruins (mile 4), Ponderosa Picnic Area (mile 14.5), or Bandelier (mile 20.4) and skip the leg to Overlook Park.

If you've never visited Los Alamos, take the detour at mile 9.9 to find out more about what took place in the 1940s in the Secret City. At the Bradbury Science Museum, you can study up on the Manhattan Project, the mission to develop the first atomic bomb. A team of scientists was assembled at a remote

THE BASICS

Start: Overlook Park in White Rock, a bedroom community of Los Alamos.

Length: 28.8-mile loop.

Terrain: Long climbs and descents, plus some fun rollers.

Traffic and hazards: There are few shoulders on this route, but traffic is usually light.

Getting there: From the intersection of U.S. Highway 285/84 and New Mexico Route 502 in Pojoaque, travel west on New Mexico Route 502 toward Los Alamos for about 12 miles. At the Y, take the right fork, following New Mexico Route 4 west, and continue 4.5 miles to White Rock. At the first traffic light, turn left on Rover Boulevard, and take the next left onto Meadow Lane. Drive 0.8 mile and turn left on Overlook Road. You'll reach parking on the right at Overlook Park after another 0.3 mile.

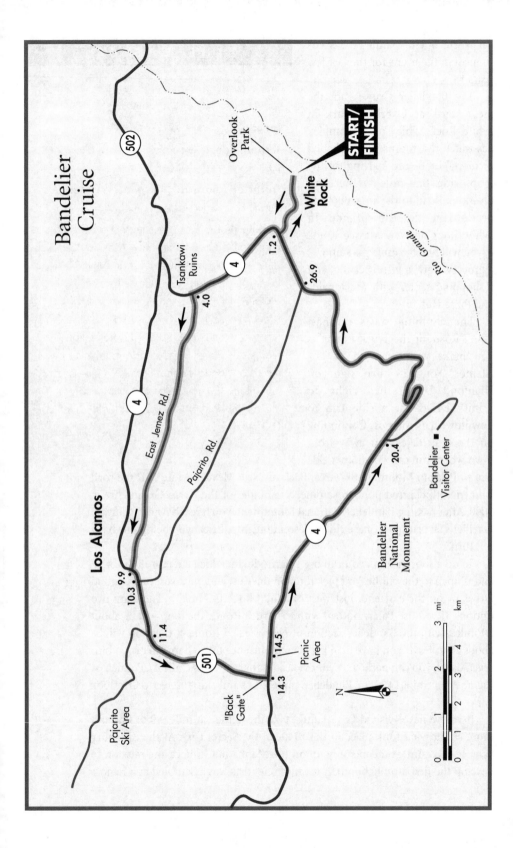

Bandelier Cruise

Los Alamos

Pajarito Ski Area

502

Tsankawi Ruins

4

East Jemez Rd.

Pajarito Rd.

4

9.9
10.3

11.4

501

4.0

4

1.2

26.9

20.4

Bandelier
Visitor Center

Bandelier
National
Monument

"Back Gate"

14.3

14.5
Picnic
Area

Overlook
Park

White
Rock

START/
FINISH

Rio Grande

N

0   1   2   3 mi

0   1   2   3   4 km

0.0 After a trip to the Rio Grande overlook, cycle out Overlook Road the way you drove in.

0.3 Turn right on Meadow Lane.

1.1 Turn right on Rover Boulevard.

1.2 Reach the traffic light at New Mexico Route 4 and turn right.

4.0 Reach a traffic light and turn left on East Jemez Road (also referred to as the Truck Route). The climbing begins-long and gradual! There is a shoulder on parts of this stretch. (*Note:* The parking at Tsankawi Ruins is just past the light on New Mexico Route 4.)

9.9 Road that veers to the right leads to Los Alamos; continue straight.

10.0 Reach the traffic light at Diamond Drive and continue straight, cycling on what is now New Mexico Route 501, or West Jemez Road. A small shoulder comes and goes. There are several cross streets with traffic lights in the next half mile. Continue climbing for 1.5 miles.

10.3 Pajarito Road on left creates cuts through to New Mexico Route 4 north of White Rock for a shorter loop.

11.4 Pass the road to Pajarito Mountain Ski Area on the right; enjoy rollers for the next 3 miles. (If you want some extra climbing, turn right on Camp May Road and ascend about 1,400 feet in 4 miles to the ski area.)

14.3 Turn left on New Mexico Route 4 at what locals call the Back Gate of LANL.

14.5 Ponderosa Picnic Area on the right (vault toilet and water); begin a gradual descent toward Bandelier.

20.4 Entrance to Bandelier National Monument on the right.

21.6 Steep descent into Ancho Canyon—one of the coolest spots on the ride. Climb out!

26.9 Traffic light at Pajarito Road, the east end of the road that creates the two shorter loops.

27.6 Return to White Rock; at the traffic light, turn right on Rover Boulevard.

27.7 Take the first left onto Meadow Lane.

28.5 Turn left on Overlook Road.

28.8 Reach Overlook Park.

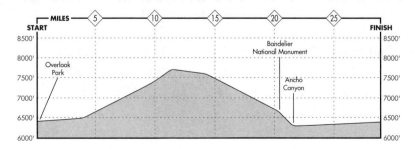

and nearly inaccessible ranch school here in 1943 for this top-secret project that would help bring an end to World War II. The city wasn't open to the public until 1957, and the scientific research that continues today is what we call LANL, a world-renowned institution that employs about 10,000 people.

The main attraction on the route is the striking cliff dwellings of the Anasazi, "the Ancient Ones." Until the 1500s the largest settlement of these peaceful basketmakers was situated in Frijoles Canyon, now part of Bandelier National Monument. A 3-mile paved road leads down to the visitor center (elevation 6,066 feet) in the base of the canyon. (*Note:* There are bike racks in front of the building.) You can learn about Swiss anthropologist Adolph Bandelier who discovered the ruins in the 1880s and hike to view what remain of multistory mud houses, ceremonial kivas, and intricate caves built into sheer cliffs. Most of the park's 33,000 acres are wilderness, and there is an extensive network of hiking trails, one of which leads to a beautiful waterfall. The ninety-four-site Juniper Campground sits at the top of Frijoles Mesa. The first-come, first-served developed sites include water and rest rooms only. For about $3.00, campers can shower in Los Alamos at the YMCA (505–662–3100) or Larry R. Walkup Aquatic Center (505–662–7665).

LOCAL INFORMATION

♦ White Rock Tourist Information Center, 125 State Road 4, White Rock, NM 87544; (505) 672–3183 (open daily from 9:00 A.M. to 4:00 P.M.).
♦ Los Alamos Chamber of Commerce and Visitor Center, 109 Central Park Square, Los Alamos, NM 87544; (505) 662–8105 (open Monday through Saturday from 9:00 A.M. to 4:00 P.M. and Sunday from 9:00 A.M. to 3:00 P.M.).
♦ Area information at www.visit.losalamos.com.

EVENTS/ATTRACTIONS

♦ Tour de Los Alamos, Roadrunners Cycling Club (tourdela.home. mindspring.com), P.O. Box 1261, Los Alamos, NM 87544; (505) 672–1927.
♦ Bradbury Science Museum, Mailstop C330, LANL, Los Alamos, NM 87544; (505) 667–4444 (free; open Tuesday through Friday from 9:00 A.M. to 5:00 P.M. and Saturday through Monday from 1:00 to 5:00 P.M.).
♦ Bandelier National Monument (www.nps.gov/band), HCR 1, Box 1, Suite 15, Los Alamos, NM 87544; (505) 672–0343 ($5.00 per cyclist/$10.00 per vehicle for seven days; open in summer from dawn to dusk).

RESTAURANTS

♦ Katherine's Fine Dining, 121 Longview Drive, White Rock, NM 87544; (505) 672–9661 (Tuesday through Friday 11:30 A.M. to 2:30 P.M. and Tuesday to Saturday 5:30 to 9:30 P.M.).

◆ Central Avenue Grill, 1789 Central Avenue, Los Alamos, NM 87544; (505) 662–2005 (Monday through Saturday 11:00 A.M. to 8:00 P.M. and Sunday 11:00 A.M. to 3:00 P.M.; stone-fired pizza and a large selection of microbrews).
◆ Hill Diner, 1315 Trinity Drive, Los Alamos, NM 87544; (505) 662–9745 (daily 11:00 A.M. to 8:00 P.M.; old-fashioned diner food).

ACCOMMODATIONS

◆ Bandelier Inn, 132 State Road 4, Los Alamos, NM 87544; (800) 321–3923 (in White Rock).
◆ Juniper Campground at Bandelier National Monument has sites for $10, and there are several hotel/motel chains and B&Bs in Los Alamos.

BIKE SHOPS

◆ D.O.M.E. (www.domemountainshop.com), 3801-A Arkansas Avenue, Los Alamos, NM 87544; (505) 661–3663.

REST ROOMS

◆ Mile 0.0: Overlook Park.
◆ Mile 9.9: Detour into downtown Los Alamos; gas stations, fast food, and shopping centers.
◆ Mile 14.5: Ponderosa Picnic Area (vault toilet).

MAPS

◆ USGS 7.5-minute quads Frijoles, White Rock, and Guaje Mountain.
◆ Delorme *New Mexico Atlas & Gazetteer,* map 23.

Jemez Mountain Trail Challenge

The Jemez Mountain Trail has it all—history, culture, recreation, and outstanding scenery. This national scenic byway is known as one of the most spectacular drives in the state—and it's even better on a bike. Along the way you can picnic, swim, sightsee, and visit some ancient ruins. The final destination—a soak in the healing waters at Jemez Springs Bath House. The route cuts through the Jemez Mountains, a range where the earth is still warm. The mountains and canyons were formed by volcanic explosions millions of years ago. There are waterfalls, hot springs, unusual geologic formations, a huge caldera, and more. You can plan your bike trip as a short out-and-back between recreation sites, as an all-day adventure with lunch in Jemez Springs, or as a leisurely overnighter.

The Jemez Mountain Trail National Scenic Byway incorporates 163 miles along New Mexico Route 4, New Mexico Route 126, and New Mexico Route 44, and this 26.5-mile bike ride is in the heart of it. For the entire ride you will be surrounded by national forest, 20 miles of which is designated as the Jemez Recreation Area. There are dozens of sites popular with hikers, campers, fishermen, rock climbers, mountain bikers, and cross-country skiers. You can stop and picnic at several spots along the road and overnight at one of two forest service campgrounds located about halfway to Jemez Springs.

One of the best-known landmarks along New Mexico Route 4, and first of this ride, is the Valle Grande, a large collapsed volcano. From the roadside you can see the vast open valley stretching 15 miles across, a good place to spot herds of elk. The forest, peaks, meadows, and rivers of the area are now part of the Valles Caldera National Preserve, nearly 90,000 acres of land acquired in the summer of 2000. A board of trustees is currently in the process of designing a management plan that will hopefully include recreational access. A number of limited tours have been offered, but there is no public access to the preserve at the time of this writing.

Of the many interesting geologic formations along New Mexico Route 4, Battleship Rock and Soda Dam definitely stand out. Battleship Rock looks like the prow of a ship and marks the beginning of the Jemez River, where the East Fork of the Jemez joins San Antonio Creek. Soda Dam was formed over thousands of years from the mineral deposits of an underground hot springs. A 15-foot waterfall is created as the Jemez River flows through a hole in the dam, and the swimming hole at the base is a popular spot for cooling off.

At Jemez State Monument you can visit what remains of an ancient Indian village and a seventeenth-century Spanish mission. The excavated adobe ruins are 400–600 years old. Learn about the history of the Spanish revolt at the visitor center, and walk the self-guided interpretive trail. There is also a large picnic area at the monument.

The tiny village of Jemez Springs, which is famous for its historic bathhouse, is home to about 400 residents. A dozen or so galleries and several good restaurants line the main road through town. There are a handful of lodging choices, including B&B, cabins, cottages, and inns that range from $40 to $180. With only about 50 rooms, reservations are definitely recommended if you decide to do an overnighter.

The reason we rode? Soaking at the Jemez Springs Bath House! This state historic building (built in the 1870s) is one of the oldest structures in the area. A small outdoor gazebo encircles the famous spring that erupted as a geyser in

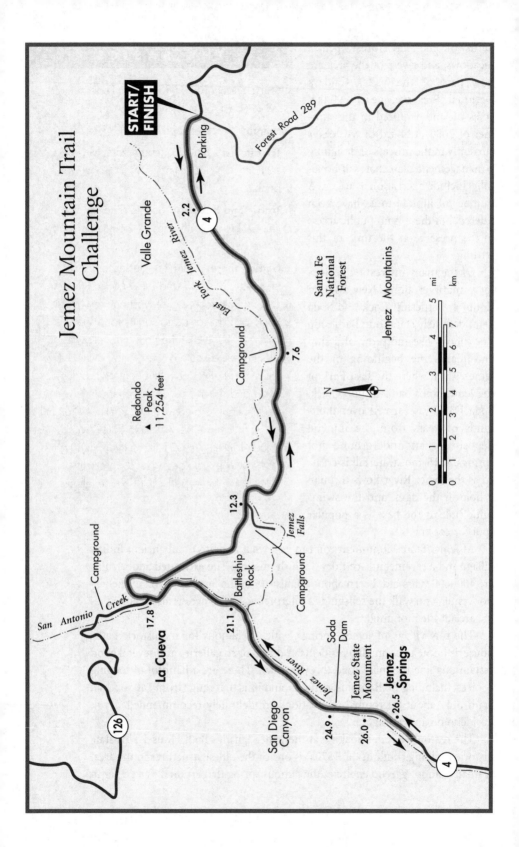

Jemez Mountain Trail Challenge

START/FINISH

Parking

Forest Road 289

4

2.2

Valle Grande

East Fork Jemez River

Campground

7.6

Santa Fe National Forest

Jemez Mountains

Redondo Peak
11,254 feet

N

12.3

Jemez Falls

Campground

Battleship Rock

Campground

San Antonio Creek

La Cueva

17.8

21.1

Soda Dam

Jemez State Monument

Jemez Springs

24.9

26.0

26.5

San Diego Canyon

Jemez River

126

4

mi
0   1   2   3   4   5
km
0   1   2   3   4   5   6   7

0.0 From the parking lot, head west on New Mexico Route 4.

0.9 Gain a small shoulder and descend.

2.2 Reach the Valle Grande. Pull over to read the information board and take in the view. You'll have level riding along the caldera for 3 miles.

5.4 Enter the Jemez Recreation Area.

7.2 Las Conchas Fishing Access on the right (vault toilet; day-use $4.00).

7.6 Reach the recreation area along the East Fork of the Jemez. Hikers, fishermen, mountain bikers, and rock climbers play here. You may see climbers on the roadside Cattle Call Wall. A trail leads from the small parking area along the shaded creek. Climb a short hill and begin a long descent.

11.4 Parking on the right for the East Fork Trail. View Redondo Peak (elevation 11, 254 feet), one of the highest peaks in the area.

11.9 Another parking area on the right. Cross the East Fork and ascend a short hill.

12.3 The paved road on the left leads 1.3 miles to a picnic area with a water pump, vault toilets, tables, and grills. You will pass Jemez Falls Campground ($9.00) on the way in. A short gravel trail leads to Jemez Falls. Bring a lock for your bike so you can walk down for a look and a dip. Another trail accesses McCauley Warm Springs.

15.5 Overlook on the left for San Diego Canyon; short leg-stretcher with overgrown view and roadside vault toilet. Redondo Campground ($8.00) is close on the right. Enjoy a long descent to La Cueva.

17.8 Junction with New Mexico Route 126; High Country Mountain Store (no public rest rooms). Spike's serves breakfast, burgers, and Mexican fare Wednesday through Sunday, and La Cueva Lodge is a small roadside motel. The shoulder is chewed up here then eventually disappears.

17.9 La Cueva Picnic Area on the left; tables along the San Antonio River (vault toilet; no fee). Begin riverside riding with views of the high red walls of San Diego Canyon.

19.0 Dark Canyon on the left; a fishing pull-off with a vault toilet.

(continued)

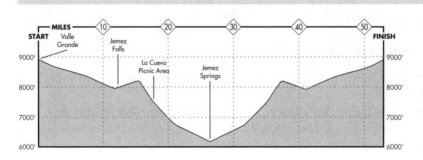

19.3 A large gravel parking lot on the left marks the popular Spence Hot Springs. A quarter-mile, steep trail leads down across the river and up to the natural pool.

20.3 Rincon Fishing Access on the left; a fishing pull-off.

20.9 Large paved parking lot on the left; roadside vault toilet.

21.1 Battleship Rock Picnic Area ($4.00) on the left provides shade, vault toilets, and water. A trail leads 2 miles to McCauley Warm Springs.

24.9 Soda Dam on the left; roadside swimming hole.

25.3 Cross the Jemez River.

25.4 Jemez Ranger Station on the left; porta-potty outside.

26.0 Jemez State Monument on the left.

26.5 Village of Jemez Springs. A municipal area on the right has picnic tables and porta-potties. The Jemez Springs Bath House sits back from the road behind the park. Then Los Ojos on the left and Deb's on the right; a bit farther, Laughing Lizard on the left. So, have lunch or stay the night before heading back toward Los Alamos.

53.0 Return to your car at the parking area on New Mexico Route 4.

1860. The healing mineral water is piped directly from the spring a short distance to the facility, where there are large concrete tubs for individuals and a cedar tub outside for groups.

You might consider parking at the municipal lot at the springs and riding this out-and-back in reverse, climbing first and returning for a soak. Tubs start at $9.00, and massage and other therapeutic treatments are available. Call ahead to guarantee a spot. Drinks and snacks are available in the gift shop.

LOCAL INFORMATION

♦ Sandoval Tourism Department (www.sctourism.com), P.O. Box 40, Bernalillo, NM 87004; (800) 252–0191.

♦ Jemez Ranger District (www.fs.fed.us/r3/sfe), P.O. Box 150, Jemez Springs, NM 87025; (505) 829–3535 (Monday through Friday from 8:00 A.M. to 5:00 P.M. and Saturday from 8:00 A.M. to 2:00 P.M.).

EVENTS/ATTRACTIONS

♦ Valles Caldera Trust, P.O. Box 1689, Santa Fe, NM 87504-1689; (505) 438–7892.

♦ Jemez Springs Bath House and Motel (www.jemez.com/baths), P.O. Box 112, Jemez Springs, NM 87025; (505) 829–3303 (summer hours, 9:00 A.M. to 9:00 P.M. daily).

♦ Jemez State Monument, P.O. Box 143, Jemez Springs, NM 87025; (505) 829–3530 (8:30 A.M. to 5:00 P.M. daily except major holidays; cost $3.00).

RESTAURANTS

♦ Deb's Deli, 17607 Highway 4, Jemez Springs, NM 87025; (505) 829–3829 (all-you-can-eat breakfast on summer weekends).
♦ Los Ojos Restaurant & Saloon, 17596 Highway 4, Jemez Springs, NM 87025; (505) 829–3547 (steaks, Mexican fare, and full-service bar).
♦ Laughing Lizard Inn & Cafe, 17526 Highway 4, Jemez Springs, NM 87025; (505) 829–3108 (healthy meals, great desserts, and lodging).

ACCOMMODATIONS

♦ Dancing Bear B&B, 314 San Diego Loop, Jemez Springs, NM 87025; (505) 829–3336.
♦ Riverdancer B&B, 16445 Highway 4, Jemez Springs, NM 87025; (505) 829–3262.

Taking a break along the East Fork of the Jemez River. (Photo courtesy of Enchanted Lands Enterprise)

◆ Desert Willow B&B, 15975 Highway 4, Jemez Springs, NM 87025; (505) 829–3410.
◆ Giggling Starr Riverfront Cabins, 40 Abouselman Loop, Jemez Springs, NM 87025; (505) 829–9175.
◆ Jemez Mountain Inn, 17555 Highway 4, Jemez Springs, NM 87025; (505) 829–3926.

BIKE SHOPS

◆ D.O.M.E. (www.domemountainshop.com), 3801-A Arkansas Avenue, Los Alamos, NM 87544; (505) 661–3663.

REST ROOMS

◆ Mile 7.2: Las Conchas Fishing Access.
◆ Mile 15.5: Roadside vault toilet at San Diego Canyon Overlook.
◆ Mile 19.3: Roadside vault toilet at large paved parking lot.
◆ Mile 25.4: Jemez Ranger Station (porta-potty outside).
◆ Mile 26.5: Porta-potties at municipal lot in Jemez Springs.
◆ Several other recreation sites along the way have vault toilets.

MAPS

◆ USGS 7.5-minute quads Bland, Redondo Peak, Seven Springs, and Jemez Springs.
◆ Delorme *New Mexico Atlas & Gazetteer,* map 23.

Cochiti Lake Ramble

Cochiti Lake, about halfway between Albuquerque and Santa Fe, offers camping, fishing, swimming, and picnicking—plus some great roads to get in a relatively flat ride. The lake is located at the foot of the Jemez Mountains along the Rio Grande and is surrounded by high-desert mesas. Most of the immediate landscape is open plains with scrub vegetation and grasses. You will notice the lush green ribbon of cottonwoods lining the Rio Grande. Stunning views include several mountain ranges—the Jemez, Sangre de Cristos, and northern edge of the Sandias. It's best to ride in the fall or winter because spring is windy and summer is pretty hot. (Of course you can always go for a swim after your ride.) Mountain breezes generate good conditions on Cochiti Lake for sailing and windsurfing. Riding early in the day is always a good idea.

At 5.5 miles long and 251 feet high, Cochiti Dam is one of the largest earth-fill dams in the country, and you have the option of riding across it. The original purpose of the spillway, which impounds the waters of the Rio Grande and the Santa Fe River, was to solve flooding problems, but state officials pushed to provide recreational use as well. The lake, which is located on Cochiti Pueblo land, opened to the public in 1975 and was named after the Cochiti Indians. Native Americans have inhabited the area for centuries. You can learn more about the cultural history, as well as the reservoir, at the visitor center at the start of the ride.

Recreation areas (Cochiti Lake and Tetilla Peak) are located on either side of the lake. They have a campground, picnic tables, a boat ramp, and an overlook.

Start: Cochiti Lake Recreation Area, off Interstate 25 about halfway between Albuquerque and Santa Fe.

Length: 31.1-mile loop.

Terrain: Not a mountainous ride. Fairly flat riding with a couple gradual 1-mile climbs.

Traffic and hazards: Traffic is fairly light except summer weekends when recreationalists are headed for the lake, although New Mexico Route 16 has some truck traffic and narrow shoulders. I-25 has a large shoulder, but interstate riding always comes with some hazards. If you choose to take Dam Crest Road or the road out to Tetilla Recreation Area, be prepared for a rougher surface.

Getting there: From Santa Fe, head south on I-25 for about 15 miles to exit 264. Turn right on New Mexico Route 16, travel 8 miles, and turn right on New Mexico Route 22, which becomes Cochiti Highway. The recreation area will be on the right after 4 miles. From Bernalillo (just north of Albuquerque), head north on I-25 for about 17 miles to exit 259. Turn left on New Mexico Route 22 and travel 13 miles to the recreation area on the right. Park at the visitor center on Dam Crest Road, and check out the road surface to decide whether you'll want to take the option over the spillway at the end of the loop.

Cochiti Lake has a small beach, a mile down Cochiti Road from the visitor center; and Tetilla Peak is closed in winter (November 1 to April 1). The campgrounds have rest rooms, showers, and electricity. Prices range from $5.00 to $12.00 depending on site and season. The cost for a shower is $0.25 for five minutes. The visitor center at Cochiti Lake is open on weekdays from 8:00 A.M. to 3:30 P.M., Saturday from 10:00 A.M. to 2:00 P.M.; and Sunday from noon to 4:00 P.M. (closed Thanksgiving, Christmas, and New Year's Day).

This ride, which is a variation on New Mexico Touring Society's Cochiti Calamity, is a lollipop loop. You will cycle the first 3.8 miles, then begin the actual 23.5-mile loop, and finally retrace the initial 3.8 miles at the end. To make a true loop, consider riding over the spillway on Dam Crest Road. You won't have to retrace any mileage, but the surface is "chip and seal," which is a bit rougher. Many cyclists love the Dam Crest Road and feel the scenery and lack of traffic make it more desirable.

Before heading out on the ride, take a spin (left out of the parking lot at the visitor center) on this end of Dam Crest Road and decide if you want to come back that way. Being up on top of the dam makes interesting riding, plus the vantage point is great. This option is only 0.7 mile longer. The Dam Crest Road is open to vehicles from 7:30 A.M. to 3:30 P.M. Cyclists can ride it anytime. After a heavy snow cross-country skiers have been known to head out across the spillway.

You can add 20 miles to the ride with an out-and-back to Tetilla Peak Recreation Area. The road is gated from November to March, so you won't have

You'll ride across the Rio Grande twice on the Cochiti Lake Ramble.

to share it with cars, although traffic is almost nonexistent anyway. The surface is similar to the Dam Crest Road, and you will have relatively flat riding except a 0.5-mile climb as you near the recreation site. The shaded overlook makes a great picnic spot; rest rooms and water nearby. (*Note:* You might consider camping and starting your ride here.)

LOCAL INFORMATION

♦ Sandoval County Department of Tourism (www.sctourism.com), P.O. Box 40, Bernalillo, New Mexico Route 87004; (505) 867–8687.

EVENTS/ATTRACTIONS

♦ Cochiti Lake Recreation Area, 82 Dam Crest Road, Pena Blanca, NM 87041-0000; (505) 465–0307.

RESTAURANTS

Convenience stores on I–25 at the turnoff for Santa Domingo Pueblo and in the town of Cochiti Lake have a vendor offering subs and pizzas; otherwise find restaurants in Albuquerque or Santa Fe.

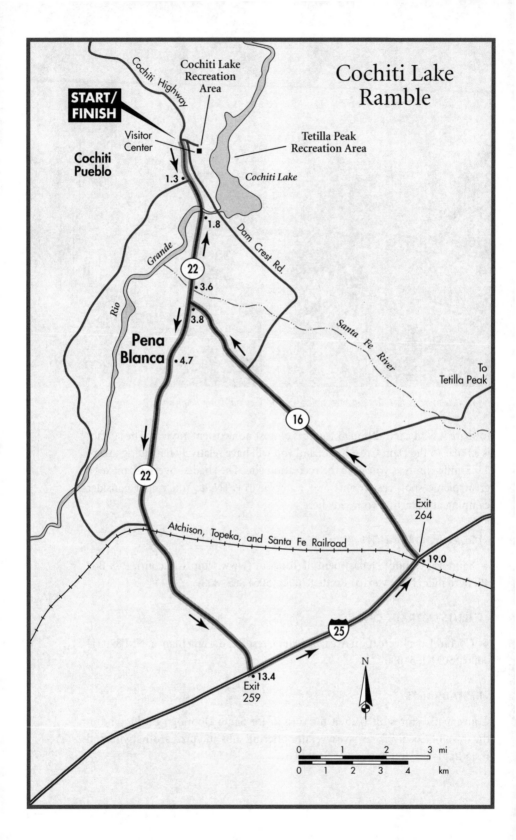

Cochiti Lake Ramble

START/FINISH

Cochiti Highway

Cochiti Lake Recreation Area

Visitor Center

Cochiti Pueblo

Tetilla Peak Recreation Area

Cochiti Lake

1.3

1.8

Dam Crest Rd.

Rio Grande

22

3.6

3.8

Pena Blanca

4.7

Santa Fe River

To Tetilla Peak

16

22

Exit 264

Atchison, Topeka, and Santa Fe Railroad

19.0

25

13.4
Exit 259

N

| 0 | 1 | 2 | 3 | mi |

| 0 | 1 | 2 | 3 | 4 | km |

0.0 Leave Cochiti Recreation Area, turn left on Cochiti Highway (BIA 90), and descend for 2 miles. There is a rough shoulder if you need it. (*Note:* For snacks before the ride, turn right and reach a Phillips 66 in the town of Cochiti Lake after 0.3 mile.)

1.3 Junction with New Mexico Route 22. To the right, New Mexico Route 22 heads north to Cochiti Pueblo. Continue straight on what is now New Mexico Route 22 heading south. You will gradually climb to I–25; shoulder improves.

1.8 Pass Al Black Recreation Area on the left, and cross the Rio Grande.

3.6 Cross the Santa Fe River.

3.8 Junction with New Mexico Route 16 on the left-your return route. Continue straight; view the electronic towers on the top of the Sandias and the incredibly green Rio Grande valley down to the right.

4.7 Reach the community of Pena Blanca. Limited services here; you may find a small grocery store open. Lose the shoulder.

5.0 Post office on the right.

6.3 Leave Pena Blanca. Begin a gradual 1-mile climb and gain a rough shoulder.

9.1 Mateo Overpass and road access to the Santo Domingo Pueblo, one of the state's largest pueblos. Begin another 1-mile climb.

12.2 Pass Santo Domingo Elementary and Junior High School.

13.1 Phillips 66 on the right. In addition to snacks and drinks, this convenience store has a vendor offering subs and pizza. Indians often sell jewelry or fruit and vegetables at the roadside stands next to the gas station.

13.3 Cross over I–25.

13.4 New Mexico Route 22 ends. Turn left to get on I–25 and descend for most of 5 miles to New Mexico Route 16. A sign notifies cyclists that they must remain on the shoulder. View the Sangre de Cristos above the mesa.

17.3 County line.

17.8 Sign indicates exit for New Mexico Route 16. The shoulder narrows here and becomes rough.

(continued)

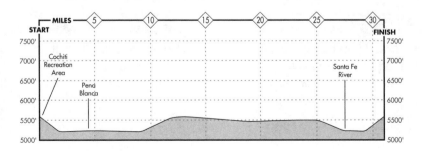

18.6 Exit the interstate.

19.0 At the top of the ramp, reach a stop sign and turn left. Go over the interstate, heading west on New Mexico Route 16. The shoulder is 3–4 feet wide. After a 1-mile gradual climb, this road is flat or descending to the base of the dam.

22.8 Road to the right leads to Tetilla Peak Recreation Area (optional out-and-back of 20 miles).

23.3 Enter the Cochiti Indian Reservation.

25.3 Turnoff for Cochiti Dam. Turn right on Dam Crest Road if you want to ride across the spillway. Remember, total distance is about the same, but the road is rougher.

27.3 At the T intersection, New Mexico Route 16 ends. Turn right and retrace the first 3.8 miles of the ride.

27.5 Cross the Santa Fe River.

29.3 Pass the Al Black Recreation Area on the right and cross the Rio Grande.

29.8 Pass the turnoff (north on New Mexico Route 22) for Cochiti Pueblo.

31.1 Back at Cochiti Lake Recreation Area.

ACCOMMODATIONS

Camp at Cochiti Lake Recreation Area or Tetilla Peak Recreation Area; otherwise lodging is available in Albuquerque or Santa Fe.

BIKE SHOPS

There are four bike shops in Santa Fe, about 40 miles away, and more than a dozen bike shops in Albuquerque, about 50 miles away.

REST ROOMS

♦ Mile 0.0: Visitor center at Cochiti Lake Recreation Area.
♦ Mile 1.8: Al Black Recreation Area (vault toilets).
♦ Mile 13.1: Phillips 66 at I–25.

MAPS

♦ USGS 7.5-minute quads Tetilla Peak, Santo Domingo Pueblo, Cochiti Dam, and San Felipe Pueblo NE.
♦ Delorme *New Mexico Atlas & Gazetteer*, map 23.

High Road to Taos Classic

Cycle into New Mexico's colonial past. The High Road to Taos, one of the most popular scenic drives in the state, passes through old Spanish villages, one after another, where you can experience a bit of the eighteenth century. The things that attract the car tourist make for a great bicycle tour as well—photographing beautiful colonial-era churches and visiting artisans where they live and work. The High Road is actually several rural back roads that follow along the foothills of the Sangre de Cristo Mountains between Santa Fe and Taos. The scenery includes chamisa- and sage-covered hills, juniper-pinon woodlands, cottonwood-lined river valleys, ponderosa forests, and mountain views of some of the highest peaks in the state.

Although this ride is described starting at the Plaza in Santa Fe, you can just as easily start at the Plaza in Taos. Twin Hearts Express, a shuttle service located in Taos, will pick you up at any area lodging in either town and run you to the other town. If you cycle toward your home base, you won't have to worry about timing your finish to catch a shuttle. The shuttles leave about every two hours starting at 7:00 A.M. When you call, be sure to let them know you have a bicycle.

Most of the small communities along the High Road were settled in the seventeenth and eighteenth centuries through communal land grants and developed in isolation during the Spanish-colonial period. The towns are not very large, and services are limited, but there are dozens of studios and galleries. In Chimayo you will find restaurants and lodging; in Truchas, a general store, a cafe, and several B&Bs; and in Penasco, a grocery, a pizza place, and a few gas stations.

Climbing on the High Road with the Truchas Peaks in the background.

The ride starts on a busy four-lane, but once you are through Pojoaque, there are no traffic lights or fast food all the way to Taos. In Nambe your route follows a winding road along the Rio Nambe, where big cottonwoods line the banks, then climbs to a high desert plateau of dry hills and eroding, red cliffs. A side road takes you to Nambe Falls, a recreation area run by the Nambe Pueblo.

In Chimayo the largest town along the High Road, apple orchards line the road, weavers have produced hand-woven blankets and other wool products for generations, and the Plaza del Cerro (built around 1740) is considered to be the last surviving fortified Spanish plaza in the Southwest. The Santuario de Chimayo is known for the curative powers of its sacred earth. On Good Friday thousands make a religious pilgrimage to this chapel, walking from as far as 300 miles away. Don't miss Leona's, next door to the Santuario, for fresh tamales, *posole* (hominy stew), and her famous thick tortillas. Once a roadside stand, Leona's has grown over the last forty years into a successful restaurant and commercial tortilla business.

A spur off the High Road circles down into Cordova, famous for its wood carvers, where you can buy New Mexican folk art carved from

THE BASICS

Start: The Plaza in Santa Fe (can be ridden from the Plaza in Taos).

Length: 72.1 miles one-way (arrange a shuttle to make this an enjoyable one- or two-day ride).

Terrain: Challenging and mountainous with one major pass.

Traffic and hazards: U.S. Highway 84/285 is a busy four-lane with a 2- to 4-foot shoulder that is in bad shape in spots. This is a dangerous stretch of road (15 miles). Otherwise, the High Road is rural, with little or no shoulder and light traffic. You'll have to deal with several traffic lights in Santa Fe, Pojoaque, and Taos and with tourist congestion around both plazas.

Getting there: In Santa Fe, take exit 284 off Interstate 25, travel north on U.S. Highway 84/285 (St. Francis Drive) for about 3 miles, and turn right on Cerrillos Road. Continue straight through the intersections at Guadalupe Street and Paseo De Peralta; after about 0.5 mile on Cerrillos, be sure to bear right at the Y intersection. You will reach a four-way stop at Alameda Street after another 0.2 mile; continue straight and begin one-way. Go two blocks and turn right on San Francisco Street. You will reach the southwest corner of the Plaza within a block. The mileage for the ride starts at the northeast corner of the Plaza, the junction of

cedar and aspen. (A sign on the door of an artist's home that says CARVINGS is an invite to knock). Then the road climbs to a beautiful mesa and the hilltop village of Truchas, where Robert Redford filmed *Milagro Beanfield War* (definitely rent this one). New Mexico Route 76 makes a sharp left, and the town itself is straight ahead. The spectacular views across the canyons include Truchas Peak (elevation 13,101 feet), New Mexico's second highest mountain.

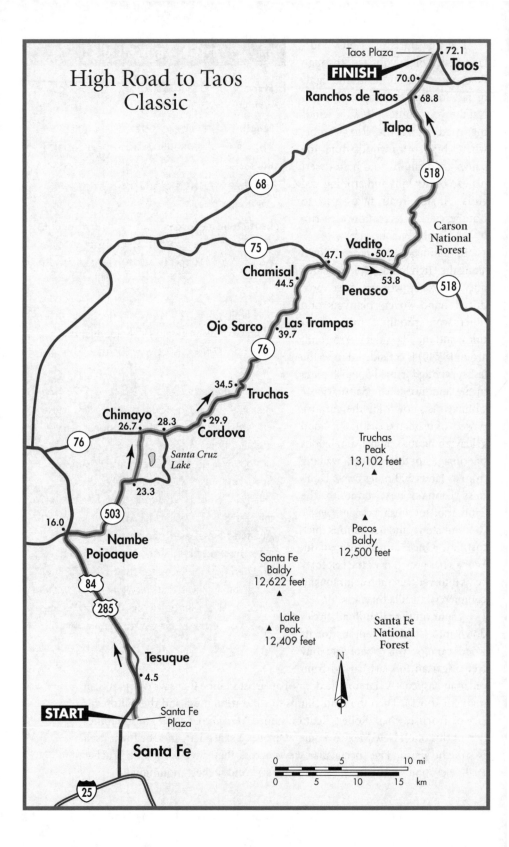

MILES AND DIRECTIONS

0.0 Leave the Plaza, cycling down Washington Street past the Burrito Company.

0.1 Pass the Santa Fe Public Library on the right at the first traffic light (Marcy Street); bike rack out front, rest rooms inside. Continue to the next light and turn left on Paseo De Peralta (small shoulder).

0.9 At the third light, turn right on Guadalupe Street and head out of town, veering right onto U.S. Highway 84/285. You will start with a mile climb.

3.3 The high point on U.S. Highway 84/285; enjoy the view and descend to Pojoaque.

4.5 Road to the right leads into the village of Tesuque.

14.5 Reach the first traffic light in Pojoaque; if you need a rest stop, turn right to reach the Phillips 66 station. Other services include a visitor center, grocery store, and Dairy Queen. As you leave town, be sure to stay on U.S. Highway 84/285 when New Mexico Route 502 veers off to the right.

16.0 Junction with New Mexico Route 503; turn right and head for Nambe.

19.2 Road to the right leads to Nambe Lake. Enjoy views of the Sangre de Cristos for the next few miles as you ride through a badlands of sorts, eroding rock that creates unusual shapes in the landscape.

23.3 Turn left onto the narrow County Road 98, and descend into Chimayo.

25.8 Turn right to visit the Santuario and Leona's. A traditional and historic restaurant, Rancho de Chimayo, is just a bit farther on the right.

26.7 T intersection; turn right on New Mexico Route 76 (Ortega's Weaving Shop on the left). Begin a steady climb toward Truchas.

28.3 Junction with New Mexico Route 503 on the right, the turn for Santa Cruz Lake (camping). High Road continues straight ahead.

29.9 The spur road down into Cordova (County Road 0800) on the right.

34.5 New Mexico Route 76 makes a sharp turn to the left. View Pecos Baldy and the Truchas Peaks. (For a detour on the main street through Truchas, continue straight. Tafoyo's General Store—rest rooms for customers only—ahead on the right and a small cafe across the street.)

36.0 Enter Carson National Forest.

(continued)

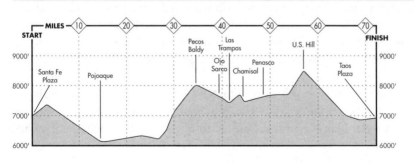

39.7 Descend into and climb out of Ojo Sarco.

41.5 Las Trampas, a beautiful eighteenth-century church on the right.

44.5 Long descent into Chamisal.

47.1 T intersection with New Mexico Route 75; turn right and cycle through Penasco. Enjoy an incredibly smooth section of road for 6.5 miles.

47.9 A-1 Auto on the right (sodas and rest rooms).

48.4 Penasco Valley Food Store, ice cream and coffee, on the right.

48.9 Camino Real Ranger Station (weekdays 8:00 A.M. to 4:30 P.M.) on the left.

50.2 Vadito, where the road levels out for a few miles along the Rio Del Pueblo.

53.8 T intersection with New Mexico Route 518; turn left and begin climbing U.S. Hill.

57.0 The top! Pass a forest service outhouse on the right, then an overlook with views north and east. Descend!

65.7 Leave Carson National Forest and the ponderosas; view the Taos Plateau as you head into Talpa.

68.8 T intersection with New Mexico Route 68 at Ranchos de Taos. Turn left to visit San Francisco de Asis Mission Church, just down on the left. Turn right (four-lane with shoulder) to head for the Plaza.

70.0 Taos Visitor Center on the right at the first traffic light in town, and the junction with New Mexico Route 585; continue straight.

70.5 Next light, Wal-Mart; then road narrows to two lanes with tourist congestion and some shoulder.

71.7 Traffic light at Quesnel Road and Placita Road, then Gearing Up Bicycle Shop on the right.

72.1 Traffic light at the junction with U.S. Highway 64; the Plaza to the left.

Continue riding rolling terrain, descending into and climbing out of the river valleys of Ojo Sarco, Las Trampas, and Chamisal. Along the way you will pass adobe homes, artist studios, old apple orchards, and small farms yielding corn and chiles. Worth a stop is the Church of Iglesia Jose de Gracia in Las Trampas, one of the most beautiful churches in the Southwest. Still in use after 200 years, it is a great example of the architecture of the time—note the hand-made altar and wooden bell towers. Penasco, a small farming community on the Picuris Indian Reservation, has a small grocery store with an ice-cream and coffee bar.

After Vadito you will turn onto New Mexico Route 518 and begin the biggest climb on the trip, U.S. Hill. A pullout at the top affords great views of the Wheeler Peak Wilderness. Descend through Talpa to Ranchos de Taos and visit the most painted and photographed church in the state, and a Georgia O'Keeffe favorite, San Francisco de Asis Mission Church. The Plaza in Taos is just a few miles north.

I highly recommend riding the High Road in the fall when the cottonwoods along the rivers and the aspens on the ridges turn bright yellow. The apples are ripe, green chiles are being roasted, and roadside stands sell fruits and vegetables from the harvest. Warm days turn to cool nights. And a bonus? The crowds thin out.

To make this an overnighter, contact a B&B or inn in Chimayo (about a third of the way into the trip) or Truchas (about halfway). For camping, there is Santa Cruz Lake, just a couple miles off-route near Chimayo. Take New Mexico Route 503 at mile 28.3, and after a couple miles, turn right and descend to the campground. This recreation area, managed by the Bureau of Land Management (BLM), is popular with boaters, fishermen, and hikers.

LOCAL INFORMATION

♦ Santa Fe County Chamber of Commerce (www.santafechamber.com), 510 North Guadalupe Street, Santa Fe, NM 87501; (505) 983–7317.
♦ Taos County Chamber of Commerce (www.taoschamber.com), P.O. Drawer 1, Taos, NM 87571; (800) 732–8267.
♦ Twin Hearts Express and Shuttle, 203 Dimas Lane, Taos, NM 87571; (505) 751–1201 (cost about $35).

EVENTS/ATTRACTIONS

♦ Ortega's Weaving Shop, P.O. Box 325, Chimayo, NM 87522; (505) 351–4215 (open daily in the summer; includes a working loom).
♦ Santuario de Chimayo, County Road 94C and Santuario Road, Chimayo, NM 87522; (505) 351–4889 (daily in the summer from 9:00 A.M. to 5:00 P.M.).

RESTAURANTS

♦ Leona's Restaurant, P.O. Box 280, Chimayo, NM 87522; (800) 453–6627 (9:00 A.M. to 5:00 P.M. daily in the summer).
♦ Rancho de Chimayo, County Road 98, Chimayo, NM 87522; (505) 351–4444 (in the summer, lunch and dinner daily and breakfast on weekends; also lodging).

ACCOMMODATIONS

♦ Casa Escondida B&B (www.casaescondida.com), County Road 0100, House 62, Chimayo, NM 87522; (505) 351–4805 (history of catering to cyclists).
♦ La Posada de Chimayo (www.laposadadechimayo.com), P.O. 463, Chimayo, NM 87522; (505) 351–4605 (located in an isolated corner of the village).

♦ Rancho Manzana, 26 Camino de Mission, Chimayo, NM 87522; (505) 351–2227 (elegant with hot tub; on the old plaza).
♦ Hacienda de Chimayo, County Road 98, Chimayo, NM 87522; (505) 351–2222 (across from the Rancho de Chimayo).
♦ Rancho Arriba B&B (www.ranchoarriba.com), Box 338, Truchas, NM 87578; (505) 689–2374.
♦ Truchas Farmhouse Inn, P.O. Box 410, Truchas, NM 87578; (505) 689–2245.
♦ Santa Cruz Lake Recreation Area, BLM/Taos Field Office, 225 Cruz Alta Road, Taos, NM 87571; (505) 758–5851.

BIKE SHOPS

♦ Ace Mountain Bikes, 825 Early Street, Santa Fe, NM 87505; (505) 982–8079.
♦ New Mexico Bike 'N Sport, 1829 Cerrillos Road, Santa Fe, NM 87505; (505) 820–0809.
♦ rob and charlie's, 1632 St. Michaels Drive, Santa Fe, NM 87505; (505) 471–9119.
♦ Santa Fe Mountain Sports, 607 Cerrillos Road, Santa Fe, NM 87501; (505) 988–3337.
♦ Gearing Up Bicycle Shop, 129 Paseo Del Pueblo Sur, Taos, NM 87571; (505) 751–0365.

The High Road, one of the most scenic roads in the state.

Enchanted Lands Enterprise (ELE)

ELE is a local business—one of the few bicycle touring companies located in New Mexico. Suellen Browersock has been traveling the globe for twenty-four years and her love of finding special places culminated in incorporating ELE in 1997. She offers tours in all of the Four Corner States—Arizona, Utah, Colorado, and New Mexico. They are fully supported with great routes, accommodations, and attractions. Some of the trips have a camping option.

The ELE tour names are enticing—Magic of New Mexico, High Country Borderlands, and Georgia O'Keeffe Country. Many of them follow scenic byways that are included in the routes in this book such as the Turquoise Trail, Jemez Mountain Trail, High Road to Taos, and Enchanted Circle. Although it was hard to pin her down, Suellen said one of her favorite stretches of road was New Mexico Route 17 heading out of Chama to Cumbres Pass. For more information, contact Enchanted Lands Enterprise (www.enchantedlands.com), P.O. Box 1222, Los Alamos, NM 87544; (505) 661–8687.

REST ROOMS

◆ Mile 0.1: Santa Fe Public Library.
◆ Mile 14.5: Phillips 66 in Pojoaque.
◆ Mile 25.8: Santuario in Chimayo.
◆ Mile 34.5: Tafoya's General Store (customers only) in Truchas.
◆ Mile 47.9: A-1 Auto, one of several gas stations in Penasco.
◆ Mile 57.0: Forest service outhouse atop U.S. Hill.
◆ Mile 70.0: Taos Visitor Center.

MAPS

◆ USGS 7.5-minute quads Santa Fe, Tesuque, Horcado Ranch, Espanola, Cundiyo, Chimayo, Truchas, Trampas, Penasco, Tres Ritos, Ranchos De Taos, and Taos.
◆ Delorme *New Mexico Atlas & Gazetteer,* maps 16 and 24.

Capital City Cruise

T his local favorite starts at the beautifully landscaped State Capitol and makes a big loop around Santa Fe, incorporating the smooth pavement in Las Campanas, the historic village of La Cienega, and one of the area's best cycling roads (Bonanza Creek) out in Lone Butte. I can't imagine a cyclist living in Santa Fe that doesn't know about this ride. It is the city's unofficial perimeter loop, what locals call the Prison Loop because it goes out and around the New Mexico Penitentiary. While you will get in a small amount of city street riding, the majority of the loop is rural countryside and quiet, newer residential areas. You will find a wide variety in the type of roads and the scenery this ride provides, and there are some interesting attractions— one of the most historic ranches in the Southwest and a famous "Old West" movie set. You can plan this as an overnight trip with a stay at the Sunrise Springs Inn and Retreat, mile 21.5—almost halfway.

I put this ride together in pieces when I first moved to Santa Fe using the book *Santa Fe Street Maps* by Horton Family Maps, which details all maintained roads in the county. (I highly recommend this map book if you live and cycle in Santa Fe.) Later I found out that locals had been using this loop for years. It's a classic for Saturday morning.

The ride starts at the State Capitol, called the Roundhouse because of its circular design, which was based on the Zia Pueblo's sun symbol. New Mexico boasts the oldest and the newest capitol buildings in the country. This is a long story, but the first capitol, the Palace of the Governors (a few blocks away on the Plaza), was built in 1610 and remained the seat of government for almost three centuries. The most recent capitol building was dedicated in 1966. You can take a tour of the State Capitol, which houses excellent exhibits. The historic and cultural artworks highlight New Mexican artists—Indian, Hispanic, and Anglo. And for the rest of the story on New Mexico's capitol buildings, check out www. sos.state.nm.us and click on "general information," then "blue book," then "state capitols."

After zigzagging here and there to get away from downtown, you will cycle smooth roads with big views in Las Campanas, a 4,700-acre club community. Residents enjoy such amenities as tennis, golf, a spa and pool, and an equestrian center. Large homesites are tucked into the juniper-pinon landscape.

A stretch on the new Santa Fe Bypass (New Mexico Route 599) takes you out to another community—La Cienega, which means "the marsh" in Spanish. This historic village lies in a narrow river valley. You can visit El Rancho de las Golondrinas (Ranch of the Swallows), a living history museum that depicts the hacienda life of Spanish-colonial New Mexico. The ranch, established in the early 1700s, was an important stop for travelers on the famous

THE BASICS

Start: The State Capitol, downtown Santa Fe.

Length: 50.5-mile loop.

Terrain: Gently rolling with a fair amount of flat riding; a couple of short climbs and good rollers.

Traffic and hazards: The biggest challenge is getting out of downtown. For a few miles, expect city traffic, narrow roads, and congestion. A majority of the loop has little traffic and some shoulder. You will encounter truck traffic along the Santa Fe Bypass and New Mexico Route 14, both of which have large shoulders. Be especially careful on the bumpy, narrow pavement in La Cienega. There is a higher possibility of dogs here.

Getting there: In Santa Fe take exit 284 off Interstate 25, travel north on U.S. Highway 84/285 (St. Francis Drive) for about 3 miles, and turn right on Cerrillos Road. Continue straight through the intersection at Guadalupe Street, and turn right at the next intersection, Paseo De Peralta. Go straight at the next two traffic lights (Galisteo Street and Don Gaspar Avenue). The State Capitol will be on your left. Pass by the ramp going down to the underground parking, then turn left into the parking lot before the next light. A sign indicates VISITOR AND EMPLOYEE PARKING, but it's hard to see from this direction. A thirty-minute limit applies to this lot only when legislature is in session in January. (Note: There is additional parking at the New Mexico and Santa Fe Visitor Center. Continue to the next traffic light. Turn left on Old Santa Fe Trail and immediately right into the parking lot.)

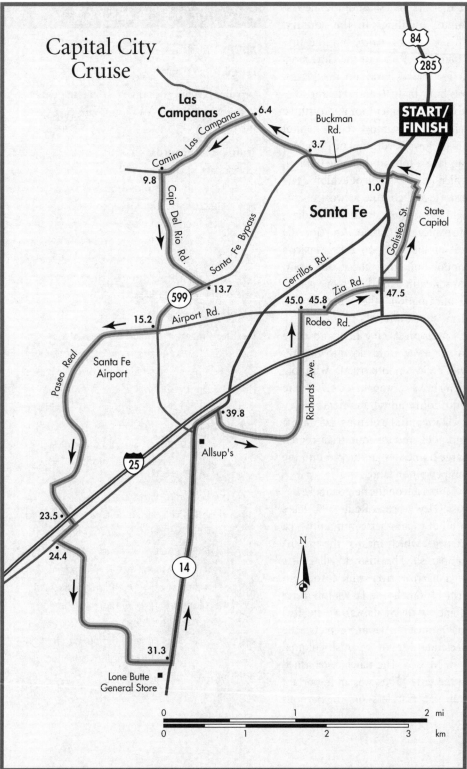

Capital City Cruise

Las Campanas

Buckman Rd.

START/ FINISH

6.4

3.7

Camino Las Campanas

9.8

1.0

Santa Fe

State Capitol

Galisteo St.

Caja Del Rio Rd.

Santa Fe Bypass

Cerrillos Rd.

599

13.7

45.0 45.8

Zia Rd.

47.5

15.2

Airport Rd.

Rodeo Rd.

Paseo Real

Santa Fe Airport

Richards Ave.

39.8

25

Allsup's

23.5

24.4

14

N

31.3

Lone Butte General Store

| 0 | | 1 | | 2 mi |
| 0 | 1 | 2 | 3 | km |

Horton Family Maps

0.0 Leave the State Capitol parking lot and walk your bike around to the west side of the building, down the steps to Don Gaspar Avenue, and across the street to South Capitol Road. Hop on and roll.

0.1 Turn right at the stop sign on Galisteo Street. Merge onto Cerrillos Road at the stop sign.

0.2 At the four-way stop, turn left on Alameda Street.

0.3 At the traffic light turn right on Sandoval Street and get in the left lane.

0.4 At the traffic light turn left on West San Francisco Street.

0.5 At the traffic light continue straight, crossing Guadalupe Street and entering a quiet neighborhood.

1.0 Reach Paseo De Peralta and turn left. You will be crossing several lanes. As you near the next light, get into the third lane from the left.

1.1 Reach the traffic light at St. Francis Drive and continue straight. The road becomes El Camino De Las Crucitas, which travels through a residential area. There are several road humps and a four-way stop.

1.6 The four-way stop at Alamo Drive marks the beginning of a short climb.

1.9 Pass Frank S. Ortiz Park, or the Dog Park, the only off-leash park in the city.

2.0 Turn right on Buckman Road and climb, then enjoy a mile of rollers and great views of the Jemez Mountains.

3.3 Cross a cattleguard and descend; gain a shoulder for a short distance.

3.7 At the stop sign turn right on Camino La Tierra, go under the Santa Fe Bypass, and head for Las Campanas.

4.6 At the four-way stop, continue straight. The road becomes one-way here with a small shoulder.

6.2 Follow signs to Las Campanas Clubhouse; go right at the Y intersection.

6.4 Go left at this Y intersection and under a rock bridge. The road is now Camino Las Campanas.

7.9 Pass the clubhouse and begin a long descent.

(continued)

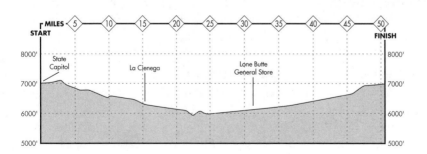

9.8 At the three-way stop, turn left on Caja Del Rio Road, tackle a short climb, and then enjoy long gentle rollers. This road has a 3-foot shoulder. You will pass the city's eighteen-hole golf course, Marty Sanchez Links, the Caja Del Rio Landfill, and the playing fields at the Municipal Recreation Complex.

13.7 At the stop sign turn right on the frontage road that parallels the Santa Fe Bypass. The large shoulder has loose gravel in places.

14.5 Look for a break in the fence on the left and get on the Santa Fe Bypass (New Mexico Route 599), which also has a large shoulder.

15.2 At the traffic light, turn right on Paseo Real (County Road 56). For water and rest rooms, turn left and head for the Shell station on the right. Paseo Real is relatively flat and passes a sewage treatment plant and the Sante Fe Airport. You will ride along the Santa Fe River for a while and across several cattleguards as you head for La Cienega. There is little or no shoulder on this quiet road.

19.0 A sharp curve to the left marks a short climb. At the top, you'll have views back toward Santa Fe of the Sangre de Cristo Mountains.

21.0 Pass a water tower on the right and descend.

21.5 Los Pinos Road (County Road 54) leads left to El Rancho de las Golondrinas and Sunrise Springs Inn and Retreat. Continue straight and for the next mile you will ride on a narrow, bumpy road with no yellow line. Watch for dogs here.

22.5 The road curves left and you will pass a sign for I–25. The yellow line is back, and the road becomes County Road 50 (County Road 54 goes right).

22.8 At the stop sign County Road 50 goes right; continue straight and up Entrada La Cienega.

23.5 Cross over I–25.

23.7 At the stop sign turn right on the frontage road that parallels I-25.

24.4 Turn left on Bonanza Creek Road (County Road 45), one of the best stretches of road for cycling in Santa Fe.

30.3 On the right, Rancho Alegre, the gravel road that leads to JW Eaves Movie Ranch.

30.6 Pass beside the small, rocky hill called Lone Butte.

31.3 Reach New Mexico Route 14, the Turquoise Trail (very wide shoulder). Turn right to reach Lone Butte General Store (0.1 mile) or turn left to continue the ride.

32.2 San Marcos Cafe on the left.

36.6 Pass the New Mexico Penitentiary, a maximum security unit.

38.4 At the traffic light (Santa Fe Bypass), continue straight. Allsup's convenience store on the right.

(continued)

39.8 Turn right on Rancho Viejo Boulevard, just before you reach I–25. You won't have a shoulder for the next 5 miles.

41.4 At the three-way stop, turn left on Avenida Del Sur.

42.1 Another three-way stop; turn left on Richards Avenue.

42.7 Pass Santa Fe Community College. For the next 2 miles, expect heavy traffic during the week. There is no shoulder. Also, be aware of traffic on Sunday when the church lets out at 11:00 A.M. and 1:00 P.M.

43.2 Santa Maria De La Paz Catholic Community on the left.

45.0 At the traffic light turn right on Rodeo Road. Conoco on the left. You will pass the Santa Fe Rodeo Fairground where the Farmer's Market takes place on Thursdays in the summer from 3:00 to 7:00 P.M. In addition to several traffic lights, you will also pass the Genoveva Chavez Community Center, the city's premier recreation facility ($4.00 day pass). You will have a good shoulder until Siringo Road.

45.8 At the traffic light Rodeo Road veers off to the right. Stay with the main road — Zia Road.

45.9 At Rodeo Plaza on the right, you will find Subway, Java Joes, Domino's Pizza, and other businesses.

46.7 Reach the traffic light at Yucca Street and continue straight. Ragel Park, on the right, has a picnic area.

47.5 Reach the traffic light at St. Francis Drive, and turn left. There are two left turn lanes; the right one sets you up to get on the shoulder of St. Francis Drive.

47.8 At the first traffic light on St. Francis Drive, turn right on Siringo Road, and do a short climb.

48.3 At the stop sign turn left on Botulph Road and enjoy one roller.

48.7 Reach the traffic light at St. Michaels Drive and continue straight, which is Hospital Drive.

49.0 The road curves left; at the stop sign, turn right on Galisteo Street.

49.1 At the four-way stop (San Mateo Road), continue straight.

49.7 Reach the traffic light at Cordova Road and continue straight. Cornell Park, which is commonly known as the Rose Park, is on the left.

50.0 At the four-way stop, continue straight.

50.4 Reach the traffic light at Paseo De Peralta and continue straight.

50.5 Turn right on South Capitol Road and return to the parking lot.

Visit El Rancho de las Golondrinas, a living history museum on the Capital City Cruise.

Camino Real, or Royal Highway, that linked Santa Fe and Mexico City.

This 200-acre facility comprises thirty-three buildings, all restored, rebuilt, or relocated from other sites. The authentic structures include a blacksmith shop, one-room schoolhouse, winery, and water-powered grist mill. You can watch interpreters dressed in period costumes making tortillas, stringing chiles, spinning wool, and shearing sheep. The museum is open Wednesday through Sunday from April to October (10:00 A.M. to 4:00 p.m; cost, $5.00 to $7.00). I recommend visiting during one of the special festival days or on a "harvest" weekend.

To make this a two-day trip, contact Sunrise Springs Inn and Retreat, which is also located on Los Pinos Road. This country inn sits on a lovely sixty-nine acres with large cottonwood trees and gardens. Sunrise Springs offers guest rooms, hot tubs, hiking trails, and natural cooking (sometimes with fresh food grown on the property).

Pedaling along the outskirts of town on Bonanza Creek Road, where the cycling couldn't be better, there is an unusual attraction—JW Eaves Movie Ranch. This authentic "Old West" town was built in 1969 as a movie set and used in many popular Westerns. Al Cantu, who has been there from the start, can brief you on the movies and movie stars, which include big names like Henry Fonda, John Wayne, and Kevin Costner. There is a Victorian-style chapel, a saloon and dance hall, and an ice cream parlor. You need to call ahead to schedule a visit (cost $10), and you must ride a hard-packed dirt road for about 0.8 mile to reach the ranch.

The next leg is on New Mexico Route 14, the Turquoise Trail. There are two good places to eat in Lone Butte. At the Lone Butte General Store, you may be surprised by the amazing aroma coming from the East Indian buffet. The San Marcos Cafe, which serves country cooking, offers an excellent breakfast and daily specials such as green chile lasagna.

After 8.5 miles on the large shoulder of New Mexico Route 14, Rancho Viejo Boulevard will take you to yet another quiet residential area with smooth pavement and little traffic. The views of the Sangre de Cristos are splendid. You will pass Santa Fe Community College, which was established in 1983. The Continuing Education Department offers short courses and workshops that deal with the Southwest, such as a walking tour of Santa Fe's Plaza, a New Mexican cooking class, and a horseback riding trip to study the geology of the Cerrillos hills. A few miles after the college, it's back to city streets. These last 5 miles, while not as scenic, follow a good route back to the State Capitol.

LOCAL INFORMATION

♦ Santa Fe County Chamber of Commerce (www.santafechamber.com), 510 North Guadalupe Street, Santa Fe, NM 87501; (505) 983–7317.
♦ Santa Fe Convention and Visitor Bureau (www.santafe.org), 201 West Marcy Street, Santa Fe, NM 87504; (800) 777–2489.

EVENTS/ATTRACTIONS

♦ State Capitol, 411 State Capitol, Santa Fe, NM 87501; (505) 986–4589.
♦ El Rancho de las Golondrinas (www.golondrinas.org), 334 Los Pinos Road, Santa Fe, NM 87505; (505) 471–2261 (New Mexico residents free on Wednesdays; call for details).
♦ JW Eaves Movie Ranch, 105 Rancho Alegre, Santa Fe, NM 87505; (505) 474–3045.

RESTAURANTS

♦ Lone Butte General Store, 3815 Highway 14, Santa Fe, NM 87505; (505) 471–5002 (buffet 11:00 A.M. to 8:00 P.M. daily).
♦ San Marcos Cafe, 3877 Highway 14, Santa Fe, NM 87505; (505) 471–9298 (8:00 A.M. to 2:00 P.M. daily).

ACCOMMODATIONS

♦ Sunrise Springs Inn and Retreat (www.sunrisesprings.com), 242 Los Pinos Road, Santa Fe, NM 87505; (800) 955–0028.

BIKE SHOPS

♦ Ace Mountain Bikes, 825 Early Street, Santa Fe, NM 87505; (505) 982–8079.
♦ New Mexico Bike 'N Sport, 1829 Cerrillos Road, Santa Fe, NM 87505; (505) 820–0809.
♦ rob and charlie's, 1632 St. Michaels Drive, Santa Fe, NM 87505; (505) 471–9119.
♦ Santa Fe Mountain Sports, 607 Cerrillos Road, Santa Fe, NM 87501; (505) 988–3337.

REST ROOMS

♦ Mile 0: State Capitol.
♦ Mile 15.2: Airport Road Shell station.
♦ Mile 21.5: El Rancho de las Golondrinas (visitors only).
♦ Mile 31.1: Lone Butte General Store.
♦ Mile 38.4: Allsup's convenience store.
♦ Mile 45.0: Conoco Quik Stop.

MAPS

♦ USGS 7.5-minute quads Santa Fe, Agua Fria, Tetilla Peak, Picture Rock, and Turquoise Hill.
♦ Delorme *New Mexico Atlas & Gazetteer,* maps 23 and 24.

Santa Fe Century Classic

More than 2,000 bicyclists ride the annual Santa Fe Century in the spring. Some participants try to complete their first century—a 100-mile ride that is a rite of passage for many cyclists—while racers and long-distance riders use the loop as a training ride. This century is held each year on the third Sunday in May and is the biggest one-day cycling event in the state. The route is beautiful—rural countryside, farmlands, scenic views, old mining towns, and small villages.

One of the best (and toughest) parts of the loop is the first third—along the Turquoise Trail (New Mexico Route 14), an ancient trading route dotted today with revived ghost towns. After leaving Santa Fe one of the first places to stop is the village of Cerrillos. Explore the dirt roads of this historic mining town and get a taste of the Old West. In its heyday during the 1880s, Cerrillos boasted twenty-one saloons and four hotels. This mining district produced gold, silver, lead, zinc, and world-famous turquoise. You can't miss the next town, Madrid, where old mining shacks are now colorful studios and galleries. You'll ride right through the main drag where you can stop for coffee, ice cream, or pizza. Lock up your bike and check out all the arts and crafts.

After a long climb into the Ortiz Mountains, you'll descend into Golden, the site of the first gold rush this side of the Mississippi River. It is the last town before you leave the Turquoise Trail. Stop in at the general store on the left and get ready for the 0.5-mile steep climb on New Mexico Route 344. The famous Heartbreak Hill will take you up and out of the Ortiz into Estancia Valley, where it will seem as if you can see all the way to Texas. The farms in the area produced tons of pinto beans until the droughts of the 1940s. Enjoy the fairly level riding through the tiny ranching communities of Cedar Grove and

Start: Capshaw Junior High School in Santa Fe.

Length: 101.6-mile loop.

Terrain: Century organizers describe it as "a medium difficult [ride] with rollers, ascents, and descents, but with a major stretch of flats and easy rollers."

Traffic and hazards: Getting out of Santa Fe is a bit of a challenge because of traffic and the frustration of intersections. Most of the rural sections have good road conditions with a small shoulder and little traffic, except the stretch between Lone Butte and Golden—be careful here. U.S. Highway 285 and Interstate 25 have large shoulders.

Getting there: In Santa Fe take exit 284 off I-25 and travel north on U.S. Highway 84/ 285 (St. Francis Drive) to the second traffic light, Zia Road. Turn right and go 0.3 mile to Capshaw Junior High on the left. The school is the official start for the Santa Fe Century, but unless you are riding the day of the event, it is best to park at the large lot in front of the Albertson's grocery store, immediately on the right when you turn onto Zia Road.

Stanley. There are no services out here.

My favorite part of the ride is between Stanley and Galisteo (New Mexico Route 41). You get great views of the Sangre de Cristo Mountains and super-fun rollers, mostly downhill. Look for the basalt walls called "hogbacks," narrow rocky ribs intersecting your route. The green oasis of Galisteo is almost a suburb of Santa Fe now. Cottonwoods line the dirt roads, and there are orchards of fruit trees and large adobe homes. Read the historic marker to learn about the site of a nearby pueblo abandoned in the late 1700s, after which Spanish settlers recolonized the village over the next hundred years. There is a tiny grocery store across from the Catholic church.

You'll be getting close to Santa Fe when you pass the turnoff for Lamy. The village dates back to 1870, when the Santa Fe Railroad Company decided to build a train station here. The route was too steep to take the line (Raton to Albuquerque) up through Santa Fe. You can turn left on County Road 533 for a round-trip of 3.2 miles to the station, or just ride 0.9 mile to the Santa Fe County Lamy Park, and use the shaded tables along the tracks for a picnic. The remainder of the ride takes you past Eldorado, a large housing community outside Santa Fe, then along I–25. With 100-plus miles behind you, you'll be back in the capital city.

This loop is considered a moderate century—easier than the Enchanted Circle Century in Taos. The hardest climb is Heartbreak Hill, one of the steepest roads in the state. You'll encounter this 0.5-mile climb after passing through Golden. Otherwise, you can enjoy gently rolling hills with some modest climbs, a long downhill after Heartbreak Hill, and a great flat stretch between Cedar Grove and Stanley. If you do the loop in a day, you'll likely face a headwind in the afternoon, about the time you reach Stanley.

Riding a leg of the Santa Fe Century through one of the many small communities on the route.

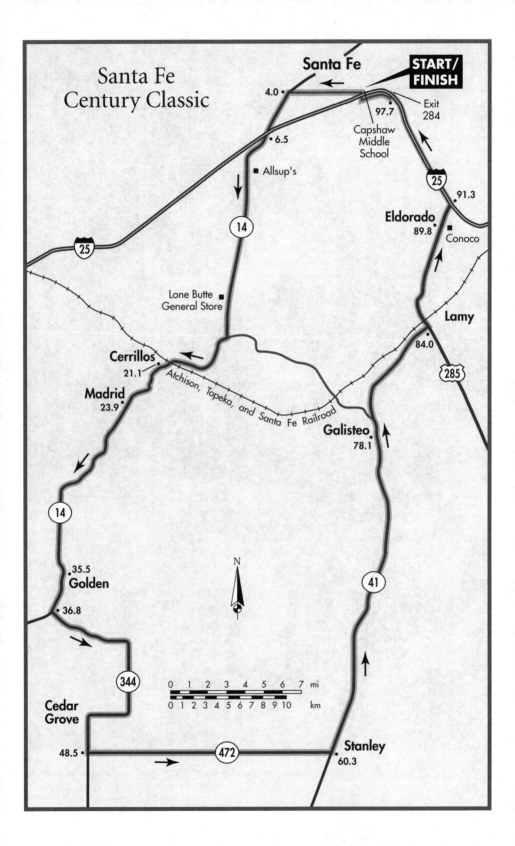

0.0 The start of the Santa Fe Century, Capshaw Junior High School on Zia Road (County Road 71A). You'll have a good shoulder through Santa Fe and a very wide shoulder once you reach New Mexico Route 14.

0.3 Intersection at St. Francis Drive (U.S. Highway 285/84); Albertson's grocery and Office Max on the left. Go straight, continuing on Zia Road. Expect a dozen or so lights before getting out of town.

2.1 Zia Road merges with Rodeo Road (New Mexico Route 300); continue straight.

3.6 Proceed through traffic light at Zafarano Road; Villa Linda Mall on the left.

4.0 Get into the left lane at this major intersection, and turn left on Cerrillos Road (New Mexico Route 14), the southern end of a commercial strip (motels, gas stations, etc.).

6.0 Traffic light at the frontage road for I–25; continue straight. Be alert for traffic getting on the interstate while you remain on New Mexico Route 14.

6.5 Go under I–25. A sign indicates TURQUOISE TRAIL.

8.3 Traffic light at New Mexico Route 599; Allsup's convenience store on the left.

9.9 Pass the New Mexico Penitentiary.

14.9 Lone Butte General Store on the right. The road narrows and is winding; soon the shoulder is almost nonexistent.

18.3 Check out the cool rock formations called the Garden of the Gods.

21.1 Cross over railroad tracks, and reach the turnoff for Cerrillos.

23.9 Ride down the mile-long "main street" of Madrid, a must stop. When you continue, be ready for a gradual climb (about 5 miles) into the Ortiz Mountains.

28.9 Reach Stagecoach Pass and descend, taking in the view of the ski area on the east side of the Sandias and Mt. Taylor, far in the distance on the western horizon.

35.5 Arrive in Golden; store on the left with limited snacks and bottled water (no public rest rooms; closed Sunday and Monday).

36.8 Turn left onto New Mexico Route 344 and climb for about 1.5 miles, the last 0.5 mile is Heartbreak Hill.

(continued)

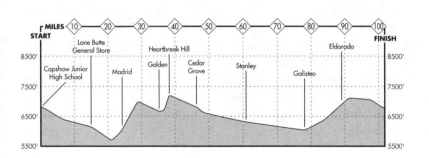

38.3 The top! Enjoy the payoff; descend for miles.

46.5 Ride through Cedar Grove. No elevation change for about 20 miles.

48.3 Pass South Mountain Elementary School.

48.5 Turn left onto New Mexico Route 472 toward Stanley. (Continue straight on New Mexico Route 344 to reach Edgewood—overnight stop. Travel 5 miles on New Mexico Route 344, go under I–40 to a four-way stop, and turn left on old U.S. Highway 66. Alta Mae's Heritage Inn is 0.2 mile on the right, and Red Arrow Campground is 0.3 mile on the left.)

60.3 Turn left onto New Mexico Route 41 and ride through Stanley. A wide shoulder exists for about 8 miles.

78.1 Reach Galisteo; Catholic church on the left and Anaya's Country Store (no rest rooms) on the right. The store is open daily if you can catch the owner around. Sometimes you must go around back and knock at the residence. The Galisteo Inn is just a bit farther on the right.

79.6 Vista Clara Ranch on the right.

84.0 Turn left (north) on U.S. Highway 285, and gain a wide shoulder.

84.5 Optional turnoff for Lamy (County Road 553). Turn right and travel 0.9 mile to the shaded picnic tables along the railroad tracks. To continue the century, cross the railroad tracks on U.S. Highway 285 and begin a 1-mile moderate climb.

89.8 Reach a traffic light at Eldorado; Conoco on the right. For groceries, pizza, or Thai food, turn left and go about 0.2 mile to a shopping center on the right.

91.3 Get in the left lane and turn left onto I–25 (south); large shoulder continues.

97.7 Get off I–25 at exit 284, Old Pecos Trail (New Mexico Route 466), and turn left at the top of the ramp to cross over the interstate.

98.1 Turn right on Rabbit Road and parallel the interstate (no shoulder).

99.9 Turn right on St. Francis Drive (shoulder), and go under the interstate.

101.3 Traffic light at Zia Road; turn right.

101.6 Return to Capshaw Junior High School.

The actual century ride is organized by the Santa Fe Century Committee, a nonprofit corporation headed up by Willard Chilcott. This retired business-man and touring cyclist from California took over the event in the mid-1980s from a local cycling club that had been running it for a few years. In 1999 the Leukemia-Lymphoma Society of America adopted this century as one of its fund-raising cycling events. Maybe there is a chapter in your area that is getting people ready for the big day. Teams in Training are assigned a coach and meet for weekly rides.

If you are not riding the loop as part of the official century, you won't have the luxury of food stops with volunteers supplying water, fresh fruit, and energy bars; and there won't be a sag wagon for support with a mechanic on duty. The route is fairly remote, so refer to the mileage description to plan for food and water stops. You will definitely need two bottles for the section between Golden and Galisteo.

You can divide this century in half with an overnight in Edgewood, which adds 10 miles because the town is off-route. The lodging choices are limited to an interstate RV campground (tents allowed) or a lovely inn with guest rooms that include a whirlpool bath and fireplace. There are several places to stay in Madrid as well as two resort properties in Galisteo. If you plan your trip around these towns, you'll have three riding days—25, 55, and 20 miles. To leave your vehicle in Santa Fe, contact the city of Santa Fe. The city lots permit overnight parking at a rate of $5.00 per day.

LOCAL INFORMATION

♦ Santa Fe County Chamber of Commerce (www.santafechamber.com), 510 North Guadalupe Street, Santa Fe, NM 87501; (505) 983–7317.
♦ Santa Fe Convention and Visitor Bureau (www.santafe.org), 201 West Marcy Street, Santa Fe, NM 87504; (800) 777–2489.
♦ City of Santa Fe, Public Parking, P.O. Box 909, Santa Fe, NM 87504-0909; (505) 955–6581 (free map of city lots).

EVENTS/ATTRACTIONS

♦ Santa Fe Century (www.santafecentury.com), 885 Camino Del Este, Santa Fe, NM 87501; (505) 982–1282.
♦ Madrid has the largest concentration of "sights." Check out www.turquoisetrail.org/madrid.htm for information on galleries, museums, and theater.

RESTAURANTS

♦ Backroad Pizza, 2849 Highway 14, Madrid, NM 87010; (505) 474–5555 (great "pies!").
♦ Java Junction, 2855 Highway 14, Madrid, NM 87010; (505) 438–2772.
♦ For places to eat in Lone Butte, see the Capital City Cruise; and in Eldorado, see the Eldorado Ramble.

ACCOMMODATIONS

♦ Alta Mae's Heritage Inn (www.altamae-nm.com), 950 Old Route 66, Edgewood, NM 87015; (505) 281–5000.

♦ Red Arrow Campground (www.redarrowrv.com), P.O. Box 1750, Edgewood, NM 87015; (505) 281–0893.

BIKE SHOPS

♦ Ace Mountain Bikes, 825 Early Street, Santa Fe, NM 87505; (505) 982–8079.
♦ New Mexico Bike 'N Sport, 1829 Cerrillos Road, Santa Fe, NM 87505; (505) 820–0809.
♦ rob and charlie's, 1632 St. Michaels Drive, Santa Fe, NM 87505; (505) 471–9119.
♦ Santa Fe Mountain Sports, 607 Cerrillos Road, Santa Fe, NM 87501; (505) 988–3337.

REST ROOMS

♦ Mile 15.0: Lone Butte General Store.
♦ Mile 24.6: Porta-potty across from Backroad Pizza in Madrid.
♦ Mile 91.5: Conoco in Eldorado.
♦ There are several gas stations before leaving Santa Fe. No rest rooms from Madrid to Eldorado—more than 60 miles. It's possible to get water in Golden and Galisteo if the small stores are open.

MAPS

♦ USGS 7.5-minute quads Santa Fe, Agua Fria, Turquoise Hill, Picture Rock, Madrid, Golden, San Pedro, King Draw, Stanley, Ojo Hedionda, Galisteo, and Seton Village.
♦ Delorme *New Mexico Atlas & Gazetteer,* maps 23 and 24.

Old Santa Fe Trail Cruise

T his ride begins where the Santa Fe Trail ended. A plaque on the southeast corner on the Plaza in Santa Fe marks the western terminus of this historic trail and reminds us that wagon caravans loaded with goods arrived here from Missouri in the 1800s, opening up the first major trade route with the West. What took the pioneers more than two months to travel, we can cycle in a couple weeks. While you have the option of going all the way to Missouri, this out-and-back follows the paved-road Old Santa Fe Trail, which roughly parallels the last miles of the original Santa Fe Trail.

The story of the Santa Fe Trail began in 1821 when Mexico won its independence from Spain, and New Mexico became part of Mexico. A trader from Missouri, William Becknell, gets the credit for opening the Santa Fe Trail. Deep in debt and facing jail, he left Missouri and ended up in Santa Fe, where he exchanged his goods for silver coins. For the next 60 years, the trail was an important trade route; in addition to marking a pivotal point in the development of Santa Fe, it played a big role in the Mexican-American War (1846) and the Civil War (1862). In 1880 the railroad reached Santa Fe and the train gradually replaced the trail.

Today, the Santa Fe Trail is remembered by historic landmarks and relived in books and movies. Hundred-year-old wagon ruts are still apparent in places. Congress designated the route a National Historic Trail in 1987 and, along with the Santa Fe Trail Association, works to preserve it.

Start your ride with a big New Mexican–style breakfast—*huevos rancheros* (eggs with chile sauce) and *papas fritas* (home fries with chili and cheese). The

Start: The Plaza in Santa Fe.

Length: 19 miles round-trip.

Terrain: Gradual climbing for half the ride with 2 miles that will work you, plus a very steep mile out of Canada de los Alamos. You will have an almost continuous descent back to the Plaza.

Traffic and hazards: The area around the Plaza is very congested, especially in the summer. Watch for pedestrians, parked cars, and general chaos. You'll find confusing intersections and one-way streets. The rest of the ride is almost traffic-free.

Getting there: In Santa Fe take exit 284 off Interstate 25, travel north on U.S. Highway 84/285 (St. Francis Drive) for about 3 miles, and turn right on Cerrillos Road. Continue straight through the intersections at Guadalupe Street and Paseo De Peralta; after about 0.5 mile on Cerrillos, be sure to bear right at the Y intersection. You will reach a four-way stop at Alameda Street after another 0.2 mile; continue straight and begin one-way. Go one block and turn right on Water Street; go another block to the intersection at Don Gaspar Avenue and continue straight. Enter the city's public parking lot immediately on your right. Water Street Parking Lot has a bike rack and public rest rooms behind the fee station. The fee is $5.00 for the day, the best rate downtown close to the Plaza. (*Note:* Street parking is free on Sundays.) To reach the Plaza leave the parking lot, turn right on Water Street, and go half a block to Old Santa Fe Trail. Turn left and go one block to a traffic light, the southeast corner of the Plaza (San Francisco Street and Old Santa Fe Trail). There is a bike rack across from the northwest corner of the Plaza at the intersection of Lincoln Avenue and Palace Avenue.

Plaza Restaurant is located on the west side of the Plaza and is open from 7:00 A.M. to 9:00 P.M. daily (breakfast served until 11:00 A.M.). After taking some photos at the monument to the Santa Fe Trail, head out of downtown and enjoy the cycling, saving the sightseeing for after the ride.

You will ride on Old Santa Fe Trail from the Plaza to the road's end in the village of Canada de los Alamos. This is one of the most popular short rides in the city. After negotiating the maze near the Plaza, you'll gradually climb a moderate grade into the foothills of the Sangre de Cristo Mountains. The hillsides are covered with juniper and pinon, and some of Santa Fe's largest homes are visible here and there. After the first few miles, you'll have local traffic only, which is very light.

Old Santa Fe Trail turns to gravel just past the village of Canada de los Alamos (no services). The 1-mile climb back out of the village is steep, but the

Participants in the Santa Fe Trail Bicycle Trek on Day 1 heading out of town—their destination, Missouri.

rewards far outweigh the work. This long descent is a personal favorite, as much for the ride as for the expansive views.

There is a lot to stop and see in the first (or last) 2 miles of this ride. A history buff may never leave the Plaza. The NPS (National Park Service) Southwest Office is located in one of the largest adobe buildings in the country. This National Historic Landmark is worth a stop. Follow the self-guided tour to fully appreciate the outstanding Spanish–Pueblo Revival architecture. The next stop—the museums. A turn onto Camino Lejo takes you to the Museum of International Folk Art, the Museum of Indian Arts and Culture, and the Wheelwright Museum of the American Indian (cost $5.00 each; $1.00 for New Mexico residents on Sunday).

At the intersection of Camino Corrales, there is a city park that is a certified site of the Santa Fe National Historic Trail. The main route of the trail crossed here at Amelia E. White Park, and faint wagon ruts are still visible. As you near the Plaza, there are three historic churches within a couple blocks of each other—San Miguel Mission, Loretto Chapel, and St. Francis Cathedral. Don't miss the Miraculous Staircase at the Loretto Chapel.

If you want to follow the northern route of the Santa Fe Trail all the way to its eastern terminus in Missouri (about 1,100 miles), you can join the Santa Fe Trail Bicycle Trek. For eleven years, a group of cyclists has left the Plaza in

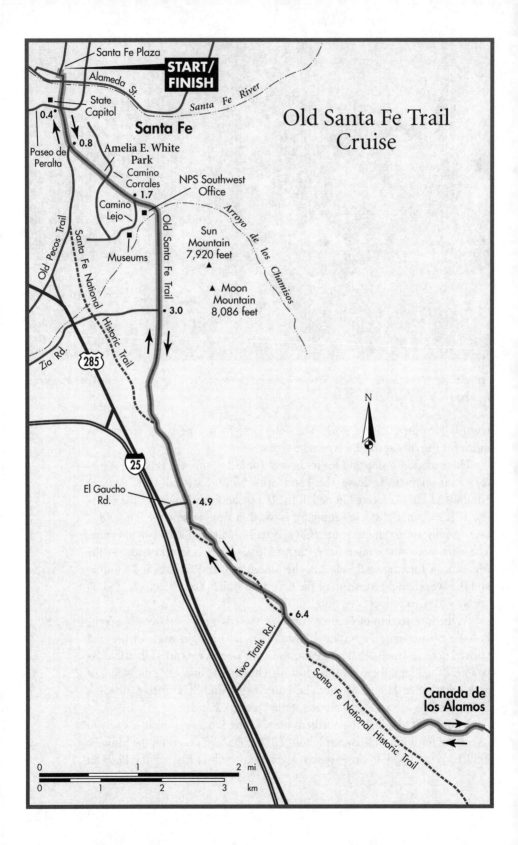

Santa Fe Plaza

START/ FINISH

Alameda St.

Santa Fe River

State
Capitol

0.4

0.8

Santa Fe

Old Santa Fe Trail Cruise

Paseo de
Peralta

Amelia E. White
Park

Camino
Corrales

NPS Southwest
Office

• 1.7

Arroyo de los Chamisos

Camino
Lejo

Old Santa Fe Trail

Old Pecos Trail

Santa Fe National

Museums

Sun
Mountain
7,920 feet
▲

▲ Moon
Mountain
8,086 feet

• 3.0

Historic Trail

Zia Rd.

285

25

N

El Gaucho
Rd.

• 4.9

• 6.4

Two Trails Rd.

Santa Fe National Historic Trail

**Canada de
los Alamos**

0   1   2 mi

0   1   2   3 km

MILES AND DIRECTIONS

0.0 Start at the southeast corner of the Plaza, the intersection of Old Santa Fe Trail and San Francisco Street, where you'll find a monument dedicated to the historic trail. Head south, walking your bike on the sidewalk because Old Santa Fe Trail is one-way for a block and a half.

0.1 Turn left on Water Street and take an immediate right to continue on Old Santa Fe Trail, which is now a two-way street. You can hop on your bike here.

0.2 Reach the traffic light at Alameda Street and continue straight, crossing over the Santa Fe River. Garrett's Desert Inn is on the left.

0.3 Upper Crust Pizza (right)—good stop for the return trip.

0.4 Pass the New Mexico and Santa Fe Visitor Center on the left; Guadalupe Cafe and the State Capitol on the right. Then cross Paseo De Peralta (traffic light).

0.8 Watch for a left turn to stay on Old Santa Fe Trail. Signs read ST. JOHN'S COLLEGE and MUSEUMS. Leave the craziness of downtown behind you. A good shoulder exists for the next 2 miles.

1.3 Reach Amelia E. White Park (left), where you'll find shaded benches under a grape arbor. At the four-way stop (Camino Corrales), continue straight.

1.7 For a side trip to the museums, turn right on Camino Lejo. There is a large parking lot on the left in 0.2 mile. You'll find a green bike rack out front, straight ahead as you enter the lot.

1.8 Pass the NPS Southwest Office, where there is a visitor information desk, rest rooms, and a water fountain (no bike rack).

1.9 Take a sharp curve to the right and cross Arroyo de los Chamisos. Enjoy views of Sun Mountain (Monte Sol), the small, rounded hill on the left.

3.0 Reach a three-way stop (Zia Road), and continue straight. Barely any paved shoulder from here to the road's end.

4.7 Pass New Mexico Academy.

4.9 County Road 36 (El Gancho Road) on the right leads to Old Las Vegas Highway; continue straight.

5.4 A bridge marks the start of a 0.5-mile gradual climb, which is followed by a steeper 0.2-mile climb.

(continued)

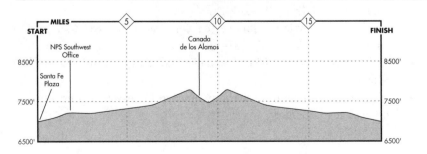

6.4 Sign reads TO I-25. County Road 67C (Two Trails Road) on the right leads to Old Las Vegas Highway. Another sign reads NO OUTLET. Continue straight ahead, gradually climbing for 2 miles. The last 0.2 mile is a grunt.

8.5 Reach the high point of the ride, and view the rocky Shaggy Peak and Glorieta Baldy behind and to the left. Begin a fast descent.

9.0 Enter the village of Canada de los Alamos (watch for dogs), continuing your descent.

9.5 Pavement ends. Change into a climbing gear before you turn around and retrace your route. The first mile is the steepest part of the ride, then enjoy a long descent, practically downhill all the way back to the Plaza. You'll have incredible views to the west of the Jemez Mountains.

19.0 Return to the historic Plaza.

September and ridden paved roads that closely trace the original route. The twenty-day trip is fully supported and limited to fifty riders. Your breakfast, dinner, and campsite are covered for $30 per day. All gear is transported by truck. You can choose to ride with the group for part of the trip (a minimum of four days starting in Santa Fe). Contact the Santa Fe Bicycle Committee for more information.

LOCAL INFORMATION

♦ City of Santa Fe, Public Parking, P.O. Box 909, Santa Fe, NM 87504-0909; (505) 955–6581 (free map of city lots).

♦ Santa Fe County Chamber of Commerce (www.santafechamber.com), 510 North Guadalupe Street, Santa Fe, NM 87501; (505) 983–7317.

♦ Santa Fe Convention and Visitor Bureau (www.santafe.org), 201 West Marcy Street, Santa Fe, NM 87504; (800) 777–2489.

EVENTS/ATTRACTIONS

♦ Santa Fe Trail Association (www.santafetrail.org), Santa Fe Trail Center, RR 3, Larned, KS 67550; (316) 285–2054.

♦ Santa Fe Trail Bicycle Committee (chilcott1@aol.com), 885 Camino Del Este, Santa Fe, NM 87501; (505) 982–1282.

♦ NPS Southwest Office, 1100 Old Santa Fe Trail, Santa Fe, NM 87504; (505) 988–6011.

♦ For general information on the museums, go to www.nmculture.org and click on "alphabetical order."

RESTAURANTS

◆ Plaza Restaurant, 54 Lincoln Avenue, Santa Fe, NM 87501; (505) 982–1664.
◆ Upper Crust Pizza, 329 Old Santa Fe Trail, Santa Fe, NM 87501; (505) 982–0000.
◆ Guadalupe Cafe, 422 Old Santa Fe Trail, Santa Fe, NM 87501; (505) 982–9762.

ACCOMMODATIONS

◆ Garrett's Desert Inn, 311 Old Santa Fe Trail, Santa Fe, NM 87501; (505) 982–1851 (on-route).

BIKE SHOPS

◆ Ace Mountain Bikes, 825 Early Street, Santa Fe, NM 87505; (505) 982–8079.
◆ New Mexico Bike 'N Sport, 1829 Cerrillos Road, Santa Fe, NM 87505; (505) 820–0809.
◆ rob and charlie's, 1632 St. Michaels Drive, Santa Fe, NM 87505; (505) 471–9119.
◆ Santa Fe Mountain Sports, 607 Cerrillos Road, Santa Fe, NM 87501; (505) 988–3337.

REST ROOMS

◆ Mile 0.4: New Mexico and Santa Fe Visitor Center.
◆ Mile 1.8: NPS Southwest Office (mile 17.2 on the return).

MAPS

◆ USGS 7.5-minute quads Santa Fe, Seton Village, and Glorieta.
◆ Delorme *New Mexico Atlas & Gazetteer,* map 24.

Santa Fe Hill Climb Challenge

*A*re you ready for a real challenge? This hill climb will put your granny gear to work. The road up to the Santa Fe Ski Area is a local favorite. The Santa Fe National Forest Scenic Byway (New Mexico Route 475) starts near the historic Plaza and climbs into the Sangre de Cristo Mountains, gaining a total of about 3,400 feet in elevation. For most of the ride, you'll be surrounded by the Santa Fe National Forest, the city's backyard where hikers, backpackers, cross-country skiers, and snowshoers recreate. If this climb is too easy, you can always race up it. Locals hold a race to the top in August called the Santa Fe Hill Climb. The record is around 54 minutes. Contact Stephen Newhall at rob and charlie's for more information.

In addition to the climb, this ride has many highlights—incredible views, cool mountain air, picnic sites, and some of the largest stands of aspen in the country. You will climb from hilly juniper-pinon country through stands of ponderosa pine and mixed conifers into a beautiful alpine forest with spruce and fir. The ride starts at Fort Marcy/Magers Field Complex, one of the city's most popular parks. The facility includes an indoor pool, a gymnasium, racquetball courts, a weight room, and outdoor playing fields. There is a bike rack out front, and you can get bottled water, sports drinks, and granola bars from the vending machines inside. (*Note:* For $1.85 you can use the pool and/or showers. Call ahead for information on lap and recreational pool times.)

New Mexico Route 475 changes names three times from Artist Road to Hyde Park Road to Ski Basin Road. The wide shoulder at the start only lasts for

Start: Fort Marcy/Magers Field Complex on Washington Avenue, downtown Sante Fe.

Length: 30 miles round-trip.

Terrain: A fairly continuous climb from about 7,000 feet to 10,000-plus feet; and of course, a screaming descent.

Traffic and hazards: Dangers vary from leaf-lookers and RVs to rockfall and sudden mountain thunderstorms. You'll have to share the road with other outdoor enthusiasts, especially on summer weekends and during aspen viewing season. New Mexico Route 475 is winding and narrow, but there is a small shoulder and most drivers go relatively slowly. Use extreme caution on the descent. I have a friend who almost took out a line of Girl Scouts crossing the road in Hyde State Park. This area can be very congested.

Getting there: In Santa Fe take exit 284 off Interstate 25 and travel north on U.S. Highway 84/285 (St. Francis Drive) for about 3 miles to the major intersection at Cerrillos Road. Continue straight on St. Francis Drive for another 0.8 mile to Paseo De Peralta and turn right. Bank of America is on the corner. (Do not turn on Paseo De Peralta at the traffic light right after Cerrillos Road. Paseo De Peralta is a horseshoe that intersects St. Francis Drive twice.) At the fifth traffic light on Paseo De Peralta, after 1.1 miles, turn left on Washington Avenue. At the first traffic light, Artist Road, turn left into Fort Marcy/Magers Field Complex. (Note: On Sunday, Fort Marcy doesn't open until 12:00 p.m. If you need water or a rest rooms, stop at one of the gas stations on St. Francis Drive, or turn left into the De Vargas Mall at the first light on Paseo De Peralta and go into Starbucks.)

0.3 mile. Through the residential section (the first 3 miles), there is little or no shoulder, and this is where you need it. There is a 1-foot shoulder that comes and goes throughout the rest of the ride. The road is fairly smooth with patchy sections, loose rock, and small potholes that are easy to avoid.

You can plan your day a number of ways. The 350-acre Hyde Memorial State Park marks the halfway point on the climb—time for a picnic? It's New Mexico's highest state park, located at 8,400 feet and surrounded by national forest. Hyde makes a great base for visiting the area; and if you cycle in, you can use the facilities free of charge. Log shelters are available for picnicking or as camping spots, and vault toilets and water pumps are located near every site.

I highly recommend doing this ride in the fall when the ski area offers

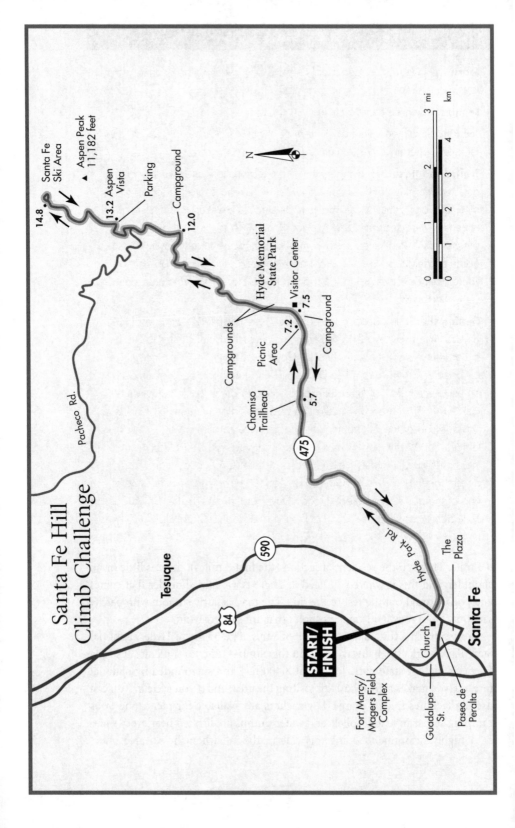

Santa Fe Hill
Climb Challenge

Tesuque

84

590

Pacheco Rd.

Santa Fe Ski Area

14.8

13.2 Aspen Vista

Parking

▲ Aspen Peak
11,182 feet

Campground
12.0

N

Campgrounds

Hyde Memorial
State Park

Visitor Center
7.5

7.2

Picnic Area

Campground

Chamiso Trailhead

5.7

475

Hyde Park Rd.

The Plaza

START/FINISH

Church

Santa Fe

Fort Marcy/
Magers Field
Complex

Guadalupe St.

Paseo de Peralta

0   1   2   3 mi

0   1   2   3   4 km

0.0 Pedal out of the parking lot and go straight at the traffic light to begin cycling on New Mexico Route 475, or Artist Road. The workout begins with a 0.5-mile climb. When the road flattens out, look for the towers on top of Tesuque Peak to locate the ski area.

0.3 Prince Avenue on the right leads to Fort Marcy Compound.

2.6 Sierra Del Norte on the left with alternative parking. The large dirt lot is for Dale Ball Trails (hiking and mountain biking).

3.5 Ten Thousand Waves on the left. At the top of the next hill, enjoy a 1-mile descent and check your brakes. The sharp curve during the descent is called Nun's Corner.

5.2 Roadside parking on the right at the sign that reads SANTA FE NATIONAL FOREST.

5.7 Chamiso Trailhead, with parking on both sides of the road.

7.2 Little Tesuque Picnic Ground on the left offers shaded tables.

7.3 Black Canyon Campground on the right (no picnicking).

7.5 Reach Hyde Memorial State Park. Be sure to top off your water bottles here. If the visitor center (small building on the right) is open, you can use the rest rooms and get something from the vending machines. From here you will cycle a very steep mile called "the Wall." Little Tesuque Creek parallels the road through the park.

8.5 Borrego Trailhead, the small parking lot on the left, offers access to a popular 4-mile hiking loop. From here views open up and continue to get better and better as you climb.

9.8 Did the road just level out for a second?

11.0 The break you've been waiting for-some flat and downhill total 1 mile!

12.0 Big Tesuque Campground is situated along a creek.

13.2 Aspen Vista, where it seems everyone and their dog comes during aspen viewing season.

14.2 A must stop—overlook on the left affords the best view around. Relax on the benches and take it all in.

(continued)

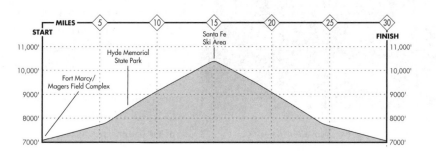

14.3 Parking for the cross-country ski track on the left and the start of 0.5-mile descent.

14.8 Santa Fe Ski Area, the second highest ski area in the country. Circle the loop to the left to reach picnic tables near the famous Windsor Trail, great for hiking into the wilderness area or mountain biking down to Tesuque.

15.0 Reach the top of the climb and the bottom of the ski area (elevation 10,400 feet; summit, 12,053 feet). Retrace your route, and enjoy the descent!

30.0 Return to Fort Marcy.

chairlift rides for aspen viewing. The Super Chief Quad Chair will take you to Aspen Peak (about 11,000 feet), where you can get a better look at the spectacular patches of gold on the mountainside. The chairlift operates from 10:00 A.M. to 3:00 P.M. daily, late-September to mid-October. You can buy your lift

Enjoying the descent from the Santa Fe Ski Area.

ticket for about $7.00 from Skier's Services, the small building on the right near the Quad. The Base Lodge is open during this time (water and rest rooms), and La Casa Cafe Grill serves soups, burgers, and lunch specials out on a large deck. (*Note:* You will have to lock your bike to the ski racks or a railing.)

A soak in an outdoor tub may be in order after the ride. Drive up to Ten Thousand Waves, Santa Fe's Japanese-style health spa, when you finish. You will need a reservation for treatments—massages, facials, and wraps—as well as for lodging at the Houses of the Moon, but you can walk in and use the communal tub or the women's tub for as long as you like for $13. These public tubs include a wet/dry sauna, cold plunge, and sun deck. The Waves sells fresh fruit, healthy snacks, bottled water, and sodas.

Trek for Trash

Every year since 1994, Gov. Gary Johnson and his Clean Team have cycled across New Mexico picking up trash along the highways. This state program, Trek for Trash, is raising awareness for the environment and helping to keep New Mexico's roads litter free. All ages and abilities are encouraged to participate. There are thousands of volunteers each year, and communities get involved with the project by providing meals, sponsoring rallies, and staging cleanups in their area. The number of trash bags collected was as high as 18,000 one year, and the total mileage covered during the event is usually between 450 and 900. For more information, contact New Mexico Clean and Beautiful, Department of Tourism, 495 Old Santa Fe Trail, Lew Wallace Building, Santa Fe, NM 87501; (505) 827–6346.

Lodging choices in Santa Fe are endless. Check with the chamber of commerce or the visitor bureau. If you want to stay right on the route, contact Fort Marcy Compound. This ten-acre facility is a nice alternative to downtown hotels, and it's only a couple blocks from the Plaza. The one-, two-, and three-bedroom suites have fireplaces and kitchens; the amenities include indoor pool, hot tub, and continental breakfast. Also, guests have free use of the facility at Fort Marcy/Magers Field Complex.

LOCAL INFORMATION

♦ Santa Fe County Chamber of Commerce (www.santafechamber.com), 510 North Guadalupe Street, Santa Fe, NM 87501; (505) 983–7317.
♦ Santa Fe Convention and Visitor Bureau (www.santafe.org), 201 West Marcy Street, Santa Fe, NM 87504; (800) 777–2489.

EVENTS/ATTRACTIONS

♦ Fort Marcy/Magers Field Complex, 490 Washington Avenue, Santa Fe, NM 87501; (505) 955–2500 (opens 6:00 A.M. weekdays, 8:00 A.M. Saturdays, and 12:00 P.M. Sundays).
♦ Hyde Memorial State Park, 740 Hyde Park Road, Santa Fe, NM 87501; (505) 983–7175.
♦ Santa Fe National Forest, 1220 St. Francis Drive, Santa Fe, NM 87504; (505) 988–6940.
♦ Ski Santa Fe (www.skisantafe.com), 2209 Brothers Road, Suite 220, Santa Fe, NM 87505; (505) 982–4429.

◆ Ten Thousand Waves (www.tenthousandwaves.com), 3451 Hyde Park Road, Santa Fe, NM 87501; (505) 992–5025.

RESTAURANTS

◆ La Casa Cafe Grill at the ski area in the fall when chairlift is running.
◆ Endless choices in and around the Plaza. Leave Fort Marcy and take a right on Washington Avenue. Go straight through the traffic lights at Paseo De Peralta and Marcy Street to Palace Avenue, the northeastern corner of the Plaza.

ACCOMMODATIONS

◆ Fort Marcy Compound (www.fortmarcy.com), 320 Artist Road, Santa Fe, NM 87501; (800) 745–9910.

BIKE SHOPS

◆ Ace Mountain Bikes, 825 Early Street, Santa Fe, NM 87505; (505) 982–8079.
◆ New Mexico Bike 'N Sport, 1829 Cerrillos Road, Santa Fe, NM 87505; (505) 820–0809.
◆ rob and charlie's, 1632 St. Michaels Drive, Santa Fe, NM 87505; (505) 471–9119.
◆ Santa Fe Mountain Sports, 607 Cerrillos Road, Santa Fe, NM 87501; 505-988-3337.

REST ROOMS

◆ Mile 0: Fort Marcy/Magers Field Complex (just inside on the right).
◆ Mile 7.5: Visitor center at Hyde State Park.
◆ Mile 15.0: Santa Fe Ski Area (inside main building at far end on the left; only open when chairlift is running in the fall).
◆ Vault toilets are located at Little Tesuque Picnic Ground, Hyde Memorial State Park, Big Tesuque Campground, Aspen Vista, and the Windsor Trailhead.

MAPS

◆ USGS 7.5-minute quads Santa Fe, McClure Reservoir, and Aspen Basin.
◆ Delorme *New Mexico Atlas & Gazetteer,* map 24.

Tesuque Cruise

This out-and-back starts at the same place—just north of the historic Santa Fe Plaza—as the Santa Fe Hill Climb Challenge (17) and gives you about the same mileage without the continuous climbing to 10,000 feet. However, the ride out through the village of Tesuque and beyond is still challenging. This ride, in the rolling hills north of Santa Fe, offers some of the most extraordinary views in the area—from the red mesas of the Rio Grande valley, up to the forested mountain ranges, and toward the (usually) blue New Mexico sky. Enjoy sweeping vistas of the Sangre de Cristo Mountains to the northeast and the Jemez Mountains to the west. Return views include the Sandia Mountains near Albuquerque.

The ride starts at Fort Marcy/Magers Field Complex, one of the city's most popular parks. The facility includes an indoor pool, a gymnasium, racquetball courts, a weight room, and outdoor playing fields. There is a bike rack out front, and you can get bottled water, Powerade, and granola bars from the vending machines inside. (*Note:* For $1.85 you can use the pool and/or the showers. Call ahead for information on lap and recreational pool times.)

Fort Marcy is a common starting point for several area rides. The Santa Fe Road Riders meet here for their weekday afternoon rides, which might involve climbing up to the ski area or following Old Santa Fe Trail, and sometimes they head out through Tesuque. You can sign up to get weekly e-mail announcements about the club's rides by going to www.clubs.yahoo.com/clubs/sfroadriders.

Start: Fort Marcy/Magers Field Complex on Washington Avenue, downtown Santa Fe.

Length: 24.4 miles round-trip.

Terrain: Rolling foothills of the Sangre de Cristo Mountains provide some good, short climbs. The steepest grade is on the switchback coming out of Chupadero on the return.

Traffic and hazards: No shoulders on any of the route. The road through Tesuque is very narrow with blind curves and congestion; in contrast, New Mexico Route 592 is more open with little to no traffic.

Getting there: In Santa Fe take exit 284 off Interstate 25 and travel north on U.S. Highway 84/285 (St. Francis Drive) for about 3 miles to the major intersection at Cerrillos Road. Continue straight on St. Francis Drive for another 0.8 mile to Paseo De Peralta and turn right. Bank of America is on the corner. (Do not turn on Paseo De Peralta at the traffic light right after Cerrillos Road. Paseo De Peralta is a horseshoe that intersects St. Francis Drive twice.) At the fifth traffic light on Paseo De Peralta, after 1.1 miles, turn left on Washington Avenue. At the first traffic light, Artist Road, turn left into Fort Marcy/Magers Field Complex and park. (Note: On Sunday, Fort Marcy doesn't open until 12:00 P.M. If you need water or a rest rooms, stop at one of the gas stations on St. Francis Drive, or turn left into De Vargas Mall at the first light on Paseo De Peralta and go into Starbucks.)

You will begin with a 1.5-mile climb, riding into the juniper-pinon hill country north of Santa Fe, once uninhabited and now filled with hundreds of adobe-style homes. This back road (Bishops Lodge Road) becomes narrow and tree-lined as you descend into the charming creekside village of Tesuque. This old Spanish agricultural area turned artist community is lush, green, and quiet, a nice change of pace from the hustle and bustle of the Plaza. The village is adjacent to the Tesuque Indian Reservation, hence the name.

Beyond Tesuque, New Mexico Route 592 will take you into the colorful foothills of the Sangre de Cristos and through the tiny villages of Chupadero and En Medio (the end of the road). Challenging hills and big views await. This part of the ride is very rural and one of my all-time favorite stretches of road. At mile 12.2, the road turns to gravel and leads into Santa Fe National Forest.

Early in the ride you will pass by Shidoni, a bronze art foundry where you can see the sculptures in the roadside garden from your bike or stop and visit the operation and its gallery. The first bronze was poured 30 years ago, and demonstrations are held on Saturdays. You can take a self-guided tour of the outdoor sculptures in the apple orchards along the river; the sculpture gardens are open during daylight hours. At Tesuque Glassworks, which is next door, you can learn about the process of blowing glass; and there are several other galleries near the elementary school.

Tesuque Village Market, the type of place you wish was along every cycling route, acts as a restaurant, deli, bakery, grocery, and liquor store. It will fill the needs of any cyclist—pizza, salads, international brews, pastries, breakfast burritos, ice cream, even power gel. The dessert counter is decadent. You can dine in or sit outside on the deck. Be sure to plan your trip to include this favorite local hangout.

Lodging choices in Santa Fe are endless. Check with the chamber of commerce or the visitor bureau. If you want to stay right on the route, there are two beautiful resorts—Bishop's Lodge and Rancho Encantado. Both properties have excellent restaurants. Check out their Web sites for more information.

LOCAL INFORMATION

♦ Santa Fe County Chamber of Commerce (www.santafechamber.com), 510 North Guadalupe Street, Santa Fe, NM 87501; (505) 983–7317.
♦ Santa Fe Convention and Visitor Bureau (www.santafe.org), 201 West Marcy Street, Santa Fe, NM 87504; (800) 777–2489.

EVENTS/ATTRACTIONS

♦ Fort Marcy/Magers Field Complex, 490 Washington Avenue, Santa Fe, NM 87501; (505) 955–2500 (opens 6:00 A.M. weekdays, 8:00 A.M. Saturdays, and 12:00 P.M. Sundays).

Shidoni—a sculpture garden on the ride out to Tesuque and beyond.

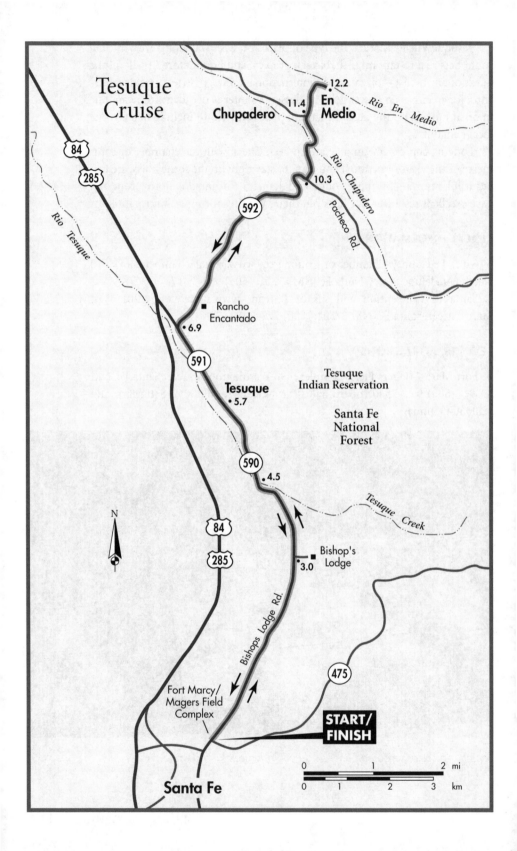

MILES AND DIRECTIONS

0.0 From the traffic light at Fort Marcy, turn left and head north on Bishops Lodge Road (New Mexico Route 590). Begin with a steady 1.5-mile climb.

1.4 Road levels off; enjoy views of the Sangre de Cristo Mountains to the northeast.

2.2 Begin the descent into the village of Tesuque.

3.0 Pass the entrance to Bishop's Lodge on the right; road narrows ahead.

4.0 Dead end road on the right leads to the parking for the Windsor Trail, well-known hiking and mountain biking trail that climbs to the Santa Fe Ski Area. Begin riding alongside Tesuque Creek.

4.5 Cross Tesuque Creek.

5.1 Pass the Shidoni Foundry on the left; see the sculpture gardens along the road.

5.6 Pass the Tesuque Elementary School on the right; several galleries nearby.

5.7 Reach a stop sign; Tesuque Village Market one block to the left. Continue straight as the road becomes one-way.

5.8 Another stop sign; El Nido Restaurant to the right. Turn right (almost straight ahead) onto Tesuque Road (New Mexico Route 591).

6.1 Pass the post office.

6.9 Turn right onto New Mexico Route 592; a sign for Rancho Encantado marks the intersection. Begin climbing into the foothills. This climb is about a mile.

9.1 Begin another mile-long climb.

10.3 Reach a stop sign and turn left. The gravel road ahead leads into the national forest, up Pacheco Canyon, to the Ski Basin Road. Descend to Chupadero—one steep switchback.

10.9 Cross the Rio Chupadero as the road levels out for a half mile.

11.4 Side road on the left leads into the tiny community of Chupadero; continue straight. Climb some more on rollers.

12.0 Flat stretch of road into the community of En Medio; watch for dogs.

12.2 Road turns to dirt ahead; turn around here, or before.

24.4 Return to Fort Marcy. (Note: On the return trip, you won't be able to legally ride the one-way stretch of road that you encountered at mile 5.7. Instead, continue a block past El Nido, reach Tesuque Village Market, and turn left through their parking area. Turn right at stop sign; you are back on Bishops Lodge Road.)

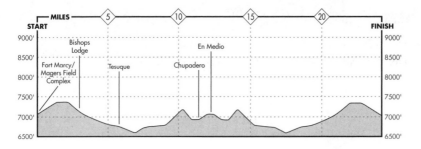

♦ Shidoni Foundry (www.shidoni.com), P.O. Box 250, Tesuque, NM 87574; (505) 988–8001 (gallery open Monday through Saturday from 9:00 A.M. to 5:00 P.M.; foundry open Monday through Friday from noon to 1:00 P.M. and all day Saturday).

RESTAURANTS

♦ Tesuque Village Market, P.O. Box 6400, Tesuque, NM 87574; (505) 988–8848 (daily 7:00 A.M. to 9:00 P.M.; until 10:00 P.M. in the summer).
♦ El Nido Restaurant, NM 591 at Bishops Lodge Road, Tesuque, NM 87573; (505) 988–4340 (dinner only Tuesday through Sunday; American and Southwest cuisine and full bar).
♦ In addition, both resorts listed under Accommodations have excellent restaurants.

ACCOMMODATIONS

♦ Bishop's Lodge (www.bishopslodge.com), P.O. Box 2367, Santa Fe, NM 87501; (800) 732–2240.
♦ Rancho Encantado (www.rancho-encantado.com), 198 State Road 592, Santa Fe, NM 87506; (505) 982–3537.

BIKE SHOPS

♦ Ace Mountain Bikes, 825 Early Street, Santa Fe, NM 87505; (505) 982–8079.
♦ New Mexico Bike 'N Sport, 1829 Cerrillos Road, Santa Fe, NM 87505; (505) 820–0809.
♦ rob and charlie's, 1632 St. Michaels Drive, Santa Fe, NM 87505; (505) 471–9119.
♦ Santa Fe Mountain Sports, 607 Cerrillos Road, Santa Fe, NM 87501; (505) 988–3337.

REST ROOMS

♦ Mile 0.0: Fort Marcy/Magers Field Complex, just inside on right (water fountain also).
♦ Mile 5.7: Tesuque Village Market.

MAPS

♦ USGS 7.5-minute quads Santa Fe and Tesuque.
♦ Delorme *New Mexico Atlas & Gazetteer*, map 24.

Eldorado Ramble

T his short loop is worth the drive out to Eldorado, a "subdivision" of Santa Fe. The terrain is perfect for any level of rider, and you will have wide open views of three different mountain ranges— the Sandias, the Jemez, and the Sangre de Cristos. The route is relatively flat, the roads are smooth, and the traffic is light. You will be riding through Santa Fe "suburbia." When this residential area was first developed, many people wondered who would want to drive twenty minutes in to work. Now Eldorado is a community in itself. Try this neighborhood ride as a warm-up in early season—you may enjoy it enough to ride it twice.

This loop begins at the Agora, a shopping center that serves Eldorado and the surrounding area. Start your trip with coffee or tea at Las Chivas; or plan your ride so when you return, you can eat lunch or dinner at Zen World Cuisine, which serves excellent Pad Thai. At the Eldorado Supermarket, you can get bottled water, energy bars, or ice cream, and relax at the tables in the lovely courtyard. A bike rack is located on the west side of the complex between Outback Video and the coffeehouse.

After a short stretch on U.S. Highway 285, where the shoulder is 6 feet wide, you'll enter Eldorado by what residents call the "third entrance," Avenida Eldorado. Views ahead include the scattered hills of the Ortiz Mountains and the big dome of the Sandia Mountains. As you roll along Avenida Casa Del Oro, the Jemez Mountains dominate the scenery. You may be able to pick out Valle

Start: Agora Shopping Center in Eldorado off U.S. Highway 285, 10 miles southeast of Santa Fe.

Length: 14-mile loop.

Terrain: Relatively flat with one gentle climb and some easy rollers.

Traffic and hazards: U.S. Highway 285 has light highway traffic but a large shoulder. The roads in Eldorado have little traffic except when residents are commuting to and from work. You will probably encounter traffic on Avenida Vista Grande, the main artery in the community; but there is a 3-foot shoulder and a bike path on this stretch. Be careful at the two railroad crossings.

Getting there: From Santa Fe, travel north on Interstate 25 for about 8 miles to exit 290. Head south on U.S. Highway 285 toward Clines Corners. Turn right at the second traffic light onto Avenida Vista Grande, which Eldorado residents call the "second entrance." There is a Chevron station on the left at this intersection. Go 0.3 mile and turn right into the parking lot at the Agora.

Grande, the remnant of a volcano that collapsed into its magma chamber a million years ago. A little over halfway into the ride, you pedal toward the southern tip of the Sangre de Cristos, the closest of the three ranges, and climb gently along the edge of the foothills before exiting Eldorado by way of the "first entrance" and turning back toward the Agora.

At many places along the ride, you will see the treelike cholla cacti—the cane cholla, which is the most common species in New Mexico. These weird-looking plants have short, tubular segments that are joined together. The flower is a brilliant red-maroon and blooms in early summer. You may also notice a barrel-shaped yellow fruit that remains on the plant for several seasons. The cane cholla can grow as tall as a person. Look for them along the road, especially where there is a large undisturbed lot.

The Eldorado Ramble incorporates most of the paved roads in the community. The roads are smooth except for a section on Avenida Vista Grande (from the small park to the railroad tracks) and the section on Avenida Del Monte Alto. You can choose to ride on the paved bike path, but you'll have to cross dirt roads and be alert for walkers, runners, and other cyclists.

When I first started work on the book, I was housesitting in the area and used the paved roads in Eldorado for my easy morning rides. I was surprised to see wildlife—hawks, jackrabbits, coyotes. When I wanted to get in more miles, I'd just ride the Eldorado Ramble twice for a total of 28 miles. You can also add an out-and-back on Avenida Azul (2 miles) and a smaller loop using Avenida Torreon (3 miles).

The Celebrated Chile

One thing that changed when I started cycling in New Mexico was the food in my handlebar bag. I found new kinds of snacks like green chile bagels and chile-lemon pistachios. The chile, one of the oldest spices in the world, is celebrated and honored. There are endless varieties—up to ninety—ranging from mild to hot. Chiles have been grown here for centuries, and today 60 percent of the nation's chile crop is harvested in the Land of Enchantment.

New Mexico has its own unique cuisine, far from the taste of Mexican or Tex-Mex. The chile is often the defining ingredient. Many rides can be combined with a traditional New Mexican meal so you can sample some of the state's best chiles—red or green. Don't miss the chance to savor some of the famous dishes such as hot tamales, stuffed *sopapillas* (fried dough), *carne adovada* (pork in red chile sauce) and blue-corn enchiladas.

LOCAL INFORMATION

♦ Eldorado Community Improvement Association, 1 Hacienda Loop, Santa Fe, NM 87505; (505) 466–4248.

EVENTS/ATTRACTIONS

♦ Eldorado offers local events such as a Fourth of July Parade and the Eldorado Studio Tour. Check out www.eldoradonet.com, a listing of services, businesses, and special events.

RESTAURANTS

♦ Las Chivas, 7 Avenida Vista Grande, Santa Fe, NM 87505; (505) 466–1010.
♦ Zen World Cuisine, 7 Avenida Vista Grande, Santa Fe, NM 87505; (505) 466–3700 (dinner entrees average about $15).

ACCOMMODATIONS

There are no accommodations in Eldorado.

BIKE SHOPS

There are four bike shops in Santa Fe, 10 miles away.

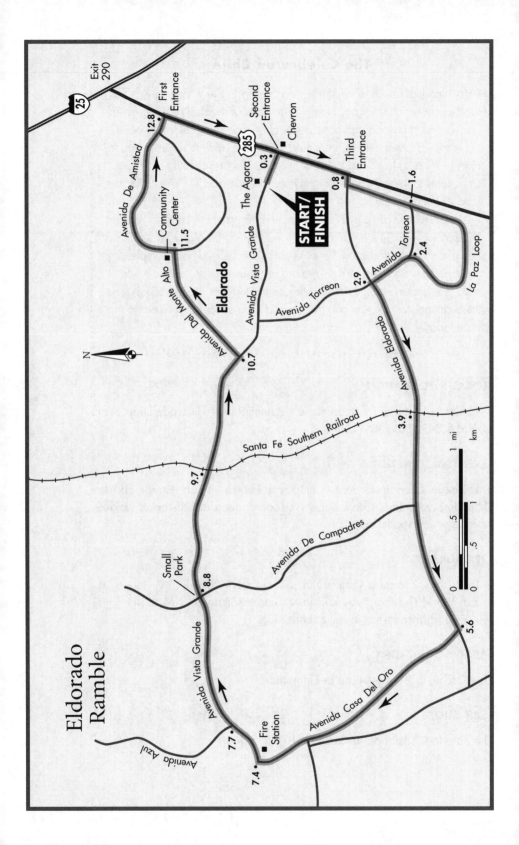

Eldorado Ramble

0.0 Leaving the shopping center, turn left on Avenida Vista Grande.

0.3 Reach a traffic light, and turn right on U.S. Highway 285. The shoulder is at least 6 feet wide.

0.8 Turn right on Avenida Eldorado, the first paved right after the light, just beyond the horse stables.

0.9 Turn left on La Paz Loop and parallel U.S. Highway 285.

1.6 When the road curves away from the highway, it becomes Avenida Torreon. Look closely for a left turn in order to stay on La Paz Loop.

2.4 Reach a stop sign at a T intersection; turn left on Avenida Torreon.

2.6 Reach another stop sign at a T intersection, and turn right. The street sign reads CARISSA ROAD, but the road is still Avenida Torreon.

2.9 At the stop sign turn left on Avenida Eldorado, where you'll have a good shoulder.

3.9 Cross the railroad tracks. Lamy Singletrack, a multiuse trail that runs from Santa Fe to Lamy, crosses here.

5.6 Pavement ends ahead. Turn right on Avenida Casa Del Oro and enjoy rolling hills.

7.4 Reach a stop sign after the El Dorado Fire and Rescue Station No. 2, and turn right onto Avenida Vista Grande. A paved bike path begins on the left side of the road.

7.7 Option: Turn left on Avenida Azul and do an out-and-back for an additional 2 miles with great views and gentle rollers.

8.8 If you need a break, turn left on Avenida De Compadres (use the bike path; road is dirt) to a small park with a picnic table, porta-potty, and trash can.

9.7 Cross the railroad tracks again.

10.7 Turn left on Avenida Del Monte Alto.

11.3 The bike path crosses to the left side of the road. (*Note:* If you get on the bike path here, you'll end up in the parking lot of the community center. There is a bike rack on your right and a porta-potty on your left. Continue into the parking

(continued)

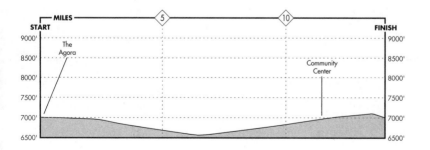

lot, and circle around to the left to locate a water pump. Leave the parking lot and turn left to continue on the ride. You will be on Avenida De Amistad.)

11.4 Community center on the left.

11.5 At the T intersection, turn left on Avenida De Amistad.

12.8 Reach a traffic light, and turn right on U.S. Highway 285.

13.7 Turn right on Avenida Vista Grande at the traffic light.

14.0 Turn right into the shopping center parking lot.

REST ROOMS

♦ Mile 0: Eldorado Supermarket (back left corner).
♦ Mile 8.8: The small park off Avenida De Compadres (porta-potty).
♦ Mile 11.4: Community center at the end of the bike path (porta-potty).

MAPS

♦ USGS 7.5-minute quad Seton Village.
♦ Delorme *New Mexico Atlas & Gazetteer,* map 24.
♦ *Santa Fe Street Maps* by Horton Family Maps (purchase at local bookstores).

Pecos River Valley Challenge

New Mexico Route 63 out of Pecos is one of two gateways to the central section of the Pecos Wilderness Area. (The other is New Mexico Route 475, the Santa Fe Hill Climb Challenge [17].) This huge wilderness area covers 233,667 acres of the Sangre de Cristo Mountains and includes the second highest mountain in the state, Truchas Peak (elevation 13,103 feet.). The dead-end road leaves town and follows the Pecos River into the beautiful high country of the Santa Fe National Forest. While we can't cycle into the wilderness, New Mexico Route 63 offers a peek at the heavily forested ridges, broad mesas, lush meadows, and rugged mountains. There are great views of East Pecos Baldy, and you can choose several turn-around points depending on how much mileage and climbing you want to get in.

I almost didn't go check out this ride because locals warned of rough pavement and terrible traffic. There is some of both, but on a weekday in the early morning, this stretch of road is one of my favorites. New Mexico Route 63 gets heavy use in the summer and on weekends for good reason. There is great fishing, hiking, horseback riding, and camping. The forest service maintains numerous campgrounds, picnic sites, and day-use areas; weekend cabins, summer camps, and private communities line the road. The canyon isn't Disney World by any means; it's just crowded sometimes.

You will follow the Pecos River for the entire ride, and the sights and sounds of the river almost make up for the scary traffic. This river is full of trout. I don't think you could ride along this road without seeing a fly fisherman.

Start: Pecos/Las Vegas Ranger Station in Pecos.

Length: 43.6 miles round-trip; Terrero makes a nice turn-around point for a mellow ride of 27.6 miles.

Terrain: Rolling with gentle climbs to Terrero, some steep sections to Cowles, and a 700-foot gain in 2 miles to Jacks Creek.

Traffic and hazards: Narrow, winding road with high recreational use on weekends. Be prepared for pickups, RVs, and horse trailers. I would not ride on New Mexico Route 63 during any holidays—Memorial Day, Fourth of July, or Labor Day. Although there are several big potholes, the pavement is relatively smooth. Please respect private property.

Getting there: From Santa Fe, travel on Interstate 25 for about 15 miles and get off at exit 299, Glorieta/Pecos. Turn left at the stop sign, drive over the interstate, and take a right at the next stop sign to pick up New Mexico Route 50. You'll reach a four-way stop, the intersection with New Mexico Route 63, in the village of Pecos after 5.7 miles. Turn right and go 0.2 mile. Park at the Pecos/Las Vegas Ranger Station on the right.

Taking a break at Holy Ghost Creek on the Pecos River Valley Challenge.

Lisboa Springs, the oldest fish hatchery in the state (built in the early 1920s), produces more than two million trout every year, most of which are released in the Pecos and its tributaries. The natural reproduction cycle just isn't enough to meet the fishing demands of this area.

For a more mellow ride, your destination is Terrero, 14 miles up the canyon where a country store is famous for its hummingbird watching. I burned a lot of film trying to get a shot of these birds hovering in flight. There were dozens of hummingbirds trying to get to the large feeders along the porch. For a bigger challenge, keep climbing to Cowles and on to Jacks Creek where the scenery gets even better. The traffic and crowds lessen, and you ride high above the river for awhile. The views of East Pecos Baldy are worth the climb. Ponderosa pines tower over you; and as you get close to Jacks, the higher elevation rewards you with stands of spruce and aspen.

The ride starts at the Pecos/Las Vegas Ranger Station, which is open Monday to Saturday from 8:00 A.M. to 5:00 P.M. You can fill up water bottles and use the rest rooms here. In addition, there are two gas stations across the road. Adelo's is a real country store, selling everything from fishing tackle and lumber to groceries and jeans-since the turn of the twentieth century. I highly recommend the Beloved Bakery on your way out of town. They have everything a cyclist needs—big-bun cinnamon rolls, sandwiches, homemade pizza, and ice cream. If you are staying overnight, you can camp at one of several forest service campgrounds, you can rent a cabin along the river, or you can stay at a B&B in town.

Don't leave town without visiting the Pecos National Historic Monument, 1.6 miles south of the ranger station on New Mexico Route 63. A trail leads to ruins of an ancient pueblo and an eighteenth-century mission church, and you can climb down a wooden ladder into a ceremonial chamber called a *kiva.* Learn about the area's Spanish, Anglo, and Native American history, including the Santa Fe Trail and the Civil War Battle at Glorieta Pass. The facility, which opens daily at 8:00 A.M. except Christmas and New Year's Day, offers a visitor center, museum, short film, and picnic area. (*Note:* The monument can be used as an alternative starting point.)

LOCAL INFORMATION

♦ Pecos/Las Vegas Ranger Station (Santa Fe National Forest), P.O. Box 429, Pecos, NM 87522; (505) 757–6121.

EVENTS/ATTRACTIONS

♦ Terrero General Store and Riding Stables, P.O. Box 12, Terrero, NM 87573; (505) 757–6193.
♦ Pecos National Historic Monument, P.O. 418, Pecos, NM 87522; (505) 757–6414 ($2.00 per person/$4.00 per carload).

RESTAURANTS

♦ Beloved Bakery, Main Street, Pecos, NM 87552; (505) 757–8717.
♦ Adelo's Town and Country Store, Main Street and NM 63, Pecos, NM 87552; (505) 757–8565.
♦ Pecos Cafe & Grill, Main Street, Pecos, NM 87552; 505-757-7020 (New Mexican food; open Tuesday through Sunday from 5:30 to 9:00 P.M.).

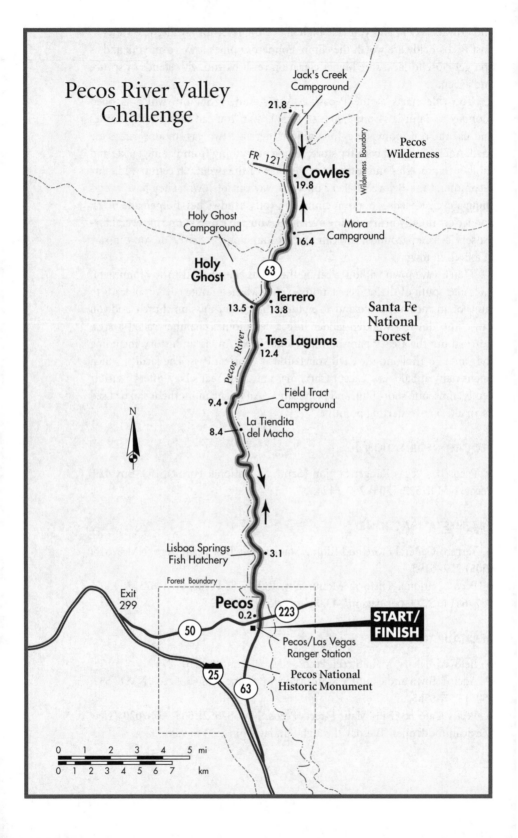

Pecos River Valley Challenge

Jack's Creek
Campground

21.8

FR 121

Cowles
19.8

Wilderness Boundary

Pecos
Wilderness

Holy Ghost
Campground

Mora
Campground
16.4

**Holy
Ghost**

63

13.5 **Terrero**
13.8

Santa Fe
National
Forest

Pecos River

Tres Lagunas
12.4

Field Tract
9.4 Campground

La Tiendita
8.4 del Macho

N

Lisboa Springs
Fish Hatchery
3.1

Forest Boundary

Exit
299

Pecos
0.2 223

50

**START/
FINISH**

Pecos/Las Vegas
Ranger Station

25

63

Pecos National
Historic Monument

0 1 2 3 4 5 mi
0 1 2 3 4 5 6 7 km

0.0 Leave the Pecos/Las Vegas Ranger Station, turn left on New Mexico Route 63, and begin riding through the northern end of the village. You will pass the Cake Stand Inn, Pecos Cafe & Grill, and Adelo's Town and Country Store.

0.2 Continue straight at the intersection with New Mexico Route 223. A 3-foot shoulder exists for a mile; you might end up sharing it with pedestrians, horses, or ATVs.

0.9 Beloved Bakery on the left. You must stop—before the ride (cinnamon rolls) and after (ice cream).

1.0 Cross the Pecos River.

1.3 From here to the road's end, there is little or no shoulder. Hopefully you are riding on a weekday morning.

1.7 Monastery Benedictine, a Catholic retreat, on the left.

2.6 Turnoff for Monastery Lake; a gravel road leads to a popular fishing spot (vault toilet).

3.1 Lisboa Springs Fish Hatchery on the left.

4.6 Enter the Santa Fe National Forest.

6.5 Dalton, a day-use area; vault toilet on the right.

8.4 La Tiendita del Macho, small grocery and fishing tackle store on the right with a covered wooden deck and a picnic table (no rest rooms).

9.4 Field Tract Campground, a fourteen-site shaded campground on the right with rest rooms and water.

10.2 Cross over the river at Windy Bridge; vault toilet at the picnic area on the left before the bridge.

10.9 Pass Brush Ranch, a residential school and summer camp on 283 acres.

12.4 Tres Lagunas, a private community with beautiful log homes and bright red roofs nestled among the ponderosa pine.

13.3 Sign indicates BERT CLANCEY RECREATION AREA NEXT 4 MILES. The 2,166 acres along the river were purchased to provide public fishing access.

13.5 Forest Road 122 on the left leads to Holy Ghost Campground.

(continued)

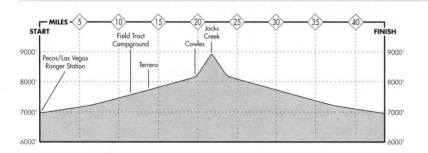

13.8 Terrero General Store and Riding Stables, a good turn-around point and the destination for most of the hummingbirds in the area. Relax on the bench behind the flower boxes and watch these funny little birds. In addition to food and water, Terrero has a post office, showers (cost $5.00), rest rooms, and a pay phone. If you are continuing, be aware that there is no center line for the next 5 miles.

16.4 Mora Campground has a roadside picnic table and a vault toilet.

19.8 Cowles, another possible turn-around point. Federal Road 121 on the left leads to a campground and Panchuelo Day-Use Area. The yellow center line is back, and the pavement is smooth to Jacks Creek.

21.8 Jacks Creek, a forty-three-site campground that has an equestrian area and trail access to the wilderness (water and vault toilet). The beautiful meadow is filled with aspen. Enjoy mostly downhill on your way back to the ranger station.

43.6 Return to the Pecos/Las Vegas Ranger Station.

ACCOMMODATIONS

♦ Cake Stand Inn (www.cakestandinn.com), P.O. Box 205, Pecos, NM 87522; (505) 757–2426 (early 1900s farmhouse with guest rooms and great food).

♦ Mark Rents Cabins (www.markrentscabins.com), 215 Washington Avenue, Santa Fe, NM 87501-1926; (505) 988–7517 (nine cabins between Windy Bridge and Terrero; three-night minimum).

BIKE SHOPS

There are four bike shops in Santa Fe, 15 miles away.

REST ROOMS

♦ Mile 0: Pecos/Las Vegas Ranger Station (closed Sundays).

♦ Mile 9.4: Field Tract Campground.

♦ Mile 13.7: Terrero General Store (customers only).

♦ There are vault toilets at several of the recreation sites including Monastery Lake, Dalton, Mora Campground, and Jacks Creek.

MAPS

♦ USGS 7.5-minute quads Pecos, Rosilla Peak, and Cowles.

♦ Delorme *New Mexico Atlas & Gazetteer,* map 24.

Mora River Valley Cruise

I f you love cycling out in the country, this route through the beautiful Mora River valley is for you. Here, the Sangre de Cristo Mountains meet the high plains. There is rolling farmland and roadside raspberry picking, plus a state park with a lake where you begin and end your trip. You will be riding along the eastern edge of the Santa Fe National Forest with some dramatic views of the mountains in the Pecos Wilderness Area. The terrain alternates between small valleys with lush green fields and forests of ponderosa pine. In addition, you will pass through several old Hispanic villages. This ride is a lollipop loop; you'll pedal out 8 miles before starting the actual loop, then repeat those 8 miles at the end.

The ride begins just north of Las Vegas at Storrie Lake State Park, a great jumping-off point for a day of cycling. Come the night before and camp right along the edge of the 1,100-acre lake, popular with water-skiers, sailboarders, fishermen, and families. In late fall you will see a variety of waterfowl including Canada geese; in the winter you might spot an eagle. The water is pretty cool—in August when I rode this loop, the water-skiers had on wet suits—but I'm sure there are days hot enough for a swim. This man-made lake was built in the early 1900s to provide irrigation for a large-scale farming project that never got off the ground. The area was dedicated as a state park in 1960.

Rest rooms with hot showers and a water fountain are located to the left of the visitor center. (*Note:* The building is locked before dark. There are portapotties in the parking lot and vault toilets throughout the park.) The visitor center also has rest rooms and water as well as a pay phone. You can choose to

Start: Storrie Lake State Park, about 4 miles north of Las Vegas.

Length: 52.6-mile loop.

Terrain: Flat to rolling farmland with one stiff climb.

Traffic and hazards: Traffic is generally light, and there is a shoulder for about two-thirds of the ride. New Mexico Route 94 is winding and narrow in a few spots.

Getting there: Exit off Interstate 25 onto Business I–25 in Las Vegas. If you are traveling from the south, take exit 343, then go about 2.5 miles to the traffic light at Mills Avenue, and turn left. At the intersection, you will find a train engine on display and a Phillips 66. From the north, take exit 347 and turn after the golf course (second right) on Mills Avenue. Travel 0.6 mile on Mills Avenue to the first traffic light (Seventh Street). Turn right, heading north on New Mexico Route 518. Pass the Las Vegas Ranger Station on the right after 0.5 mile. Continue another 2.5 miles, and turn left into Storrie Lake State Park. There is an after-hours parking lot immediately on the right (no fee).

pay for day-use (picnicking), for an overnight stay, or no fee. There is a parking lot outside the gate before the fee station. The camping options include primitive sites, shelters, and shelters with electricity. Everyone has views across the lake with the Sangre de Cristo Mountains as a backdrop. The park opens at 6:00 A.M. from April through September, otherwise 7:00 A.M., and closes at sunset, which in the summer is about 8:30 P.M.

You may notice the distinctive Hermit Peak (elevation 10,212 feet) to the west before you reach the historic marker at mile 6.0. The story goes that a hermit living up there in the 1860s carved crucifixes to trade for food. At this point in the ride, the high grassy prairies of the Great Plains stretch as far as you can see to the east; and the Sangre de Cristo Mountains rise up behind Hermit Peak.

Slow down at the intersection of New Mexico Route 442, and check out the scenic waterwheel of La Cueva Mill. From the late 1800s until 1949, this adobe mill was used to grind flour, and the waterwheel produced electricity. It was one of a number of mills in the area that supported a large wheat-farming industry. Today the restored mill and several other buildings, including San Rafael Church, are part of a national historic district—Salman Ranch.

The property is home to a famous raspberry farm. Raspberries have been grown commercially here since the 1930s. Folks come from all over to visit the outlet store, and the raspberry business is large enough to provide seasonal jobs for the county. At the store, you can purchase pints of plump, red raspberries (pesticide-free), and raspberry jam, syrup, and vinegar—even raspberry lemonade! Time your visit for after Labor Day, and you'll be able to pick your own fresh raspberries.

This peaceful little valley allows you to step back in time. The old walled-in gardens are beautifully landscaped, and willows line the canal in front of the historic mill. Across the street from the store, there are picnic tables and a rest room. You can purchase bottled water or fill up at the sink. Salman Ranch runs a big mail-order business, especially busy during the holidays, so be sure to pick up a brochure.

Next stop? Mora, a Hispanic farming village with a quaint main street. As you ride through "downtown," you may find it hard to believe that this is the county seat (founded 1835). Many buildings are boarded up now, but in the early 1900s, the area flourished with homes, mills, and mercantiles. Mora once had the third largest number of homesteads in the state. For fast food and New Mexican dishes, stop at Alfonso's just before turning onto New Mexico Route 94. You can eat outside at tables under red and white umbrellas.

The remainder of the ride is even more rural, which you'll be able to appreciate after the steep climb out of Mora. Rolling hills and long straightaways take you through some of the most scenic farming and ranching land in the state. There are no services until you reach New Mexico Route 518 again—nothing left to stop and see but plenty of great scenery to enjoy.

LOCAL INFORMATION

♦ Mora Valley Chamber of Commerce (www.moravalley.com/chamber), P.O. Box 800, Mora, NM 87732; (505) 387–6072.

EVENTS/ATTRACTIONS

♦ Storrie Lake State Park, HC 33 Box 109-2, Las Vegas, NM 87701; (505) 425–7278.
♦ Salman Ranch, P.O. Box 156, Buena Vista, NM 87712; 505-387-2900 (summer hours daily 9:00 A.M. to 5:00 P.M., except Sundays open at 10:00 A.M.).

RESTAURANTS

♦ Alfonso's Foods, Highway 518, Mora, NM 87732; 505-387-6503 (Sunday through Thursday 11:00 A.M. to 7:00 P.M.).
♦ Variety of food choices in Las Vegas just a few miles from the state park. Head south back into town on NM 518.

ACCOMMODATIONS

♦ Almanzar Motel, HC 34 Box 10, Mora, NM 87715; (505) 387–5230 (just off the bike route).
♦ Variety of lodging choices in Las Vegas. Go to www.lasvegasnewmexico.com.

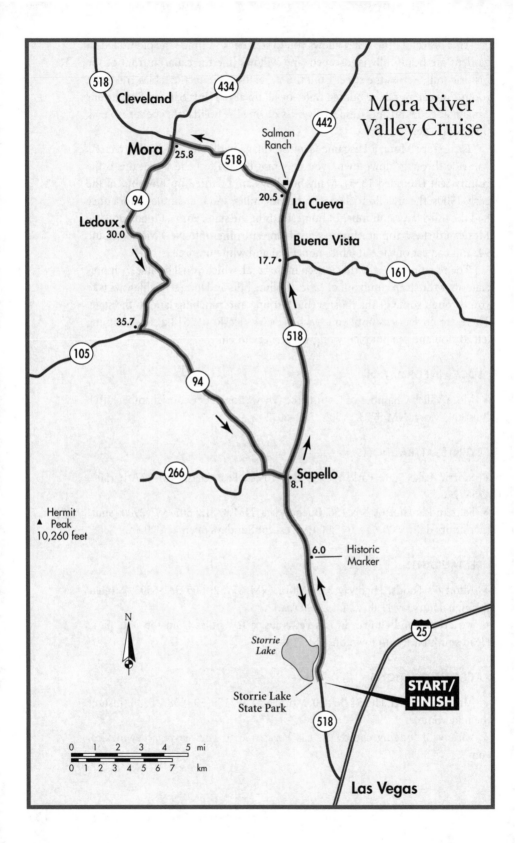

Mora River Valley Cruise

518 Cleveland
434
442

518
Mora
25.8
Salman
Ranch
518
20.5
La Cueva

94
Ledoux
30.0
Buena Vista

17.7
161

35.7
518

105

94
266

518
Sapello
8.1

Hermit
Peak
10,260 feet

6.0
Historic
Marker

N

25

Storrie
Lake

START/
FINISH

Storrie Lake
State Park

518

0   1   2   3   4   5 mi
0 1 2 3 4 5 6 7 km

Las Vegas

0.0 Leave the state park and head north (left) on New Mexico Route 518.

6.0 A historic marker on the right gives a brief story on Hermit Peak. You can see this distinctive tabletop peak directly to the west.

8.1 Reach the small community of Sapello; Chevron station on the left. You will cross the Sapello River and reach the junction with New Mexico Route 94, your return route; continue straight.

17.7 New Mexico Route 161 heads right to Golondrinas; continue straight.

18.5 Ride through the tiny town of Buena Vista; post office on the left.

19.8 Lose the shoulder and descend to La Cueva.

20.5 Cross over the Mora River, and reach Salman Ranch at the junction of New Mexico Route 442 in La Cueva. The ride continues straight on New Mexico Route 518 toward Mora. Turn right on New Mexico Route 442 to get a better view of the mill and to visit the store (0.1 mile up on left).

21.4 Regain shoulder.

24.6 Reach Mora and try to locate a steep road on the hillside (up and slightly to the left). After turning onto New Mexico Route 94, you will be climbing that hill.

25.8 Turn left on New Mexico Route 94; a sign indicates MORPHY LAKE STATE PARK. This junction is hard to see. Look left after passing Alfonso's. This rural road has no shoulder except during the steep climb.

26.5 Gain shoulder and begin the steepest climb on the ride.

27.5 The top-look right over your shoulder to view the Mora River valley. There is no shoulder until you reach New Mexico Route 518 again.

30.0 Ride through the small community of Ledoux.

33.5 T intersection; turn right.

35.7 T intersection; turn left and continue on New Mexico Route 94. New Mexico Route 105 goes to the right.

44.4 Return to Sapello; Chevron station on the right. Turn right on New Mexico Route 518, the final stretch.

52.6 Return to Storrie Lake State Park.

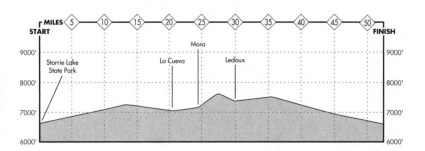

BIKE SHOPS

♦ Kortes Furniture and Bicycle Shop, 171 Bridge Street, Las Vegas, NM 87701; (505) 425–6572 (Tuesday through Friday 9:30 A.M. to 5:00 P.M. but closed for lunch between noon and 1:30 P.M.; Saturdays 9:30 A.M. to 12:00 P.M.).

REST ROOMS

♦ Mile 0.0: Storrie Lake State Park (inside the visitor center or a separate building to the left of the visitor center).
♦ Mile 8.1: Chevron in Sapello.
♦ Mile 20.5: Salman Ranch (across from store, second building to the left).
♦ Mile 44.4: Chevron in Sapello.

MAPS

♦ USGS 7.5-minute quads Mora, Lake Isabel, Rainsville, and Sapello.
♦ Delorme *New Mexico Atlas & Gazetteer,* maps 24 and 25.

El Malpais—El Morro Classic

T his out-and-back is a favorite with the New Mexico Touring Society, an annual outing they call the El Morro Picnic Ride. Their Web site describes it as a "delightful tour" because it's moderate and scenic—it's that and a whole lot more. You will cycle through a strange badlands, a massive lava flow south of Grants now preserved as El Malpais National Monument; and at the turn-around point—El Morro National Monument—you can explore the historic carvings along Inscription Rock and the ruins of two Anasazi pueblos. Other high-lights include the privately owned Ice Cave and Bandera Volcano. This moderate ride has a short climb to the Continental Divide at 7,882 feet.

New Mexico Route 53, the backroad from Gallup to Grants, is called the "Ancient Way" because it follows an old trade route between the Zuni and Acoma pueblos. The road skirts to the south of Cibola National Forest and the foothills of the Zuni Mountains, climbing to a high point at the Continental Divide. A festival is held every October to celebrate this scenic byway. Throughout the weekend, the museums, monuments, galleries, and businesses along the route host events. To find out more about the Ancient Way Fall Festival, check the link on the Web site for the Ice Cave and Bandera Volcano.

On this ride an elevation gain of about 2,000 feet is spread out over the 40 miles to El Morro National Monument. Much of this ride is newly paved; road construction was under way at the time of this writing. There is a designated bike lane for the first 20 miles, and it looks as if that might extend for most of the ride when the work is complete. If you don't want to tackle the entire 81.8 miles, you can turn around at the visitor center at El Malpais (total 44.8 miles);

Start: Grants Chamber of Commerce.

Length: 81.8 miles round-trip (several shorter options exist).

Terrain: Easy to moderate terrain with one short climb to the Continental Divide.

Traffic and hazards: Good shoulder most of the way with light traffic (some trucks).

Getting there: Take exit 85 off I-40 in Grants, and follow the business route through town. This is Santa Fe Avenue, or Historic Route 66. After you go through the traffic light at Fifth Street, look for Iron Avenue on the right (no light). Turn right on Iron Avenue; the Grants Chamber of Commerce is immediately on the right. There is parking across the street near the park (picnic tables) as well as behind the chamber of commerce building.

or you can plan an overnight, camping at El Morro, to break up the mileage into two days. Also, you can do an out-and-back between the visitor centers at El Malpais and El Morro (total 37 miles).

The ride starts on Historic Route 66 in downtown Grants, a boom or bust town founded in the late 1800s as a refueling stop for the Santa Fe steam engines. The booms included fame as the Carrot Capital of the World and later as the Uranium Capital of the Country. Don't miss the New Mexico Mining Museum, located inside the Grants Chamber of Commerce, where you can take an elevator down into a simulated mine. The Uranium Cafe is across the street—good breakfast burritos.

A few miles after crossing Interstate 40, you will pass San Rafael, a small Hispanic village supported by farming and ranching. With most signs of civilization behind you, enjoy the solitude of this high desert region. You'll ride through grassy flatlands and rolling hills covered with low-lying shrubs and juniper-pinon. Ponderosa pines grow along the slopes of the Zuni Mountains. Farther into the ride, sandstone cliffs and blackened lava fields begin to appear.

You'll pass the parking lot for the Zuni-Acoma Trail, an ancient Anasazi trade route that crosses several major lava flows, and then El Calderon Area, a place to explore some of the badlands' natural features such as Junction Cave and Twin Craters. Both sites have picnic tables and porta-potties. At the visitor center for El Malpais National Monument, you can get more information about this interesting landscape; and at the Ice Cave and Bandera Volcano, you can go underground, where the temperature remains below freezing, and hike up to the rim of the area's largest crater. After the climb to the Continental Divide, enjoy the descent and the scenery that takes you to El Morro National Monument.

El Malpais means "badlands" in Spanish. For most of the ride, you'll be cycling through an area where ancient lava flows poured across a broad valley. You can see the evidence of the past volcanic activity—lava tubes, cinder cones, arches, ice caves, and craters. The most recent eruptions were a few thousand years ago. The area is jointly managed by the National Park Service (NPS) and the Bureau of Land Management (BLM) and includes 114,000 acres contained in El Malpais National Monument and 263,000 acres contained in El Malpais National Conservation Area.

The Ice Cave and Bandera Volcano are worth the stop. For a small fee you can climb down a wooden stairway into a collapsed lava tube where the walls are covered in blue-green ice. The impressive Bandera Volcano is 200 feet across and 800 feet deep. These features are the reason the region is often referred to as "the Land of Fire and Ice." A trading post sells contemporary art and displays ancient Indian artifacts, many found nearby in the lava flow.

El Morro means "headlands" or "bluff" in Spanish. As you near the monument, you'll see the sandstone landmark of Inscription Rock. This lone butte and the watering hole at the base have been a rest stop for travelers for centuries. There are more than 2,000 carvings along the cliffside marking the passage of a variety of cultures. You will see Anasazi petroglyphs and signatures of Spanish explorers and American pioneers. A paved, 0.5-mile trail leads to the pool and the inscriptions; and a 2-mile loop takes you atop the mesa to pueblo ruins (circa 1275–1350) and a panoramic view.

Take two days to fully explore this unique area by staying overnight at El Morro. The nine-site campground operates on a first-come, first-served basis, and the fee is $5.00 in the summer. The facilities include water and pit toilets. Check with the fire department (behind the chamber of commerce and one block west) about leaving a vehicle overnight in Grants.

Inscription Rock at El Morro National Monument.

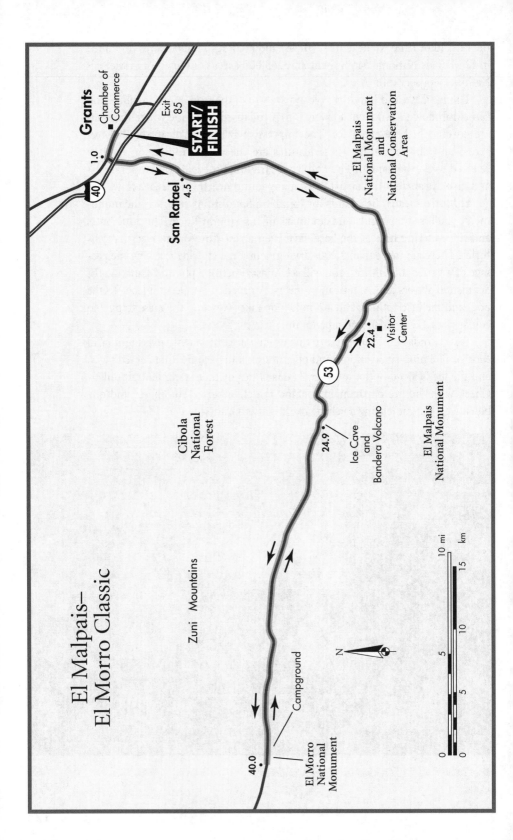

El Malpais—
El Morro Classic

Grants

Chamber of Commerce

Exit 85

START/FINISH

1.0

40

San Rafael

4.5

El Malpais National Monument and National Conservation Area

Cibola National Forest

53

Visitor Center

22.4

Ice Cave and Bandera Volcano

24.9

El Malpais National Monument

Zuni   Mountains

Campground

40.0

El Morro National Monument

N

10 mi

km

15

5   10

5   10

0   5

0

0.0 Follow Santa Fe Avenue (Historic Route 66) west riding in the bike lane.

1.0 Reach the traffic light at the west end of town (McDonalds on the right) and turn left on New Mexico Route 53, crossing over I–40. The first several miles are relatively flat. You will have a wide shoulder for most of the ride; some rough spots and loose gravel.

4.5 Village of San Rafael; post office and historic mission church to the right.

16.4 Zuni-Acoma Trailhead on the left leads 7.5 miles one-way to New Mexico Route 117. There are picnic tables and a porta-potty.

20.2 Pass El Calderon Area on the left; another trailhead with picnic tables and a porta-potty.

22.4 Reach the visitor center at El Malpais National Monument on the left. Steeper climbing toward the Continental Divide begins here.

24.9 Side trip to the Ice Cave and Bandera Volcano on the left.

25.4 Reach the sign that marks the Continental Divide at 7,882 feet and descend!

30.2 The turn for Cimarron Rose B&B is on the right between mile marker 56 and 57.

35.6 Tinaja Restaurant on the left serves Mexican food (also RV park caters to full hook-ups).

38.4 San Lorenzo Mission Church on the left.

38.8 Here, you'll get your first glimpse of the sandstone cliffs of Inscription Rock.

39.1 Pass El Morro RV park on the left (cafe and cabins). The El Morro Old School Gallery, the home of the area arts council, is across the street and open Thursday through Saturday from 11:00 A.M. to 5:00 P.M.

39.5 Cross into El Morro National Monument.

40.0 Turn left into the monument on a paved road.

40.4 The road leading to the monument's campground is on the left.

40.9 Reach the turn-around point of the ride, the visitor center of El Morro National Monument. After watching the video, checking out the museum, and hiking the trails, retrace your route with less climbing on the way back.

81.8 Return to the Grants Chamber of Commerce.

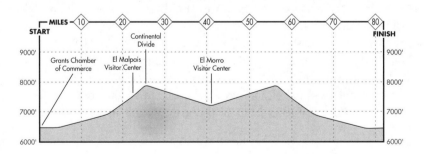

Historic carvings in Inscription Rock at El Morro National Monument.

LOCAL INFORMATION

♦ Grants Chamber of Commerce (www.grants.org), P.O. Box 297, Grants, NM 87020; (800) 748–2142 (visitor center 9:00 A.M. to 5:00 P.M. Monday through Saturday).

EVENTS/ATTRACTIONS

♦ New Mexico Mining Museum, 100 North Iron Avenue, Grants, NM 87020; (800) 748–2142 (9:00 A.M. to 4:00 P.M. Monday through Saturday; cost $3.00).
♦ El Malpais National Monument (NPS), 123 East Roosevelt Avenue, Grants, NM 87020; (505) 474–4774 (visitor center daily from 8:30 A.M. to 4:30 P.M.; closed Thanksgiving, Christmas, and New Year's Day).
♦ El Malpais National Conservation Area (BLM), P.O. Box 846, Grants, NM 87020; (505) 287–7911.
♦ El Morro National Monument, Route 2, Box 43, Ramah, NM 87321; 505-783-4226 (9:00 A.M. to 7:00 P.M. daily in the summer—must be on trails an hour before closing; cost $3.00, closed Christmas and New Year's Day).
♦ Ice Cave and Bandera Volcano (www.icecaves.com), 12000 Ice Caves Road, Grants, NM 87020; (888) 423–2283 (8:00 A.M. to 7:00 P.M. in the summer; cost $8.00).

RESTAURANTS

♦ Uranium Cafe, 519 West Santa Fe Avenue, Grants, NM 87020; (505) 287–7540 (closed Monday).

♦ Tinaja Restaurant, Highway 53, Ramah, NM 87321; (505) 783–4349 (closed Monday).

ACCOMMODATIONS

♦ El Morro RV Campground, Route 2, Box 44, Ramah, NM 87321; (505) 783–4612 (tent sites, cabins, and cafe).

♦ Cimarron Rose B&B (www.cimarronrose.com), 689 Oso Ridge Route, Grants, NM 87020; (800) 856–5776 (rooms start at $105).

BIKE SHOPS

The closest bike shops are in Albuquerque, 70 miles away.

REST ROOMS

♦ Mile 0.0: Grants Chamber of Commerce.

♦ Mile 16.4: Zuni-Acoma Trailhead (porta-potty).

♦ Mile 20.2: El Calderon Area (porta-potty).

♦ Mile 22.4: Visitor center for El Malpais National Monument.

♦ Mile 40.9: El Morro National Monument.

MAPS

♦ USGS 7.5-minute quads Grants, San Rafael, Arrosa Ranch, Ice Caves, Paxton Springs, Valle Largo, and El Morro.

♦ Delorme *New Mexico Atlas & Gazetteer,* maps 21 and 29.

Jemez Dam Ramble

T here is no shortage of ancient ruins to visit in New Mexico. Before you get on the bike and head out to Jemez Dam, you can tour Coronado State Monument and the pueblo ruins of Kuaua, both just north of Albuquerque. Bring a picnic to enjoy at the turn-around point of the ride, a small recreation area that provides views of the mesa walls along the Jemez River. This out-and-back offers a great way to get in a short, hilly ride away from the big city traffic. A majority of the ride travels a quiet two-lane road through the Santa Ana Indian Reservation. The high desert plains offer little in the way of vegetation, but you'll be rewarded with expansive mountain views of the Jemez on the way out and the Sandias on the way back.

This ride starts at Coronado State Monument, where you can discover something of what Francisco Vasquez de Coronado found on his famed expedition in 1540. He and his explorers were searching for the fabled cities of gold and found instead a number of prosperous native villages along the Rio Grande, including the Tiwa pueblo of Kuaua, which was first settled around 1300. The excavation of this site in the 1930s revealed layers of mural paintings on the walls of a *kiva*, a ceremonial structure. The monument offers an outstanding exhibit of the preserved mural segments and a self-guided trail to the reconstructed kiva, in addition to prehistoric and historic Indian and Spanish artifacts.

This ride is almost entirely on the Santa Ana Indian Reservation. These Native Americans have lived in the area since the late 1500s. The old pueblo, called Ta'ma'ya, is located upstream northwest of the dam and open for special ceremonies only. Most of the 650 or so members now live and work on a fertile strip of land along the Rio Grande near El Ranchito.

Santa Ana Pueblo is known for its blue corn. The prize crop is packaged under the brand name "Tamaya Blue," and all types of blue corn products can be purchased at the Cooking Post. There are several successful businesses on the reservation including a golf course, casino, hotel, and restaurant. The four-star Prairie Star Restaurant is worth a visit for its regional cuisine, Southwestern architecture, and patio views of the Sandias at sunset.

Your biking destination is Jemez Dam, which is operated by the Army Corps of Engineers and lies on the tribal lands of the Santa Ana Pueblo. The day-use facility includes an overlook, covered picnic tables with grills, and a couple porta-potties,

but there is no access to the lake. The ride out is enjoyable once you get off U.S. Highway 550. You'll pass the soccer fields that Santa Ana leases to the city of Bernalillo. The large tournament complex contains twenty-two fields, and the pueblo's golf course is on the other side of the road.

The remainder of the ride is just you, the road, and an uninhabited high desert landscape. You travel through a section of the reservation where there is nothing but cows and views all the way to the reservoir. You'll encounter just enough elevation change to keep the biking interesting. Cycling clubs and local riders often include this out-and-back as part of a longer ride, incorporating roads in and around the village of Corralles or using U.S. Highway 550 (heading west) where a large shoulder exists for about 20 miles to San Ysidro.

You can camp adjacent to the monument at Coronado Campground. This first-come, first-served campground provides sites along the Rio Grande with mountain views and shade from the tall cottonwoods. The facility is open year-round, and sites cost about $11.

LOCAL INFORMATION

♦ Santa Ana (www.santaana.org), 2 Dove Road, Bernalillo, NM 87004; (505) 867–3301.

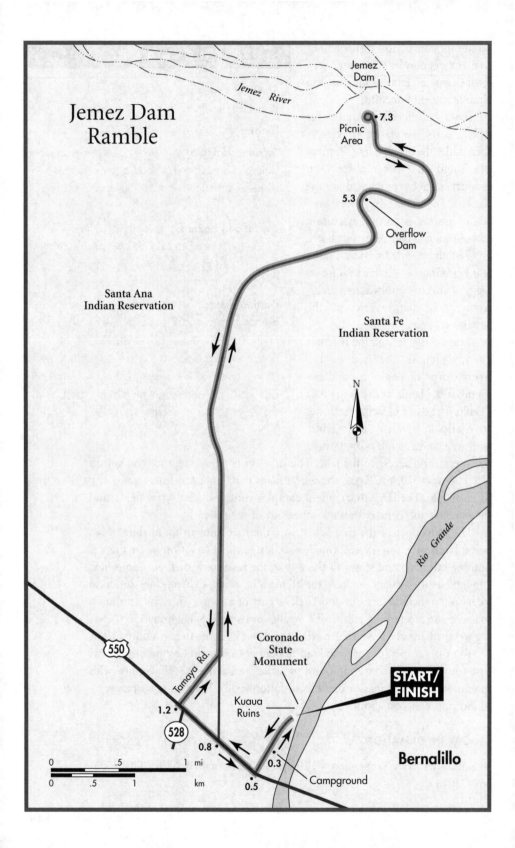

Jemez Dam
Ramble

Jemez River

Jemez Dam

•7.3

Picnic Area

5.3•

Overflow Dam

Santa Ana
Indian Reservation

Santa Fe
Indian Reservation

N

Rio Grande

550

Tamaya Rd.

Coronado
State
Monument

START/
FINISH

1.2•

528

Kuaua
Ruins

0.8•

0.3•

Campground

0.5•

Bernalillo

0   .5   1 mi

0   .5   1 km

MILES AND DIRECTIONS

0.0 Leave the parking area at Coronado State Monument, and head out to U.S. Highway 550.

0.3 Pass the campground on the left.

0.5 Reach U.S. Highway 550 and turn right. You'll have to deal with traffic for about a mile, but a good shoulder exists.

0.8 Pass Jemez Dam Road and the casino at the first traffic light. Continue west on U.S. Highway 550.

1.2 At the next intersection, there is a Texaco station on the left. Turn right on Tamaya Road, a new road that leads past the soccer fields and out to Jemez Dam.

2.2 Reach a three-way stop. Continue straight and lose the shoulder. This two-lane road is usually deserted to the overlook.

3.7 Ride through what cyclists call the "sundown gate."

5.3 Begin a steep descent, followed by a hairpin curve and a short climb.

7.3 Jemez Dam Overlook; enjoy the view and retrace your route to the monument.

14.6 Return to the Coronado State Monument.

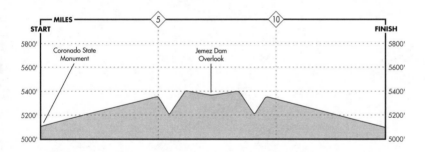

EVENTS/ATTRACTIONS

♦ Coronado State Monument, P.O. Box 95, Bernalillo, NM 87004; (505) 867–5351 (8:30 A.M. to 5:00 P.M. daily; cost $3.00).

♦ The Cooking Post (www.cookingpost.com), 2 Dove Road, Bernalillo, NM 87004; (505) 771–8318.

RESTAURANTS

♦ Prairie Star Restaurant, 255 Prairie Star Road, Bernalillo, NM 87004; (505) 867–3327 (Sunday through Thursday from 5:00 to 9:00 P.M.; Friday and Saturday until 10:00 P.M.).

ACCOMMODATIONS

◆ Coronado Campground, P.O. Box 638, Bernalillo, NM 87004; (505) 867–5589.

BIKE SHOPS

There are a dozen-plus bike shops in Albuquerque, about 10 miles away.

REST ROOMS

◆ Mile 0: Coronado State Monument.
◆ Mile 1.2: Texaco station.
◆ Mile 7.3: Jemez Dam Overlook (porta-potties).

MAPS

◆ USGS 7.5-minute quads Bernalillo and Santa Ana Pueblo.
◆ Delorme *New Mexico Atlas & Gazetteer,* map 23.

Albuquerque Bike Path Ramble

Abuquerque has a network of designated bike paths throughout the city, the longest and most scenic being Paseo Del
Bosque Trail. The city and county officials seem to be good about sup-
porting bicyclists, and the future looks bright for a high-quality inter-
connected bike system in Albuquerque. This easy ride near the banks of
the Rio Grande travels through the largest continuous cottonwood forest
in the country, called the bosque, and accesses destinations such as the
Rio Grande Nature Center, the historic Old Town Plaza, the Rio Grande
Botanic Garden, and the Rio Grande Zoo. You can zip through the city
from the North Valley to the South Valley with no traffic as many commuters do, or you can spend a day exploring all that the Rio Grande
bosque has to offer.

The Paseo Del Bosque Trail, along with the Riverside Trail and the newer
extension called the Chris Chavez Trail, offers about 16 miles one-way on
smooth pavement with practically no traffic. These urban bike paths lie just to
the east of the Rio Grande, and all the major street crossings use passages under
the roads. In this protected oasis, it's almost possible to forget you are surrounded by the largest city in the state.

Many visitors are surprised by the large green ribbon that runs north-south
through Albuquerque's high desert—the bosque of the Middle Rio Grande.
Bosque is the Spanish word for woods, and this riparian habitat is largely dominated by cottonwoods but also includes coyote willow, Russian olive, salt cedar,
and tamarisk.

Start: Trailhead at Alameda Boulevard for Rio Grande Open Space (several access points along the way give you alternative starts).

Length: 33 miles round-trip.

Terrain: Relatively flat; any elevation gain is barely noticeable.

Traffic and hazards: No vehicle traffic except for a few cross streets at the halfway point. You'll encounter other recreationalists on the bike path such as runners and in-line skaters. Hazards may include dogs, baby strollers, and even radio-controlled toys.

Getting there: Get off Interstate 25 at exit 233, about 6 miles north from I-40, and head west on Alameda Boulevard. Continue about 3.5 miles, past North Rio Grande Boulevard and South Rio Grande Boulevard, then turn left into the parking lot marked ALAMEDA/RIO GRANDE OPEN SPACE. If you cross the Rio Grande, you've just missed the trailhead. There are no rest rooms at the start, so stop at the Chevron station at North Rio Grande Boulevard on your way to the parking lot.

Here in Albuquerque the Rio Grande lies at an elevation of about 4,800 feet and splits the city in half. To the east the terrain rises gently toward the foothills of the Sandia Mountains then climbs abruptly to the Sandia Crest at 10,678 feet. To the west the terrain rises gently toward five dormant volcanic cones on a long mesa. These distinctive features will be part of the scenery on your ride.

The ride is actually an out-and-back with a small lollipop loop on the southern end. South of Bridge Boulevard, the path is called Riverside Trail and eventually heads east along the South Diversion Channel under Second Street and the railroad tracks of Burlington Northern Santa Fe. Add a couple of miles by taking the Chris Chavez Trail, a memorial to a local firefighter and avid cyclist. This trail wraps back around—north and west—to the point where the bike path initially went under Rio Bravo Boulevard. The northern portion of the ride is typically loaded with people on summer weekends, while the southern half is less crowded.

At the Rio Grande Nature Center, you can spend some time learning about the hundreds of birds, migratory waterfowl, and other wildlife that depend on the bosque. This state park includes 270 acres of riverside forest with 100-year-old cottonwoods, several nature trails, a three-acre pond, and outstanding exhibits. Farther south a short detour allows you to walk through history on the narrow streets and alleys around Old Town Plaza, laid out and founded in 1706. Today, the 300-year-old adobe buildings house shops, restaurants, and galleries. The centerpiece: the Gothic towers of the Church of San Felipe de Neri.

Another stop offers a look at the colorful seasonal gardens and permanent conservatories of the Rio Grande Botanic Garden. This great resource showcases a variety of plants including exhibits of a Southwestern desert. And finally, there is the Rio Grande Zoo, an impressive facility with more than a thousand

Sunday morning on a ride with the New Mexico Touring Society along the bike path in Albuquerque.

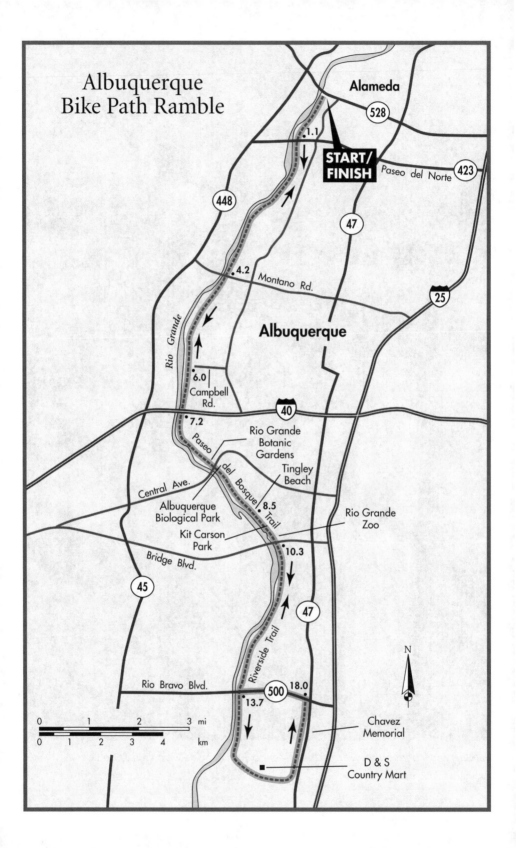

Albuquerque
Bike Path Ramble

Alameda

528

1.1

START/
FINISH

Paseo del Norte

423

448

47

4.2 Montano Rd.

25

Rio Grande

Albuquerque

6.0
Campbell
Rd.

40

7.2

Paseo

del Bosque

Rio Grande
Botanic
Gardens

Central Ave.

Tingley
Beach

Albuquerque
Biological Park

8.5

Trail

Rio Grande
Zoo

Kit Carson
Park

10.3

Bridge Blvd.

45

47

Riverside Trail

Rio Bravo Blvd.

500

18.0

13.7

N

Chavez
Memorial

D & S
Country Mart

0   1   2   3 mi
0   1   2   3   4 km

0.0 Head south on the paved bike path (left out of the parking lot).

0.2 Cross a bridge to the west side of Albuquerque Riverside Drain.

1.1 Go under Paseo Del Norte.

4.2 Go under Montano Road.

5.4 A ramp on the left leads down and across a bridge into the Rio Grande Nature Center. Ride continues straight.

6.0 Cross back to the east side of the riverside drain; Campbell Road intersects on the left.

7.2 Go under I-40.

7.5 Mountain Road on the left accesses Old Town. (Follow Mountain Road to Rio Grande Boulevard. Turn right, then left on North Plaza.)

8.3 Pass the Rio Grande Botanic Garden.

8.5 Go under Central Avenue. Ride alongside Tingley Drive, Tingley Beach, and Kit Carson Park; good picnic spot. You may see model sailboats racing on the small fishing lake.

9.5 Reach the intersection of Tingley Drive and Alcalde Court; there may be a porta-potty at this corner of the park.

9.7 Pass the Rio Grande Zoo.

10.3 Reach the first of several "bike traps," and walk your bike through. Go under Bridge Boulevard, and cross a small bridge. The bike path is now called Riverside Trail.

10.9 Pass behind a chile-packing company; good smells in the fall.

13.7 Negotiate another bike trap, go under Rio Bravo Boulevard, and reach another trap. To the west, the Rio Bravo Riverside Picnic Area has a fishing pier, nature trail, and benches. Be aware that vehicles enter here.

14.0 Cross a big wooden bridge.

15.8 The bike path splits just before Second Street. Up and left is D&S Country Mart; no rest rooms but drinks and good breakfast burritos (7:00 A.M. to 7:00 P.M.

(continued)

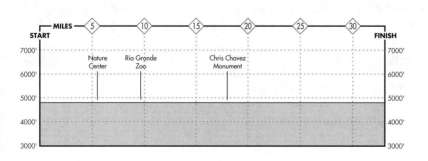

daily). Continue down and right under Second Street to follow the extension—
Chris Chavez Memorial Trail.

16.1 Cross a bridge over the confluence of Tijeras Arroyo and the South Diversion
Channel, and soon head north. Views of downtown but not the most scenic section of the ride. Members of the NMTS (New Mexico Touring Society) refer to
this area as "Tour de Junkyard."

16.5 Cross Murray Street, the first of several intersections with low-volume local traffic.

18.0 Reach the Chris Chavez Memorial (a stone sculpture of a cyclist) on the right.
Head left over a bridge, and ride along Rio Bravo Boulevard. A couple side
streets intersect the bike path here.

18.5 Giant Convenience Store on the other side of the highway.

19.3 Return to the dirt lot (Rio Bravo Riverside Picnic Area), and head right under Rio
Bravo Boulevard. Now just retrace your first 13.7 miles in reverse.

33.0 Return to the trailhead at Alameda Boulevard.

animals—exotic, native, and endangered. Concert performances take place in
the summer, and the Cottonwood Cafe is open every day but Monday.

LOCAL INFORMATION

♦ Albuquerque Convention and Visitor Bureau (www.abqcvb.gov), 20 First
Plaza NW, Suite 601, Albuquerque, NM 87125; (800) 284–2282.

EVENTS/ATTRACTIONS

♦ Rio Grande Nature Center State Park, 2901 Candelaria Road, Albuquerque,
NM 87107; (505) 344–7240 (10:00 A.M. to 5:00 P.M. daily; cost $1.00).
♦ Old Town Visitor Center, 303 Romero NW, Albuquerque, NM 87104; (505)
243–3215 (9:00 A.M. to 5:00 P.M. daily in the summer).
♦ Rio Grande Zoo, 903 Tenth Street SW, Albuquerque, NM 87102; (505)
764–6200 (9:00 A.M. to 5:00 P.M. Tuesday through Sunday; cost $5.00).
♦ Rio Grande Botanic Gardens, 2601 Central Avenue NW, Albuquerque, NM
87104; 505-764-6200 (9 A.M. to 5 P.M. Tuesday through Sunday; cost $5.00).

RESTAURANTS

Two of many options in Old Town:
♦ Rolling in Dough Cafe, 203 Romero Street NW, Albuquerque, NM 87104;
(505) 248–1786 (great bakery).

♦ Frybread Mama's Restaurant & Coffee Bar, 303 Romero, Albuquerque, NM 87104; (505) 246–2817 (Navajo owned).

ACCOMMODATIONS

Choose from a wide variety of lodging in and around the city. Log on to the Web site of the Albuquerque Convention and Visitor Bureau at www.abqcvb.gov and click on "visitors," then "accommodations." A hostel near Old Town offers a low-cost alternative in a historic building.
♦ Route 66 Hostel, 1012 Central Avenue SW, Albuquerque, NM 87102; (505) 247–1813.

BIKE SHOPS

There are more than a dozen bike shops in Albuquerque. The following shops rent bikes and are close to Old Town Plaza and the bike path:
♦ Absolutely Recumbent Bike Shop (www.absolutelyrecumbent.com), 8225 Fourth Street NW, Albuquerque, NM 87114; (505) 243–5105 (offers guided recumbent tours on the bike path with lunch).
♦ Old Town Bicycles (www.oldtownbicycles.com), 400 Rio Grande Boulevard, Albuquerque, NM 87104; (505) 247–4926 (also has lodging on-site).
♦ Rio Mountainsport, 1210 Rio Grande Boulevard NW, Albuquerque, NM 87104; (505) 766–9970.

REST ROOMS

♦ Mile 5.4: Rio Grande Nature Center.
♦ Mile 7.5: Detour to the Old Town Visitor Center (about a mile).
♦ Mile 9.5: Corner of Alcalde Place and Tingley Drive (possibly a porta-potty).
♦ Mile 18.5: Giant Convenience Store (must leave bike path and cross Rio Bravo Boulevard).

MAPS

♦ USGS 7.5-minute quads Los Griegos and Albuquerque West.
♦ Delorme *New Mexico Atlas & Gazetteer,* maps 23 and 31.

Albuquerque Perimeter Loop Challenge

"*O*ne learns more by going around than by cutting across."
This is the motto of the Perimeter Bicycle Association of America, an organization that has accepted this loop around Albuquerque as a perimeter ride. Tom Sullivan, the president of New Mexico Touring Society (NMTS), developed this ride using streets and bike paths around the city. Albuquerque is big, but Sullivan took advantage of some roads at the edge of town to create a fairly scenic route that avoids the busiest sections of the city. You'll bike along the foothills of the Sandia Mountains, through part of the cottonwood bosque of the Rio Grande, and up on the volcanic escarpment on Albuquerque's west side.

The Perimeter Bicycle Association of America (PBAA), based in Tucson, Arizona, organizes perimeter events and encourages the idea of perimeter bicycling-around towns, cities, states, countries, etc. Tom Sullivan put a loop together called the East Perimeter and sponsored the inaugural ride for the NMTS in October of 1999. He submitted this ride to the PBAA, but it was not accepted. The ride needed to be longer and follow more of the perimeter of Albuquerque. He resubmitted the following ride in the summer of 2000, which is now registered with the PBAA as a perimeter ride. There is not a formal event on this loop, but the NMTS schedules a ride around it every fall.

The 52-mile shorter version (East Perimeter) uses Paseo Del Bosque Trail (bike path) and cuts out the miles around the volcanoes on Albuquerque's West Mesa. The details here use the Volcano Excursion and give you the additional

15 miles. For the East Perimeter check out the NMTS Web site and click on "Ride Maps," or follow the mileage here, then flip to the Albuquerque Bike Path Ramble (24) in this book.

Albuquerque, which lies in the sunny Rio Grande Valley, is the biggest city in New Mexico, home to a third of the state's population. You'll find old historic districts, modern high rises, and everything in between. There are freeways, airports, shopping malls, and the usual sprawl, but bicycling in and around the city can be an enjoyable experience if you know where to go. This perimeter loop is a good way to start exploring the streets and bike paths of Albuquerque.

The Rio Grande splits the city in half. To the east the desert foothills of the Sandia Mountains rise abruptly to the Sandia Crest at 10,678 feet. To the west five dormant volcanic cones sit atop the 17-mile-long West Mesa. You will ride alongside the foothills and the volcanoes, as well as through sleepy neighborhoods, new housing developments, business strips, and industrial parks. The ride is quite diverse.

You will start cycling beneath the pink granite west face of the Sandias, where Tramway Boulevard parallels the rugged foothills for about 10 miles-a mix of open space and subdivisions. This area has long been popular with hikers and mountain bikers because of its proximity to the city and the wilderness. You can take a ride on the Sandia Peak Tramway, known as the world's longest single-span tramway. The tram covers the 2.7 vertical miles up to Sandia Peak in fifteen minutes. Highlights include panoramic views, a visitor center, and a fine-dining restaurant.

The five extinct volcanoes on the West Mesa that dominate your view for much of the ride are part of Petroglyph National Monument. This 7,200-acre park preserves thousands of petroglyphs carved in the volcanic rock—some are thought to be 2,000 years old. Self-guided trails at three main locations provide

THE BASICS

Start: Tramway and Central in Albuquerque.

Length: 65.2-mile loop

Terrain: Fairly easy with some gentle climbing and a couple long downhill stretches. The total elevation gain is about 1,500 feet.

Traffic and hazards: City riding that varies from quiet bike paths to extremely congested areas. A majority of the street riding includes bike lanes, and the 15-mile stretch out near the volcanoes is two-lane with little traffic.

Getting there: Take exit 167 off Interstate 40 on the east side of Albuquerque. If you are eastbound, turn right at the bottom of the ramp onto Tramway Boulevard, and cross Central Avenue to reach the shopping center. If you are westbound, take exit 167 and drive down Central Avenue for 1 block. Turn left on Tramway Boulevard to reach the shopping center. Four Hills Village is on the right, and Smith's is on the left; either area has a large parking lot. You'll find Einstein Brothers Bagels and Starbucks Coffee in the shopping center.

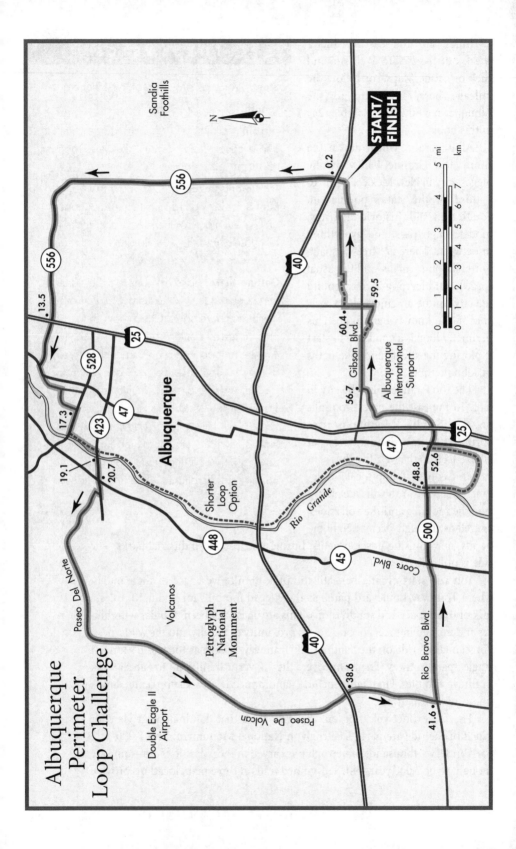

0.0 Leaving Four Hills Village, turn left (north) on Tramway Boulevard, and cross over Central Avenue at the traffic light.

0.2 Ride under I–40 and choose between the wide shoulder or jogging right onto the bike path that parallels Tramway Boulevard for 8 miles.

0.6 Traffic light at Cloudview Avenue and Encantado Road. This is the first of more than a dozen intersections that you'll encounter as you travel Tramway Boulevard.

0.9 Copper Avenue and the first of the cool pedestrian bridges across Tramway.

5.2 Bear Canyon Arroyo.

6.4 Road on the right leads to Elena Gallegos Picnic Area.

8.5 The bike path ends here. Reach a stop sign and continue straight on Tramway Boulevard, which curves to the west and affords views of the five volcanoes on the horizon, as well as the high-rises downtown. Enjoy a long downhill and a large shoulder.

13.0 Traffic light at Sandia Casino.

13.5 Ride under I–25, where Tramway becomes Roy Avenue (shoulder continues); Phillips 66 on the left.

15.0 Curve left and the road becomes Fourth Street (New Mexico Route 313).

15.4 Historic marker on the right describes the eighteenth-century Spanish settlement of Alameda. Shoulder narrows to about a foot as Fourth Street curves to the south.

16.3 Watch for a right turn onto Guadalupe Trail. This one-way side street is immediately after a light pink house. Narrow residential road; no shoulder.

16.6 At the stop sign, turn left to stay on Guadalupe Trail (now two lanes).

17.3 Traffic light at Alameda Boulevard; turn right into the bike lane.

17.6 Traffic light at North Rio Grande; Chevron station on the right. Continue straight here and at the next light, South Rio Grande.

18.1 A green sign indicates RIO GRANDE (the river, not the road). Turn right at the "bike pass-through." Continue down and right across a footbridge and under Alameda Boulevard. You are now on the Paseo Del Bosque Trail, one of Albuquerque's urban bike paths.

(continued)

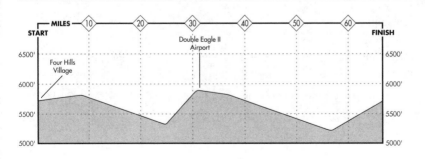

19.1 Pass under Paseo Del Norte, continue about 40 feet (uphill), and take the sharp U turn to the right, then an immediate left turn. This is Paseo Del Norte Trail. Continue across the Rio Grande. (If you want the East Perimeter—shorter option—pass under Paseo Del Norte and continue straight on the main bike path. See Albuquerque Bike Path Ramble mile 1.1 to 13.7. Rejoin this route at Rio Bravo Boulevard, mile 48.9.)

20.2 Bike path ends; follow the road to the right.

20.7 At the stop sign (Phillips 66 station on the right), turn right. Turn right again at the traffic light (Coors Boulevard) and head immediately for the left turning lanes—get into the one on the outside (right). Sign indicates WEST PASEO DEL NORTE—LEFT LANE.

21.0 Travel under Paseo Del Norte and up the ramp.

21.4 Veer to the right off Paseo Del Norte onto Eagle Ranch Road at the first light. Phillips 66 on the right.

21.6 At the next traffic light, turn left onto Paradise Boulevard and begin a gradual climb.

22.3 Continue straight at the traffic light for Golf Course Road; Conoco on the left. The bike lane that starts here only lasts 0.8 mile.

23.5 Continue straight at the traffic light for Lyon Boulevard; Phillips 66, then Texaco stations, on the right.

24.1 Paradise Hills Park on the right; shade and picnic tables.

24.9 Be alert! There is some construction and new development going on here. Get into the left turn lane when it appears, and turn left. The road becomes Paseo Del Norte, but it may not be marked. Soon you'll be riding in wide open grasslands.

28.3 Road curves to the left (south); still climbing. View the volcanoes to the southwest.

30.9 Stop sign at Double Eagle II Airport. Turn left (only way to go) and stop for a break at the Prop Wash Cafe (food, water, and rest rooms). Come back out to this stop sign, and turn right (only way to go).

31.5 Turn right at the next corner, past the wind sock. Road becomes Paseo De Volcan. Begin riding fairly level terrain alongside the volcanoes. Good views of the Sandias.

34.3 Pick up a small, smooth shoulder.

37.0 Cattleguards!

38.2 More cattleguards!!

38.6 Cross over I-40.

38.8 Cross Central Avenue; caution—divided highway. Chevron to the left.

41.6 Paseo De Volcan ends; stop sign and road barricade. Turn left (east) on New Mexico Route 500. This new road has a wide shoulder; fast and long descent on a 6 percent grade.

(continued)

46.1 Continue straight at the traffic light for Coors Boulevard.

48.0 Continue straight at the traffic light for Isleta Boulevard.

48.5 Cross the Rio Grande.

48.8 At the first opportunity, turn right (Poco Loco Drive); then turn right again on an unmarked side road.

48.9 Proceed left through the "bike trap" onto Riverside Trail. To the west, the Rio Bravo Riverside Picnic Area has a fishing pier, nature trail, and benches. Cross a big wooden bridge. (The shorter option rejoins route here.)

50.5 The bike path splits just before Second Street. Up and left is D&S Country Mart; no rest rooms but drinks and good breakfast burritos (7:00 A.M. to 7:00 P.M. daily). Continue down and right under Second Street to follow the extension— Chris Chavez Memorial Trail.

50.7 Cross a bridge over the confluence of Tijeras Arroyo and the South Diversion Channel and soon head north. Views of downtown but not the most scenic section of the ride. NMTS members refer to this area as "Tour de Junkyard."

51.1 Cross Murray Road, the first of several intersections with low-volume local traffic.

52.6 Reach the Chris Chavez Memorial (a stone sculpture of a cyclist) on the right. Lift bike over guardrail, and head right on the shoulder of Rio Bravo Boulevard to the traffic light at Broadway Boulevard, where you'll continue straight with a small shoulder.

52.2 Traffic lights; ride under I–25; road becomes University Boulevard (lose shoulder and start climbing).

53.2 Gain bike lane and travel straight through several traffic lights.

55.2 Ride under Sunport Boulevard (airport access road) and lose bike lane.

55.5 Curve right (only way to go), and road becomes Randolph Avenue. Thomas Bell Community Center on the left (water and rest rooms).

56.0 Left at traffic light onto Yale Boulevard, then immediate right onto Alamo Avenue.

56.4 Road curves left and becomes Columbia Drive (only way to go). Take the next right onto Miles Road.

56.6 At the stop sign, turn left on Girard Road.

56.7 At the traffic light, turn right on Gibson Boulevard (rough shoulder).

57.2 Continue straight at the traffic light for Carlisle Boulevard, and jog right onto bike path.

58.1 Side street, Truman Avenue.

58.3 Turn right at San Mateo Boulevard, continue through the gate of the Veterans Administration Hospital (shade and picnic tables on right), and follow VA Road to the left.

(continued)

58.8 Stop sign at USS *Bullhead* Memorial Park (shade and picnic tables); turn left.

58.9 Turn left at the stop sign onto San Pedro Drive.

59.0 Turn right at the stop sign onto Ridgecrest Drive.

59.2 Lassetter Park on the left.

59.5 Curve left (road gated straight ahead); road becomes Louisiana Boulevard.

59.9 Continue straight at traffic light for Gibson Boulevard; Diamond Shamrock convenience store on the left.

60.4 Turn right at the traffic light onto Kathryn Avenue.

60.6 Get onto the bike path at Cesar E. Chavez Community Center.

60.8 Come out at Dallas Street, and turn right onto Southern Avenue. Cross several side streets with state names.

61.3 Turn right at the stop sign onto Utah Street.

61.4 Turn left at the stop sign onto San Joaquin Avenue.

61.6 Turn left at the stop sign onto Wyoming Boulevard.

61.7 Turn right onto Susan Avenue; gas station on the corner.

62.2 Turn right at the stop sign onto Moon Street; as the road curves to the left it becomes Southern Avenue.

62.7 Continue straight at the traffic light for Eubank Boulevard.

63.2 Gain a small, smooth shoulder.

63.7 Turn right at the traffic light onto Juan Tabo Boulevard (shoulder).

64.0 Turn left on Singing Arrow Avenue into a private community. Go through one stop sign.

64.7 Continue straight at the stop sign for Dorado Place.

64.9 Reach Singing Arrow Center, and pick up the bike path heading to the left.

65.1 Pass Burger King (path ends), and hop up on the sidewalk. Four Hills Village to the left.

65.2 The end!

you with the opportunity to view some of the petroglyphs, but start first at the visitor center on Unser Boulevard, which is accessed via I–40 at exit 154.

LOCAL INFORMATION

♦ Albuquerque Convention and Visitor Bureau (www.abqcvb.gov), 20 First Plaza NW, Suite 601, Albuquerque, NM 87125; (800) 284–2282.

♦ Perimeter Bicycling Association of America (www.pbaa.com), 2609 East Broadway, Tucson, AZ 85716; (520) 745–2033.

◆ New Mexico Touring Society (www.swcp.com/~russells/nmts), P.O. Box 1261, Albuquerque, NM 87128; (505) 237–9700.

EVENTS/ATTRACTIONS

◆ Sandia Peak Tramway (www.sandiapeak.com), #10 Tramway Boulevard, Albuquerque, NM 87122; (505) 242–9052.
◆ Petroglyph National Monument, 6001 Unser Boulevard, Albuquerque, NM 87120; (505) 899–0205 (visitor center open daily from 8:00 A.M. to 5:00 P.M.).

RESTAURANTS

◆ Einstein Brothers Bagels, 13170 Central Avenue SE #A, Albuquerque, NM 87123; (505) 296–1299.
◆ Starbucks Coffee, 13170 Central Avenue SE #2, Albuquerque, NM 87123; (505) 293–3923.
◆ Prop Wash Cafe, West Mesa Aviation, P.O. Box 66149, Albuquerque, NM 87193-6149 (8:00 A.M. to 4:00 P.M. daily except closed Tuesday; selection of baked goods plus Mexican food, pizza, and sandwiches).

ACCOMMODATIONS

◆ Choose from a wide variety of lodging in and around the city. Log on to the Web site of the Albuquerque Convention and Visitor Bureau at www.abqcvb. gov and click on "visitors," then "accommodations."

BIKE SHOPS

◆ There are more than a dozen bike shops in Albuquerque; none of them is directly on the route.

REST ROOMS

◆ Mile 0: Four Hills Village (several businesses and restaurants).
◆ Mile 39.0: Double Eagle II Airport (rest rooms near restaurant).
◆ Mile 56.7: Thomas Bell Community Center.
◆ Many gas stations along the route—at least every 8 miles, sometimes every mile.

MAPS

◆ USGS 7.5-minute quads Albuquerque East, Albuquerque West, Alameda, Los Griegos, the Volcanoes, and La Mesita Negra SE.
◆ Delorme *New Mexico Atlas & Gazetteer,* maps 23 and 31.

Sandia Crest Challenge

*S*andia Crest Scenic Byway (New Mexico Route 536) ascends to the very crest of the Sandia Mountains (elevation 10,678 feet). From the junction with the Turquoise Trail (New Mexico Route 14), this paved road gains about 4,000 feet in 13.5 miles as it snakes its way up the east slopes of the Sandias, the most visited mountains in the state. Completing this challenging hill climb gives riders a huge sense of accomplishment, and the descent is not to be missed. The Sandia Crest, with its 360-degree views, may be the highlight for most cyclists because it's "the top," but a chairlift ride will take you to another spot along the ridge that is equally amazing. This bike ride is a favorite with locals, who usually start in Tijeras or even ride from Albuquerque.

You will be riding through Cibola National Forest for most of this out-and-back, passing through several vegetation zones. The bottom is juniper-pinon country, and the top is alpine forest. Hiking trails along the way access the Sandia Mountain Wilderness Area.

The challenge starts at mile marker 0 as you begin your climb on New Mexico Route 536. Expect good road conditions and long switchbacks. A shoulder exists for 8 miles. The best views from the bike are on the way down. If you need a bite to eat before the ride, Not Just Bagels, which is located on New Mexico Route 14 on the left just before you reach the Triangle, serves breakfast bagels, sandwich bagels, and just regular bagels, plus pizza and beer.

As you cycle through the community of Sandia Park, you'll pass Tinkertown, an animated miniature museum featuring an old Western town and a three-ring circus. This unusual private museum includes a huge collection of interesting treasures and antique toys. After entering the national forest, you'll pass several picnic areas. (*Note:* While there are vault toilets at most recreation sites, the availability of water is sporadic.)

Sandia Peak Ski Area is the midpoint of the climb. Plan your ride to take advantage of the Summer Scenic Chairlift, which operates on weekends Memorial Day through Labor Day and for nine days during the Balloon Fiesta in October. The area at the "top of the chair" (elevation 10,378 feet) is not accessible by car. Other than riding the chairlift from the base lodge, you'd have to take the famous Sandia Peak Tramway from Albuquerque or hike a 1.7-mile trail from the Crest. Mountain biking up is also an option.

Bring your bike lock and stay awhile. There is a bike rack at the base outside the bike shop, which rents mountain bikes for the 24 miles of great singletrack on the slopes. The Double Eagle II Outdoor Grill is open for lunch. At the top, along with great views, you will find the High Finance Restaurant and Tavern and the Four Seasons Visitor Center.

The byway dead-ends at Sandia Crest, elevation 10,678 feet. From the observation deck, you have breathtaking views in all directions. Look west 5,000 feet down the rugged cliffs to the city and the green ribbon of cottonwoods lining the Rio Grande. Beyond, see the remnants of extinct volcanoes on West Mesa, and farther still, the 11,301-foot Mt. Taylor. To the north, south, and east, views include the Jemez Mountains, Manzano Mountains, and Estancia Valley, respectively. On a clear day, it's possible to see 100 miles. The Sandia Crest House sells gifts and serves sandwiches, burgers, and dogs. The forest service operates a small information kiosk with vault toilets.

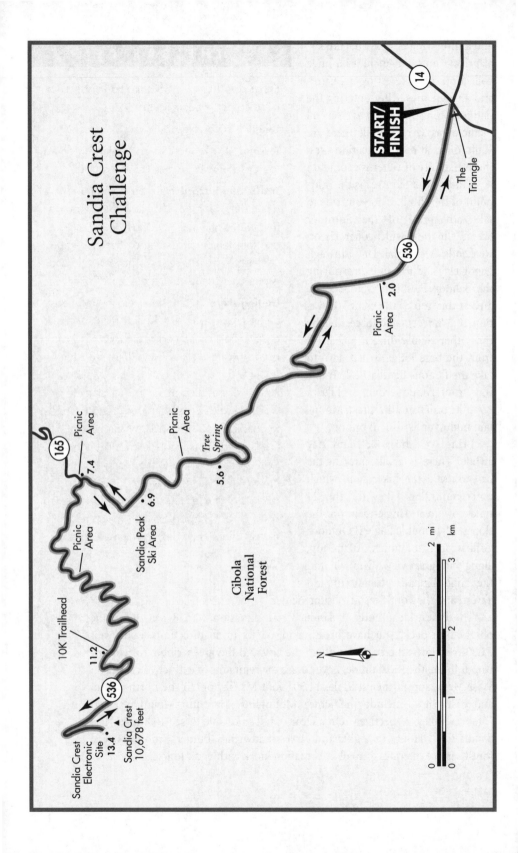

Sandia Crest Challenge

Cibola
National
Forest

START/
FINISH

The
Triangle

14

536

Picnic
Area
· 2.0

Picnic
Area
· 7.4

165

Picnic
Area

Tree
Spring
5.6

Sandia Peak
Ski Area
· 6.9

10K Trailhead
· 11.2

536
· 13.4

Sandia Crest
Electronic
Site

Sandia Crest
10,678 feet

N

0   1   2 mi

0   1   2   3   km

MILES AND DIRECTIONS

0.0 Head up New Mexico Route 536 and begin your hill climb. The shoulder starts out at about 3 to 4 feet wide.

1.2 Pass Tinkertown Museum on the left.

1.5 Enter Cibola National Forest.

2.0 Reach the first of several recreation sites along New Mexico Route 536— Doc Long. Remember, availability of water is sporadic at these areas.

5.1 A sign indicates the 8,000-foot mark and type of vegetation zone.

5.6 Tree Spring on the left.

6.0 Pass Dry Camp.

6.5 Enjoy a slight descent for 0.5 mile.

6.9 Reach Sandia Peak Ski Area. Even if you decide to skip the chairlift ride, stop in at the ski area for water, rest rooms, and an outdoor deck.

7.4 Balsam Glade, a roadside picnic area with tables and vault toilets. A dirt road along Las Huertas Creek leads 5 miles to Sandia Man Cave, an interesting archaeological site, then down to the village of Placitas.

8.1 Capulin Spring, a maze of roads leading to secluded picnic sites; several vault toilets. Lose the shoulder from here to summit.

9.0 Ninemile—mile marker and recreation site.

11.2 10K Trailhead, parking both sides of the road; vault toilet on the right.

12.0 Ellis Trailhead on the left.

12.3 A sign indicates the 10,400-foot mark.

13.4 Reach Sandia Crest Recreation Area, and enjoy the view before the steep descent back to the Triangle.

26.8 Return to the Triangle Grocery in Sandia Park.

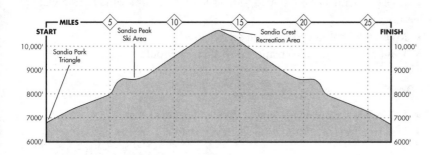

LOCAL INFORMATION

◆ Sandia Ranger District (Cibola National Forest), 11776 Highway 337, Tijeras, NM 87059; (505) 281–3304.

EVENTS/ATTRACTIONS

♦ Tinkertown Museum, 121 Sandia Crest Road, Sandia Park, NM 87047; (505) 281–5233 (April to October).

♦ Sandia Peak Ski Area (www.sandiapeak.com), #10 Tramway Boulevard, Albuquerque, NM 87122; (505) 242–9052.

RESTAURANTS

♦ Not Just Bagels, 12469 North Highway 14, Sandia Park, NM 87047; (505) 286–4300.

♦ High Finance Restaurant and Tavern, 40 Tramway Road, Albuquerque, NM 87122; (505) 243–9742.

ACCOMMODATIONS

♦ Sandia Mountain Hostel, 12234 State Highway 14 North, Cedar Crest, NM 87047; (505) 281–4117.

♦ Angel's Ascent B&B Retreat, 20 Gilbert Place, Sandia Park, NM 87047; (505) 286–1588.

BIKE SHOPS

♦ East Mountain Bikes, Boards, and Brews, 12480 North Highway 14, Sandia Park, NM 87047; (505) 286–8888 (9:30 A.M. to 6:00 P.M. Tuesday through Friday, 9:00 A.M. to 5:00 P.M. on Saturday, and 11:00 A.M. to 5:00 P.M. on Sunday—closed first Sunday of each month).

REST ROOMS

♦ Mile 0.0: Chevron or Not Just Bagels.

♦ Mile 6.9: Sandia Peak Ski Area (unlocked in the summer and during Balloon Fiesta)

♦ Mile 13.4: Vault toilets at forest service kiosk.

♦ Vault toilets at most recreation sites along the route.

MAPS

♦ USGS 7.5-minute quads Sandia Park and Sandia Crest.

♦ Delorme *New Mexico Atlas & Gazetteer,* map 23.

Oak Flat Cruise

This is one of the great rural road rides in the East Mountain area—the other side of the Sandias, east of Albuquerque. You will be making a big circle around Cedro Peak (elevation 7,767 feet) and cycling for about half the ride through part of Cibola National Forest. The roads in the area are often used in local and state road races. The highlight of the Oak Flat Cruise is the "New Mexico Route 217 Rollers." Each April the physical therapy club at the University of New Mexico, along with Two Wheel Drive, put on a benefit ride on this loop called the Get Fit Cycling Festival.

The ride starts at Oak Flat Picnic Area in hilly juniper-pinon country. This rural loop has limited services and few spots to stop and hang out, although the picnic area is a good place to relax and socialize at the end. You'll find water and vault toilets. As you descend through Cedro Canyon to the town of Tijeras, you'll pass several parking lots for what is called Cedro Peak and Otero Canyon, a 15,000-acre area with a network of multiuse trails offering incredible mountain biking.

Local road cyclists often climb up through Cedro Canyon, doing an out-and-back starting in Albuquerque. The 6-mile frontage road along Interstate 40 follows New Mexico Route 333/U.S. Highway 66 through Tijeras Canyon and allows cyclists in the city a good access route to the country roads in the East Mountain area. A popular parking spot is Smith's Food and Drug at the intersection of Central Avenue and Tramway, off exit 167 on I-40. For an extension to the Oak Flat Cruise, continue straight at mile 25.9 (not right on Gonzales Road), and follow New Mexico Route 217 until you reach New Mexico Route 337 again (then turn right).

Start: Oak Flat Picnic Area in Cibola National Forest, about 20 miles southeast of Albuquerque.

Length: 31-mile loop.

Terrain: Nice descent through Cedro Canyon, some flat stretches, and the infamous rollers on New Mexico Route 217.

Traffic and hazards: Half the ride is without a shoulder, but traffic is usually light. Locals have complained to authorities about cyclists riding two abreast. Please ride single file.

Getting there: Take I–40 east from Albuquerque to Tijeras (exit 175). Reach a traffic light at the end of the ramp, and go straight (south) on New Mexico Route 337. Pass the Sandia Ranger Station on the left after 0.5 mile. Continue a little over 8 miles, and turn left at the sign for Oak Flat Picnic Area. Follow Oak Flat Road for 1 mile to the picnic area on the left.

The 1.6 million acres of Cibola National Forest are scattered in segments throughout the mountain ranges of central New Mexico. The ranger station for this district is located on the loop and includes a nice visitor center. And just behind is building is Tijeras Pueblo Ruins, the site of an ancient pueblo inhabited in the 1300s. About 200 rooms, several small buildings, and a *kiva* (a ceremonial structure) were excavated in the 1970s then covered again to preserve them until a decision can be made about the next step. Although there is not much in the way of ruins to visit, this prehistoric site is very interesting. A short, self-guided trail is lined with educational models and displays.

If you need a place to stay in the area, check out Lazy K Ranch B&B, which is about a half mile off the route at mile 19.5. The Web site is www.geocities.com/lazykranch-bandb. Call ahead and the owners (Kwas) may let you camp on the lawn. There is a commercial campground on the route, and several forest service campgrounds are located south of the loop in the Manzano Mountains near Tajique and Torreon. Molly's Bar is on New Mexico Route 333, left at mile 9.8. The patrons are a mix of ranchers and outdoor types, and the music is usually country. You can find other lodging and food choices in Cedar Crest, a few miles north of I–40 on New Mexico Route 14.

LOCAL INFORMATION

♦ East Mountain Chamber of Commerce, P.O. 765, Cedar Crest, NM 87008; (505) 281–1999.

EVENTS/ATTRACTIONS

♦ Sandia Ranger Station, 11776 Highway 337, Tijeras, NM 87059; (505) 281–3304 (Monday through Friday 8:00 A.M. to 5:00 P.M. and weekends 8:30 A.M. to 5:30 P.M.—closed for lunch from noon to 12:30 P.M.).

Climbing the New Mexico Route 217 rollers during the Get Fit Cycling Festival at Oak Flat Picnic Area.

RESTAURANTS

♦ Molly's Bar, 414 Highway 66 East, Tijeras, NM 87059; (505) 281–9911.

ACCOMMODATIONS

♦ Lazy K Ranch B&B, 27 Autumnwood Court, Edgewood, NM 87015; (505) 281–2072.
♦ Hidden Valley Resort, 844 Highway 66 East, Tijeras, NM 87059; (505) 281–3363 (April through October).

BIKE SHOPS

♦ There are a dozen-plus bike shops in Albuquerque, about 15 miles away.
♦ Two Wheel Drive Bicycles (www.swcp.com/bicycles), 1706 Central Avenue SE, Albuquerque, NM 87106; (505) 243–8443 (for information on Get Fit Cycling Festival).

REST ROOMS

♦ Mile 0.0: Oak Flat Picnic Area.
♦ Mile 9.3: Visitor center at Sandia Ranger Station.
♦ Mile 18.1: Sedillo General Store.

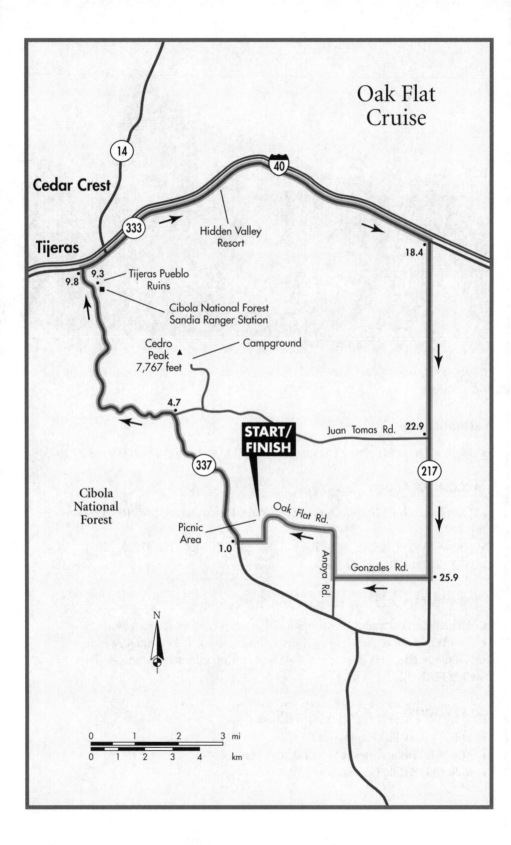

Oak Flat Cruise

Cedar Crest

Tijeras

14

40

333

Hidden Valley Resort

18.4

9.3
9.8
Tijeras Pueblo Ruins

Cibola National Forest Sandia Ranger Station

Campground

Cedro Peak
7,767 feet

4.7

Juan Tomas Rd.   22.9

START/ FINISH

337

217

Cibola National Forest

Picnic Area

Oak Flat Rd.

1.0

Anaya Rd.

Gonzales Rd.

25.9

N

0   1   2   3 mi
0   1   2   3   4 km

0.0 From the entrance to Oak Flat Picnic Area, turn right on Oak Flat Road and head for New Mexico Route 337. Begin with a descent and good shoulder.

1.0 Junction with New Mexico Route 337. Turn right and enjoy a wide shoulder as you descend through Cedro Canyon.

2.8 Pass Pine Flat Picnic Area on the right. Good views of Cedro Peak (with towers) and the Sandias beyond.

4.7 Juan Thomas Road (Federal Road 242) on the right. This gravel road cuts east through the forest to the other side of this ride.

5.9 Pass Otero Canyon; parking lot on the left.

7.2 Pass parking for Tunnel Canyon on the left; some shade trees.

8.5 Large parking area on the right at Chamisoso Canyon.

9.3 Sandia Ranger Station and Tijeras Pueblo Ruins on the right; then Tijeras Mountain Store (open daily).

9.8 Reach a traffic light at the frontage road and turn right onto New Mexico Route 333.

10.4 New Mexico Route 14 veers off to the left; stay right with New Mexico Route 333. The next 8 miles are relatively flat (good shoulder) as you parallel I-40. Within a couple miles you will pass a Chevron station and the Hidden Valley Resort (campground) on the right.

18.1 Sedilla General Store on the right (open daily).

18.4 Turn right on New Mexico Route 217 (no shoulder), and begin climbing immediately. This is the infamous stretch of steep rollers. Signs at the top of each climb indicate HILL BLOCKS VIEW.

19.5 To reach Lazy K Ranch B&B, turn left on Autumnwood Court. Bike ride continues straight.

22.9 East end of Juan Thomas Road (Federal Road 242) on the right.

25.7 Bernalillo County Fire Station on the left.

(continued)

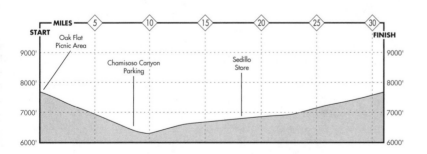

25.9 Turn right on Gonzales Road. Rough pavement for a few miles as you roll up and down.

28.0 T intersection with Anaya Road. After turning right, the pavement improves and the road becomes Oak Flat Road (little or no shoulder).

31.0 Return to Oak Flat Picnic Area.

MAPS

♦ USGS 7.5-minute quads Tijeras, Sedillo, and Escabosa.
♦ Delorme *New Mexico Atlas & Gazetteer,* map 31.

El Valle South Ramble

N ew Mexico Route 3 is a quiet, rural, and historic road in the
southern part of what locals refer to as El Valle, and it is
worth a day trip or overnighter if you aren't afraid of dogs. The ride follows the course of the Pecos River, starting at a funky cafe, passing a
winery with a tasting room in an old restored farmhouse, and ending at
a state park with neat, adobe-style shelters for camping. You will ride
through juniper-pinon hills and alongside red sandstone bluffs as you
leave and come back to the banks of the river several times. In addition,
the route passes through several old Spanish villages with historic
churches.

El Valle refers to the narrow valley formed by the Pecos River as it flows
from the headwaters in the Pecos Wilderness to the village of Villanueva. This
ride is located in the foothills southeast of the Sangre de Cristo Mountains
where New Mexico Route 3 follows the river south of Interstate 25. The route
was once used by sixteenth-century Spanish conquistadors. Today it is lined
with large cottonwoods and Russian olives and provides beautiful riverside riding. (The northern part of this area is covered in the Pecos River Valley
Challenge [20].)

The communities along the river are relatively poor, and agriculture and
ranching are a major part of the economy. Farming in the valley includes alfalfa, hay, and corn. The acequia, an irrigation ditch that you'll see right beside the
road at times, flows into the fields in the spring. Expect a pastoral setting complete with horses, fruit orchards, and old barns.

Start off your day at the Sad Cafe (named after an Eagles' song). This little
restaurant is right on New Mexico Route 3 in a 100-year-old adobe structure.

Start: Sad Cafe off I–25 between Santa Fe and Las Vegas.

Length: 24.2 miles round trip.

Terrain: Gentle descent and easy return climb along the Pecos River-plus a few rollers.

Traffic and hazards: Two-lane state road with little or no shoulder; descent road surface with some potholes. The biggest hazard is country dogs—almost a guarantee. You may be more likely to encounter a bike-chasing dog on this ride than any other in the book.

Getting there: Take exit 323 off I–25, which is 22 miles west of Las Vegas and 40 miles east of Santa Fe. The highway sign reads VILLANUEVA. Follow New Mexico Route 3 south; the Sad Cafe is 1.5 miles on the right just after you cross the railroad tracks. Please ask for permission to park here, and only if you are a patron. (Alternatively, you can start at the state park, driving the route before you ride.)

The current owners, Dennis Benjamin (an executive chef in New York) and his wife Catherine Alexander, purchased the restaurant after seeing an ad in the Santa Fe *New Mexican*. You can get breakfast burritos and omelets in the morning, and the lunch menu includes soup, salads, pasta, and green chile cheeseburgers.

The highlight is the three-course dinners on Friday night. It's theme night (prix fixe), which means one of a variety of international cuisines—Cajun, French, Asian, etc. Saturday night is a la carte. This information is only helpful if you plan to stay overnight at the state park on a weekend. The Sad Cafe also houses local artists' work, and La Sala Pottery is across the street.

There are many old Spanish settlements along the river. You'll ride through San Miguel, established in 1794 on a Spanish land grant. The white church with twin towers (1806) is the prominent building in town. Wagons along the historic Santa Fe Trail crossed the Pecos here. Toward the end of the ride, near the state park, you'll pass the hilltop village of Villanueva, founded in 1808 as an outpost to provide protection from raiding Indians. The town's centerpiece is Our Lady of Guadalupe, built in 1818. Inside, tapestry hung on the walls depicts the village's history. Villanueva General Store, across the street from the church, has been in business since before New Mexico was a state.

One of the interesting sites along the way is the Madison Winery. Bill and Elise Madison have been bottling and selling their fine wines for more than twenty years. In 1980 they started their family business, planting vines on four acres along the river in the community of El Barranco; and today they produce close to 4,000 gallons of dry and semisweet wines. You can sample their award-winning wines in the tasting room, located inside the beautiful old farmhouse right alongside the road.

Villanueva State Park, your turn-around point on this ride, is an off-the-beaten path little treasure that straddles the Pecos River. A short, steep side road leads down to it from the village of Villanueva. Hopefully you will find this 1,600-acre park with only one other camper as I did when I was there. A foot-bridge across from the visitor center provides access to both sides of the river, and a hiking trail leads to cliff-top views. There are twenty campsites (hot showers), and the day-use area has picnic tables right along the river.

LOCAL INFORMATION

♦ Las Vegas/San Miguel County Chamber of Commerce, P.O. Box 128, Las Vegas, NM 87701; (800) 832–5947.

EVENTS/ATTRACTIONS

♦ Villanueva State Park, P.O. Box 40, Villanueva, NM 87583; (505) 421–2957 (summer hours 7:00 A.M. to 9:00 P.M.; day-use $3.00 and tent sites $7.00).
♦ Madison Winery, Star Route, Box 490, Ribera, NM 87560; (505) 421–8028 (Monday through Saturday 10:00 A.M. to 6:00 P.M. and Sundays noon to 6:00 P.M.; call for winter hours).

There is wine tasting along the Pecos River on the El Valle South Ramble.

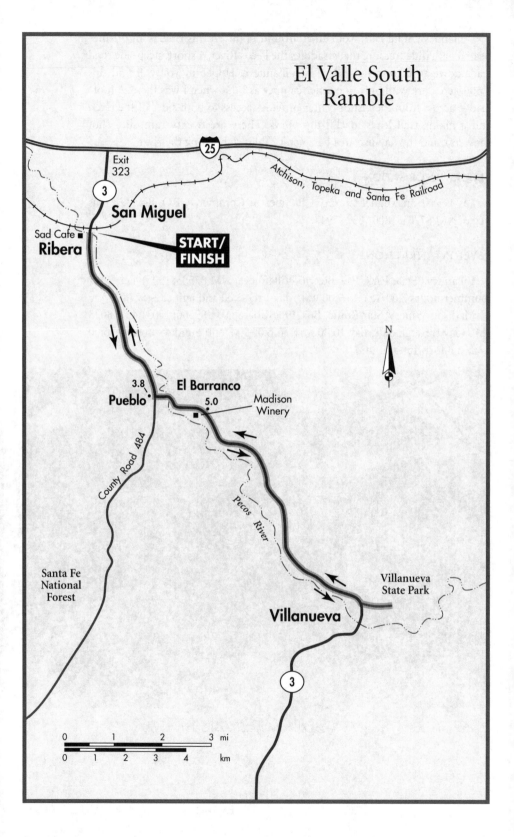

El Valle South
Ramble

Exit
323

25

3

San Miguel

Atchison, Topeka and Santa Fe Railroad

Sad Cafe ■
Ribera

START/
FINISH

N

3.8
Pueblo

El Barranco

5.0

Madison
Winery

County Road 484

Pecos River

Santa Fe
National
Forest

Villanueva
State Park

Villanueva

3

0   1   2   3 mi

0   1   2   3   4 km

0.0 Leave the Sad Cafe, turning right and continuing south on New Mexico Route 3.

0.1 Cross the Pecos River.

1.6 San Miguel Church on the right; stop to read the historic marker.

3.1 Some moderate rollers, then descend into the village of Pueblo. (This will be one of the steeper grades on the return route.)

3.8 Small gas station on the left, with the only advertisement being for beer; then County Road 484 heads off to the right. Continue straight on New Mexico Route 3.

4.2 Cross the Pecos River again.

5.0 Madison Winery on the right; visit the tasting room. The road continues to wind along the river providing fairly flat riding.

8.8 Ride through a small community where the road narrows. Watch for dogs!

10.3 Reach the junction where New Mexico Route 3 continues right to Villanueva where you'll find the post office and Villanueva General Store just down on the left. Continue straight on the entrance road to the state park and enjoy more gentle downhill along the Pecos River.

11.8 Reach the entrance station to Villanueva State Park. You'll encounter several speed humps in the park.

11.9 Visitor center on the left; rest rooms on the right.

12.1 Day-use area; road dead ends in a loop.

24.2 Retrace your route back to the Sad Cafe.

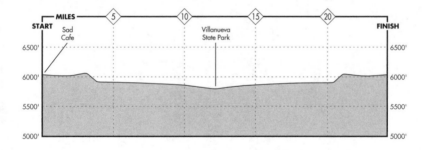

RESTAURANTS

♦ Sad Cafe, Ribera, NM 87560; (505) 421–3380 (Tuesday through Sunday 9:00 A.M. to 5:00 P.M., and until 8:00 P.M. on Friday and Saturday; closed Monday).

ACCOMMODATIONS

♦ Other than camping at Villanueva State Park, you'll have to head to Las Vegas for accommodations. Visit www.lasvegasnewmexico.com.

BIKE SHOPS

♦ There are four bike shops in Santa Fe, about 40 miles away.

REST ROOMS

♦ Mile 0.0: Sad Cafe in Ribera.
♦ Mile 12.1: Rest rooms and vault toilets at the state park.

MAPS

♦ USGS 7.5-minute quads San Jose, Sena, and Villanueva.
♦ Delorme *New Mexico Atlas & Gazetteer,* map 24.

Portales–Clovis Cruise

Credit for the contribution of this loop in eastern New Mexico goes to Ted Glasscock, a mechanic at Ace Schwinn in Clovis. Portales and Clovis lie in the sparsely populated Llano Estacado (or "staked plains"), named by the Spanish because of the numerous yuccas that looked like stakes on the prairie. The southernmost part of the Great Plains, this large expanse of land is almost featureless; and while the landscape is primarily flat and dry, you will find small hills, canyons, and mesas. The area has a famous archaeological site, very significant in human history; a state park provides a kind of oasis in this barren desert; and you may find a stark beauty in the wide open spaces.

This loop is ridden by every serious cyclist in Portales and Clovis at some time during the year because there are few paved roads in the area. It is long enough to allow the hammer dogs to get their mileage in but has enough sights and rest stops to keep the weekend warrior happy as well. Depending on the time of year, be prepared for wind and hot weather. The prevailing winds are from the southwest, often blowing at 30 mph in the spring. The wind can make it feel as if you are riding up a mountain. Temperatures are 90 to 100-plus in the summer.

You will start in Portales (*portales* means "porches" in Spanish). The name came about because the artesian springs southeast of town had holes in the cave walls that looked like little porches. Stockmen and outlaws from all over came to water their animals at the springs, the best reliable source around. Today, unfortunately, the water no longer bubbles from the ground due to lowering groundwater levels.

Start: Roosevelt County Museum on the campus of Eastern New Mexico University in Portales.

Length: 54.3-mile loop.

Terrain: Generally flat with a few small hills. The biggest challenges are the wind during the spring and the heat during the summer.

Traffic and hazards: Wide shoulders for most of the loop; however, be sure to ride U.S. Highway 70 from Portales to Clovis because the shoulder coming the other way is in terrible shape. Expect small-town city traffic in Portales and Clovis.

Getting there: Take U.S. Highway 70 through Portales until you reach Eastern New Mexico University. (All roads lead to ENMU!) Turn south onto Avenue L (right if coming from the west; left if coming from the east). This road is a block long and ends at the administration building, and there is ample street parking. You can park in front of the Roosevelt County Museum, which you can see from the highway. (*Note:* You can start this loop from a number of places in Portales and Clovis. Both communities are relatively small and friendly, so you can use public and retail parking. In Clovis, try the intersection of North Prince Street and Llano Estacado Boulevard. There are restaurants, fast food chains, drug and gift shops, and a Super Wal-Mart all within a block of this intersection.)

Portales is home to Eastern New Mexico University (ENMU); be sure to visit the numerous museums and the library. The ride begins at one of the museums on campus—Roosevelt County Museum—which provides a look at the history of the area (free). If you stay overnight, the theater or music school may be presenting a show or concert; and the Greyhound (men) or Zia (women) athletic teams may have a game.

On the way to Clovis, you pass the Blackwater Draw Museum adjacent to a highway rest area; and on New Mexico Route 467, your return route to Portales, you pass the Blackwater Draw Archaeological Site. Both are open to the public and contain many artifacts and exhibits associated with Clovis Man. These relics are evidence of human habitation in the area more than 11,000 years ago.

While Clovis is now much larger than Portales, it is the younger of the two towns. It sprang up around Riley's Switch, a site where a railroad roundhouse and switching yard were built. You can detour and visit the Clovis Depot Model Train Museum, which is housed in a historic railroad building near the old Clovis station. The detour for rock-'n'-roll buffs is the Norman Petty Studios, where local legend Buddy Holly made most of his early recordings including "Peggy Sue." Tours are given during the annual Clovis Music Festival. (These attractions are not on-route. Continue straight at mile 19.3 on U.S. Highway 70, which becomes Prince Street, and head into town to reach the museum on First Street and the studios on Seventh Street.)

West of Clovis, you'll ride alongside the Cannon Air Force Base (CAFB), where you can get up close to the fighter aircraft as they land. CAFB, a major source of income for the area, holds an open house every year for the public to visit the base. And on the way back to Portales, after the Blackwater Draw Archaeological Site, you'll pass the side road leading (2 miles) to Oasis State Park.

This state park is definitely an oasis—sandy hills, shade from large cotton-wood trees, and small fishing pond. There are picnic tables (day-use fee) and campsites with hot showers (overnight fee), but the cyclists can come and go at no charge, using the rest rooms and getting water. Hiking, fishing, and bird-watching are popular activities.

LOCAL INFORMATION

♦ Roosevelt County Chamber of Commerce, 200 East Seventh Street, Portales, NM 88130; (800) 635–8036 (for the Roosevelt County Museum, call (505) 526–2592).
♦ Eastern New Mexico University (www.enmu.edu), U.S. Highway 70, Portales, NM 88130; (505) 562–1011.
♦ Clovis/Curry County Chamber of Commerce, 215 North Main Street, Clovis, NM 88101; (505) 763–3435

EVENTS/ATTRACTIONS

♦ Blackwater Draw Museum and Archaeological Site, Station 3, ENMU, Portales, NM 88130; museum, (505) 562–2202, and site, (505) 562–5235 (during the summer, both locations are open Monday through Friday from 10:00 A.M. to 5:00 P.M. and Sunday noon to 5:00 P.M.).
♦ Oasis State Park, 1891 Oasis Road, Portales, NM 88130; (505) 356–5331.

RESTAURANTS

♦ El Rancho, 101 North Chicago, Portales, NM 88130; (505) 359–0098.
♦ The Roosevelt, 107 West Second Street, Portales, NM 88130; (505) 356–4000.
♦ Guadalajara Cafe, 916 L Casillas, Clovis, NM 88101; (505) 769–9965.
♦ Shogun Japanese Steak House, 600 Pile Street, Clovis, NM 88101; (505) 762–8577.

ACCOMMODATIONS

♦ Super 8 Motel, 1805 West 2nd Street, Portales, NM 88130; (505) 356–8518.
♦ Morning Star Inn, 620 West Second Street, Portales, NM 88130; (505) 356–2994 (B&B).
♦ There are a dozen or so choices in Clovis on "motel row," which is Mabry Drive at mile 20.7.

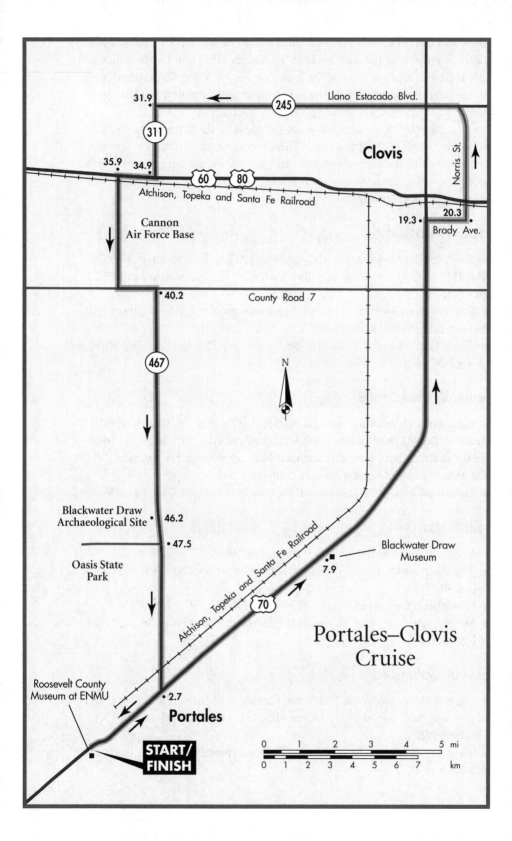

31.9

245   Llano Estacado Blvd.

311

Clovis

35.9   34.9

60   80

Atchison, Topeka and Santa Fe Railroad

Norris St.

Cannon
Air Force Base

19.3   20.3

Brady Ave.

•40.2   County Road 7

467

N

Blackwater Draw
Archaeological Site •   46.2

• 47.5

Blackwater Draw
Museum

Oasis State
Park

Atchison, Topeka and Santa Fe Railroad

7.9

70

**Portales–Clovis
Cruise**

Roosevelt County
Museum at ENMU

• 2.7

Portales

**START/
FINISH**

0   1   2   3   4   5 mi

0   1   2   3   4   5   6   7   km

0.0 Leave the Roosevelt County Museum. Go north a half block and turn right on U.S. Highway 70. You're on your way through town and on to Clovis.

0.2 Allsup's convenience store on the left.

2.7 On the outskirts of town, you'll pass the intersection with New Mexico Route 467, your return route.

7.9 Highway rest area and the Blackwater Draw Museum on the right (picnic tables); then pass the ENMU football stadium.

13.0 Cross the Roosevelt-Curry county line.

14.0 Check out the antique tractors on the west side of the road.

19.3 At the traffic light, turn right on Brady Avenue (the truck by-pass), which allows you to miss most of the traffic in Clovis. Allsup's on the left.

20.3 Turn left on Norris Street just past the Curry County Fairgrounds.

20.7 Go straight over the railroad tracks, reach the intersection with U.S. Highway 60/84 (Mabry Drive), and continue straight.

21.1 Norris Street curves to the left; just keep following it.

23.5 Turn left on Llano Estacado Boulevard.

24.5 Reach the intersection of Prince Street and Llano Estacado Boulevard; Allsup's on the right. This is the suggested starting point if you want to begin riding in Clovis. You will probably encounter the worst traffic of the ride along here. Continue west; Llano Estacado Boulevard will turn into New Mexico Route 245.

31.9 At the stop sign, turn left onto New Mexico Route 311 (Ranchvale Road). You are now heading south toward CAFB.

34.7 Housing for CAFB on the right and Allsup's on the left. There are numerous parks, rest rooms, and water fountains in this base housing area.

34.9 Turn right onto U.S. Highway 60/84.

35.9 Turn left onto Curry Road R, crossing the railroad tracks. You will be following the perimeter of CAFB.

39.1 The pavement ends; turn left (County Road 7). No road signs here.

40.1 You are a quarter mile south of CAFB's south gate; turn right.

(continued)

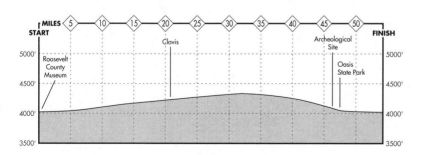

40.2 Intersection with New Mexico Route 467; turn right and head for Portales.

44.3 Cross the Roosevelt-Curry county line.

46.2 Pass the Blackwater Draw Archaeological Site.

47.5 Turnoff on the right for Oasis State Park, which is a detour of about 2 miles one-way from the highway.

51.6 Intersection with U.S. Highway 70; turn right.

54.3 After riding back through town, you will return to the museum and ENMU campus.

BIKE SHOPS

♦ Ace Schwinn, 113 North Main Street, Clovis, NM 87101; (505) 762–4848.

♦ All About Sports, 2809 North Prince Street, Clovis, NM 88101; (505) 762–6664.

REST ROOMS

♦ Mile 0.2: Allsup's convenience store.

♦ Mile 7.9: Highway rest area on U.S. Highway 70.

♦ Mile 19.3: Allsup's convenience store.

♦ Mile 24.5: Allsup's convenience store.

♦ Mile 34.7: Allsup's convenience store.

♦ Mile 49.4: Oasis State Park (detour of about 2 miles one-way).

MAPS

♦ USGS 7.5-minute quads Portales, Midway, Clovis, Portair, and Oasis State Park.

♦ Delorme *New Mexico Atlas & Gazetteer,* maps 35 and 43.

Cliff—Gila Challenge

Τ his out-and-back follows a part of one of the stages of the Tour
of the Gila, New Mexico's premier road race and one of the
most challenging in the country. Your destination—the small communities of Cliff and Gila north of Silver City in the Gila River Valley. You
will ride in high desert hills, crossing the Gila River and enjoying views
of the Gila Wilderness, the nation's first federally designated wilderness
area. Crossing the Continental Divide twice adds a challenge to this
ride.

The Tour of the Gila, which is held in Silver City every spring in May, is a
five-day stage race listed as a National Prestige Classic by the U.S. Cycling
Federation. One of the relentless courses, the Mogollon Road Race, follows this
ride, including laps around the loop through Cliff and Gila, and continues on
through Glenwood to the ghost town of Mogollon (additional 40 miles one-
way from Cliff with a big climb). If you decide to go that far, be sure to take the
side trip to the Catwalk of Whitewater Canyon. (Note: There is a great campground with a natural hot springs in Glenwood called Sundial Springs.) Two
other rides in this book are used during the Tour of the Gila–Gila Inner Loop
Classic (31) and Gila Cliff Dwellings Challenge (32).

This ride is a lollipop loop with a long stick—a 58-mile out-and-back with
a 10-mile loop on the end through Cliff and Gila. You'll ride about 24 miles out
of Silver City, do the scenic loop, and return to town the way you rode out. The
climb to the high point of the ride at the Continental Divide is right out of
town. There is another gradual climb out in the Mangas Valley.

Start: Murray Ryan Visitor Center in Silver City.

Length: 57.9 miles round-trip.

Terrain: Moderate ride with several long, gradual climbs and a couple short steep ones.

Traffic and hazards: Light traffic but trucks on U.S. Highway 180. U.S. Highway 180 has a large shoulder; New Mexico Route 211 has no shoulder.

Getting there: Silver City is located at the intersection of U.S. Highway 180 and New Mexico Route 90. U.S. Highway 180 runs east-west, and New Mexico Route 90, which is Hudson Street, heads south through the historic part of town. If you are coming from the east or the west on U.S. Highway 180, head south on Hudson Street. Signs will indicate VISITOR INFORMATION. The Murray Ryan Visitor Center is about a half mile south on the right at the corner of Broadway and Hudson.

As you near Cliff-Gila, you'll have views of Mogollon Baldy to the north and the Gila Wilderness, set aside as the country's first wilderness area in 1924. This large valley is where the Gila River exits the mountains and flows west to Yuma, Arizona, and the Colorado River. You'll find green pastures, river bottoms, and stands of cottonwoods. This section of the Gila has some of the best examples of riparian habitats in the Southwest.

After crossing the Gila River, you will reach Cliff and Gila, both too small to be considered towns. These two communities survive primarily on farming, ranching, and recreation. Cliff has a tiny commercial strip along the highway with a gas station and two restaurants. After you turn onto New Mexico Route 211, you'll reach Gila along the banks of the Gila River. The Valley Market and Supply has a deli, and you can enjoy your picnic at one of the tables at the community center. Hooker Loop leads out toward Bear Creek to a cozy B&B with a hot tub. The next mile includes rolling terrain with several short climbs. This is followed by a long descent back to U.S. Highway 180.

Several roads lead off the loop, all of which are worth the extra out-and-back miles. The road out to Bill Evans Lake is about 4.5 miles (stay left at the fork at about mile 3.5). The terrain gently rolls along the Gila River and finishes with a steep mile to the lake. This popular fishing spot, built to supply water for a copper mine, is operated by New Mexico Game and Fish and provides primitive camping sites. There is a vault toilet at the lake.

New Mexico Route 293 leads to the Gila Riparian Preserve, which protects a riparian habitat and woodlands along the Gila River. Owned by the Nature Conservancy of New Mexico, a portion of the 7,900-acre preserve is open to the public for of hiking and bird watching. Turkey Creek Road (New Mexico Route

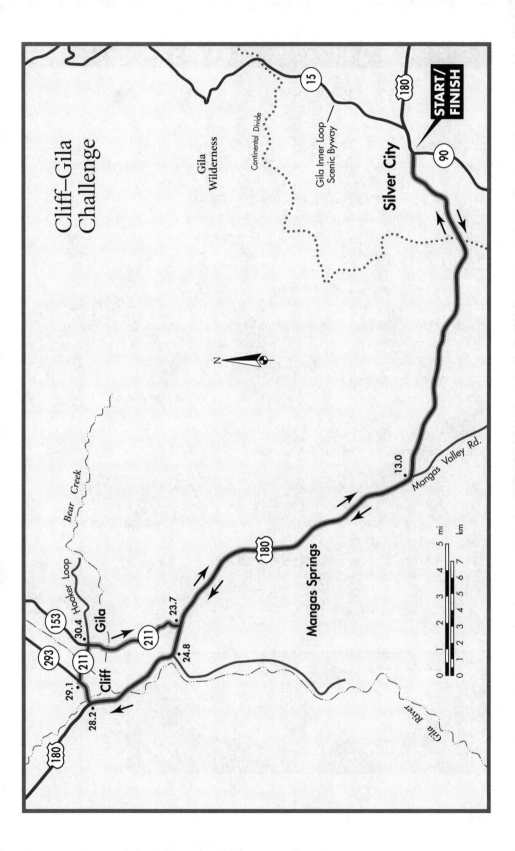

0.0 From the Murray Ryan Visitor Center, head north on Hudson Street (U.S. Highway 90).

0.2 Intersection with College Avenue; continue straight. (Turn left to reach the bike shops.)

0.4 Intersection with Thirteenth Street, the traffic light at the Food Basket. (Turn right to reach Silver City RV Park.)

0.5 Turn left at Fourteenth Street to get on U.S. Highway 180 heading west. This is before the major intersection with U.S. Highway 180.

0.6 Reach U.S. Highway 180 and turn left. You will be heading west out of town.

1.2 Your route narrows to two lanes. You will have a large shoulder all the way to Cliff.

2.3 Market Street on the left (near water tanks).

3.5 U.S. Highway 90 heads left to Lordsburg.

4.1 Reach the Continental Divide; sign indicates the elevation at 6,230 feet.

13.0 Mangas Valley Road on the left, which leads to U.S. Highway 90.

17.9 Pass through the small village of Mangas Springs; no services.

18.1 Cross Black Creek Canyon.

23.7 Pass the junction with New Mexico Route 211 on the right, where you will come out after the loop.

24.8 FR 809 on the left leads to Bill Evans Lake.

26.2 Pass through the community of Riverside; no services.

27.1 Cross the Gila River.

28.1 Reach the roadside community of Cliff; Chuck's Folly Mini Mart and the Chuckwagon Restaurant on the left and post office on the right.

28.2 Turn right on New Mexico Route 211 where there is no shoulder; Country Garden Cafe on the left.

29.1 New Mexico Route 293 on the left leads to the Gila Riparian Preserve.

29.8 Cross the Gila River again.

(continued)

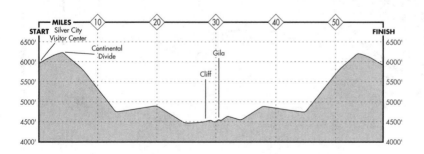

30.4 New Mexico Route 153 (Turkey Creek Road) on the left turns to gravel before reaching the wilderness area.

30.5 Reach the community of Gila; post office on the right. The Valley Market and Supply on the left has a deli.

30.8 Cross Bear Creek—usually a dry wash but sometimes you'll encounter running water. The next mile includes rolling terrain with several short climbs.

34.2 Reach U.S. Highway 180 and turn left, retracing your route to Silver City.

57.9 Return to the Murray Ryan Visitor Center.

153), which turns to gravel before reaching the wilderness area, accesses several national forest trails. The paved portion offers a total of about 6 rolling and rural miles with great views.

There are two great bike shops in town that were helpful with this ride and others in the area. To locate the shops, turn left on College Avenue (from mile 0.2 of the ride). Gila Hike and Bike is down a block on the right at the north end of Big Ditch Park. For Twin Sisters, also turn left on College, then take the next left onto Bullard Avenue, the west side of Big Ditch Park, and go several blocks.

LOCAL INFORMATION

♦ Silver City Grant County Chamber of Commerce (www.silvercity.org), 201 North Hudson, Silver City, NM 88061; (800) 548–9378.

EVENTS/ATTRACTIONS

♦ Information about the Tour of the Gila at www.tourofthegila.com.

RESTAURANTS

♦ Country Garden Cafe, 8394 Highway 180, Cliff, NM 88028; (505) 535–2545 (Monday and Tuesday from 8:00 A.M. to 7:00 P.M. and Wednesday through Friday from 8:00 A.M. to 3:00 P.M.).

♦ Chuckwagon Restaurant, 8414 Highway 180, Cliff, NM 88028; (505) 535–4100 (Wednesday through Sunday from 11:00 A.M. to 8:00 P.M.; soft-serve ice cream!).

ACCOMMODATIONS

♦ Hostelling International, 101 Copper Street, Silver City, NM 88061; (505) 388–5485 (open year-round; $12–$16).

- Silver City RV Park, 1304 Bennett Street, Silver City, NM 88062; (505) 538–2239.
- Casitas De Gila Guesthouses, 310 Hooker Loop, Gila, NM 88038; (877) 923–4827.

BIKE SHOPS

- Gila Hike & Bike, 103 East College Avenue, Silver City, NM 88061; (505) 388–3222.
- Twin Sisters Cycling and Fitness, 303 North Bullard Street, Silver City, NM 88061; (505) 538–3388.

REST ROOMS

- Mile 0.0: Murray Ryan Visitor Center.
- Mile 28.1: Chuck's Folly Mini Mart in Cliff.
- Mile 30.5: Valley Market and Supply in Gila.

MAPS

- USGS 7.5-minute quads Cliff, Mangas Springs, Circle Mesa, and Silver City.
- Delorme *New Mexico Atlas & Gazetteer,* maps 44 and 45.

Gila Inner Loop Classic

T his loop is a true classic of southwestern New Mexico. The Gila Inner Loop Scenic Byway includes some of best scenery in this corner of the state—sandstone cliffs, dense ponderosa pine forest, rivers, rugged canyons, and mountain ranges. High above the desert country, you will be surrounded by national forest, riding through the country's first designated wilderness and crossing the Continental Divide twice. Gila National Forest covers 3.3 million acres and a quarter of that is designated wilderness. The loop drive connects Silver City, Pinos Altos, Sapillo Springs, Lake Roberts, and the Upper Mimbres Valley, with a side trip to the Gila Cliff Dwellings. It is popular with recreational cyclists, touring companies, and cycling clubs; and it is part of the Tour of the Gila, New Mexico's premier stage race. Spend a day or two or three cycling this scenic byway.

The Gila Inner Loop has been called the Trail of the Mountain Spirits Scenic Byway since February 2000, but old habits are hard to break. The locals still refer to it as the Inner Loop. The name was changed to reflect the diverse heritage of those who have walked this way throughout the ages—prehistoric Indians, Spanish settlers, trappers, miners, ranchers, soldiers, and men like Aldo Leopold, a promoter for preservation of the wilderness.

You will start your journey in Silver City, the Gateway to the Gila and a great jumping-off point for a cycling tour. Nestled in the foothills of the Pinos Altos Mountains and just south of the Gila National Forest, Silver City retains its feel as an old mining town (silver was discovered in 1870). There

Start: Murray Ryan Visitor Center in Silver City.

Length: 72.9-mile loop.

Terrain: Winding, mountainous roads include steep grades, fast descents, and sections of flat to rolling terrain; more than 5,000 feet of climbing.

Traffic and hazards: Light traffic and good road surface. Extremely narrow and winding with blind curves between Pinos Altos and the junction with New Mexico Route 35. U.S. Highway 180 has a wide shoulder.

Getting there: Silver City is located at the intersection of U.S. Highway 180 and New Mexico Route 90. U.S. Highway 180 runs east-west, and New Mexico Route 90, which is Hudson Street, heads south into the historic part of town. If you are coming from the east or the west on U.S. Highway 180, head south on Hudson Street. Signs will indicate VISITOR INFORMATION. The Murray Ryan Visitor Center is about a half mile south on the right at the corner of Broadway and Hudson.

are several nationally recognized historic districts and a number of late Victorian-era buildings. This is also a university town, complete with museums, galleries, theater, festivals, etc. If you plan on spending some time here, check out the chamber's Web site or contact them for more information.

You can park at the Murray Ryan Visitor Center, which was built on the former homesite of Billy the Kid. It is located near the historic downtown. You may be able to leave your vehicle here overnight. Check with the folks at the chamber, or call the city police (505–538–3723). The police station is just up the street, and they often let visitors park overnight there. After a mile of intersections and city congestion, you'll be on the scenic byway-not another traffic light for 65 miles.

New Mexico Route 15, a narrow and winding road, climbs from the juniper-pinon hills into ponderosa pine and to the rustic village of Pinos Altos, where gold was discovered in 1859. This old mining town was once the county seat. Main Street, which looks like an old Western-movie set, is lined with many historic buildings and points of interest—a saloon and opera house, reconstructed fort, trading post, ice cream parlor, old adobe church, and several museums and galleries. If you want to visit this quaint mountaintop community, be sure to veer left shortly after mile 7. You'll rejoin the route within a mile.

Beyond Pinos Altos, the road narrows to a lane-and-a-half, and you enter the national forest and cross the Continental Divide, where a hiking and mountain biking trail now stretches from Canada to Mexico. Expect curves, switchbacks, and mountain grades for the next 15 miles. Several overlooks provide views of colorful sandstone cliffs as you travel through the dense forest. There are two campgrounds on this stretch-creekside with cottonwoods and ferns.

Riders with the New Mexico Touring Society's spring event on the Gila Inner Loop. (Photo by Peter Stirbis)

You'll reach the top of a mesa before dropping down on steep switchbacks to Sapillo Springs, the intersection with New Mexico Route 35. Here you can tackle additional miles up to Copperas Vista (the high point on New Mexico Route 15) and down into a beautiful river valley where hot springs and a national monument await. See the Gila Cliff Dwellings Challenge (32) for information on this out-and-back.

To continue on the loop, follow New Mexico Route 35 to Lake Roberts, also called the Emerald of the Gila. The seventy-five-acre lake is popular with fishermen and bird-watchers, and there are two campgrounds along the shore. The small community includes a store, a motel, and many vacation cabins. There are rolling hills through this broad valley before the climb to the second crossing of the Continental Divide.

It's easy going after the Divide as you travel through the Upper Mimbres Valley to New Mexico Route 152. This wide river valley is significant in history because the Mimbres Indians, famous potters, lived here about a thousand years ago. For more information about this branch of the Mogollon culture, read the City of Rocks Cruise (33). You'll parallel the Mimbres River for about 5 miles, passing farms and orchards. With the lower elevation the scenery changes back to juniper-pinon hills. There are a couple small grocery stores and restaurants.

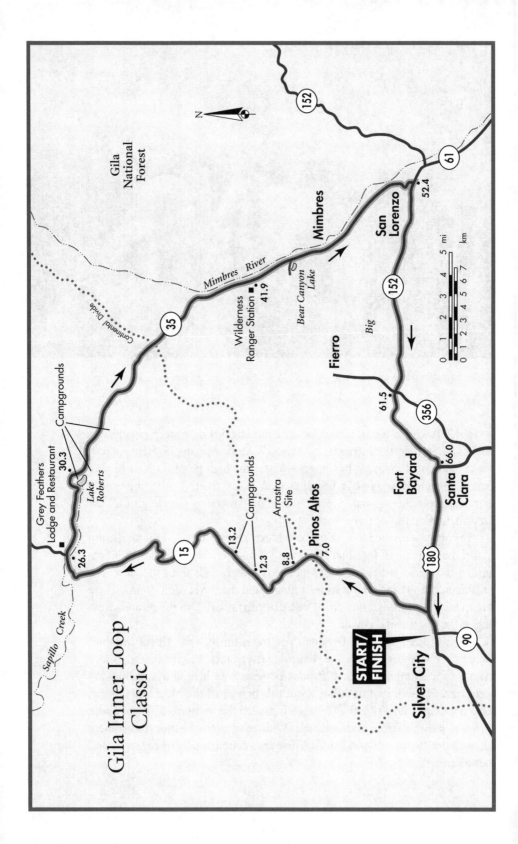

0.0 From the Murray Ryan Visitor Center, head north on Hudson (U.S. Highway 90).

0.2 Intersection with College Avenue; continue straight. (*Note:* Turn left to reach the bike shops. The Cliff–Gila Challenge provides specific directions.)

0.6 Reach the traffic light at U.S. Highway 180 and turn right, heading east from town. The next light is Swan Street; continue straight.

1.1 At the traffic light, turn left on New Mexico Route 15; Chevron station on the left. Sign indicates GILA CLIFF DWELLINGS, 44 MILES.

2.1 Reach a stop sign and continue straight across Thirty-Second Street Bypass. Small shoulder as you climb into the foothills away from town.

7.0 Historic marker for Pinos Altos. Road splits; stay right to skirt the village. You'll lose the shoulder, and the road becomes very narrow. (To visit Pinos Altos, take the left fork, cross the river, and turn right onto Main Street.)

8.1 Bear Creek Motel & Cabins on the left.

8.2 Two roads rejoin; no center line.

8.8 Arrastra Site (picnic) on the right. Enter the Gila National Forest.

11.5 Ben Lilly Monument—a memorial to one of the last great mountain men. His favorite vista is nearby, and a short trail across from the parking area leads to the monument.

12.3 Cherry Creek Campground on the right (April through October; no fee and no water). Views of magnificent sandstone cliffs just before this campground.

13.2 McMillan Campground on the right (April through October; no fee and no water).

15.3 Meadow Creek, high point of the ride.

21.5 Top out on a large plateau; gravel pullout on the left with views.

26.3 Gila Junction, the intersection with New Mexico Route 35. New Mexico Route 15 continues to the left (see Gila Cliff Dwellings Challenge for information on this out-and-back option). Continue straight on New Mexico Route 35; Grey Feathers Lodge on the left (ice cream, cafe, bakery!).

(continued)

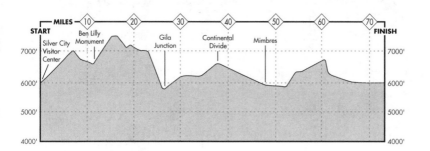

29.1 Lake Roberts General Store on the right, and Lake Roberts Motel. (The store is open daily and serves dinner on Friday nights.) After a short climb, you can see the lake. Encounter rolling hills.

30.3 Mesa Campground on the right (May through September; fee and water/rest rooms).

30.6 Lake Roberts Picnic Ground (free with water) on the right.

30.9 Upper End Campground on the right (open year-round; fee and water/rest rooms)

31.1 Spirit Canyon Lodge and Cafe (open seven days a week with German food on Saturday; also meals-to-go). Enjoy some flat miles.

32.4 Sapillo Campground (a group site) to the right. Scenery opens up and includes green meadows, tall grasses, and distant blue mountains.

36.7 Begin climbing toward the Continental Divide.

37.8 Continental Divide sign indicates the elevation at 6,599 feet.

39.5 Camp Thunderbird to the left.

40.5 Sign for Forest Lodge B&B on the left.

41.9 Wilderness Ranger Station on the right with picnic tables. You are entering the Upper Mimbres Valley.

43.3 Rio Mimbres Lodge and Turtle Works (art/antique store) on the left.

45.1 Dirt road on the right leads 1 mile to Bear Canyon Lake, another popular fishing spot.

47.7 Mimbres Store (beer and wine) and post office on the left; beautiful farmland. Enjoy flat riding as you parallel the Mimbres River for the next 5 miles.

48.9 Mimbres Valley Cafe.

51.6 La Tienda on the left, a store with gas, groceries, and camping supplies plus a Subway and a grill. Road left leads to the village of San Lorenzo; continue straight.

51.9 Turn left onto an unmarked road.

52.4 T intersection with New Mexico Route 152. Turn right and ride on a good shoulder, climbing for 2 miles.

54.4 At the top of the climb, look south to view the Kneeling Nun, a lone rock resembling a nun kneeling in prayer.

60.7 Santa Rita Mine Observation Point on the left; high point on New Mexico Route 152.

61.5 Cross the railroad tracks and New Mexico Route 356; short climb out of Hanover.

63.9 Views open up as you descend.

(continued)

66.0 Reach U.S. Highway 180 and turn right onto the four-lane highway (good shoulder).

66.4 Traffic light at Bayard Road. Sign indicates SANTA CLARA VILLAGE at 5,950 feet.

68.5 Silver City KOA on the left followed by several gas stations.

70.3 Reach the city limits of Silver City; sign indicates elevation at 5,900 feet.

71.3 First traffic light on the east edge of town; continue straight across Thirty-Second Street Bypass.

71.6 Traffic light at Wal-Mart; begin passing fast food chains and more gas stations.

72.1 Memory Lane to the left; Ranch Club Road to the right.

72.6 Traffic light where you started north on New Mexico Route 15 to Pinos Altos; continue straight.

72.3 Get in the left lane for U.S. Highway 90. Sign for VISITOR INFORMATION marks the intersection. Retrace your route down Hudson Street (U.S. Highway 90).

72.9 Return to the visitor center on the right.

New Mexico Route 152 takes you up and over some foothills of the Pinos Altos Range—more climbing. You're almost at the top when you reach the overlook for the Santa Rita Copper Mine, one of the largest open pit mining operations in the world. Copper has long been vital to the area's economy; the mine has been worked since the early 1800s. Toward the end of the ride, you'll pass Fort Bayard, an old army post dating back to the 1860s. Near the junction of Santa Clara and Fort Bayard, there is also a national cemetery and a wildlife refuge with hundreds of deer and elk. Almost home—a wide shoulder along U.S. Highway 180 takes you back into Silver City.

Several cycling clubs, including the New Mexico Touring Society (NMTS) and Silver Spokes Bicycle Club, plan annual events on the Gila Inner Loop. Both organizations welcome nonmembers on these weekend tours—NMTS in the spring and Silver Spokes in the fall. They can accommodate all ability levels because there is a sag wagon if you poop out and optional mileage if you're feeling strong. Dinner and lodging are at Camp Thunderbird (505–536–9560).

In addition to being a scenic byway and a great bicycle tour, the Gila Inner Loop is one of the stages of the Tour of the Gila, New Mexico's premier road race and one of the most challenging in the country. The Tour of the Gila, which is held in Silver City every spring in May, is a five-day stage race listed as a National Prestige Classic by the U.S. Cycling Federation. Two other rides in this book are used during the Tour of the Gila—Gila Cliff Dwellings Challenge and Cliff–Gila Challenge.

LOCAL INFORMATION

♦ Silver City Grant County Chamber of Commerce (www.silvercity.org), 201 North Hudson, Silver City, NM 88061; (800) 548–9378.
♦ Gila National Forest, 3005 East Camino Del Bosque, Silver City, NM 88061; (505) 388–8201.
♦ For information on the Gila Inner Loop, now called the Trail of Mountain Spirits Scenic Byway, log on to www.tmsbyway.com.

EVENTS/ATTRACTIONS

♦ Silver Spokes Bicycle Club, P.O. Box 2703, Silver City, NM 88062; (505) 388–5090.
♦ New Mexico Touring Society (www.swcp.com/~russells/nmts), P.O. Box 1261, Albuquerque, NM 87128; (505) 237–9700.
♦ Continental Divide Tours (www.continentaldividetours.com), P.O. Box 1771, Silver City, NM 88062; (505) 534–2953 (two- to three-day cycle tours around Silver City including the Gila Inner Loop).

RESTAURANTS

♦ Buckhorn Steakhouse, 32 Main Street, Pinos Altos, NM 88053; (505) 538–9911 (dinner starts at 6:00 P.M. but appetizers begin at 3:00 P.M.; closed Sundays).
♦ Mimbres Valley Cafe, Milepost 4, Mimbres, NM 88049; (505) 536–2857.
♦ Also along the route, Grey Feathers Lodge and Spirit Canyon Lodge have restaurants.

ACCOMMODATIONS

♦ Hostelling International, 101 Copper Street, Silver City, NM 88061; (505) 388–5485 (open year-round; $12–$16).
♦ Bear Creek Motel & Cabins (www.bearcreekcabins.com), P.O. Box 53082, Pinos Altos, NM 88053; (888) 388–4515.
♦ Grey Feathers Lodge, Junction NM 15 and 35, Silver City, NM 88061; (505) 536–3206.
♦ Lake Roberts Motel, RR 1, Box 175, Silver City, NM 88061; (505) 536–9393.
♦ Spirit Canyon Lodge, HC 68, Box 60, Silver City, NM 88061; (505) 536–9459.
♦ Forest Lodge B&B, P.O. Box 235, Mimbres, NM 88049; (505) 536–9336.
♦ Silver City KOA, 11824 Highway 180 East, Silver City, NM 88061; (505) 388–3351 (alternative starting point; bike-friendly; reservations recommended).

BIKE SHOPS

♦ Gila Hike & Bike, 103 East College Avenue, Silver City, NM 88061; (505) 388–3222.

♦ Twin Sisters Cycling and Fitness, 303 North Bullard Street, Silver City, NM 88061; (505) 538–3388.

REST ROOMS

♦ Mile 0.0: Murray Ryan Visitor Center.
♦ Mile 1.1: Chevron station on the left.
♦ Mile 12.3/13.2: Forest service campgrounds with pit toilets.
♦ Mile 26.3: Cafe at Grey Feathers Lodge (for patrons).
♦ Mile 29.1: Lake Roberts General Store.
♦ Mile 30.3–30.9: Forest service campgrounds and a picnic area with pit toilets.
♦ Mile 41.9: Wilderness Ranger Station.
♦ Mile 51.6: Mimbres Store.
♦ Mile 47.7: La Tienda.
♦ Mile 68.5: Several gas stations along the highway after the Silver City KOA.

MAPS

♦ USGS 7.5-minute quads Silver City, Fort Bayard, Twin Sisters, Copperas Peak, North Star Mesa, Allie Canyon, Hendricks Peak, San Lorenzo, and Santa Rita Mine.

♦ Delorme *New Mexico Atlas & Gazetteer,* map 45.

Gila Cliff Dwellings Challenge

This 18 miles of New Mexico Route 15, which stretches from Gila Cliff Dwellings National Monument to Gila Junction (New Mexico Route 15/35), is an out-and-back option of the Gila Inner Loop Scenic Byway. It is the "monster" in the Gila Monster stage of the Tour of the Gila, New Mexico's premier road race and one of the most challenging in the country. If you've never been to the area, the cliff dwellings, campgrounds (free!), and hot springs allow this ride to stand alone. I walked through the monument, rode the challenging terrain out to New Mexico Route 35 and back, camped at Upper Scorpion Campground, and hiked into the natural hot springs on the Middle Fork of the Gila early the following morning—a great trip. And if you are touring on the Gila Inner Loop, be sure to include this out-and-back in your plans.

New Mexico Route 15 is the road that takes you into the heart of the Gila Wilderness, an area twice as big as any wild lands in the state and the first in the country to be set aside and protected as wilderness. The Gila National Forest covers 3.3 million acres and a quarter of that is designated wilderness—a land of rivers, rugged canyons, mountain ranges, hot springs, and ponderosa pines. On this out-and-back, you will be surrounded by national forest with views into the wilderness area.

You start cycling out of the valley that is the headwaters of the Gila River, where three forks converge. The colorful sandstone cliffs and large cottonwoods are highlights at the beginning of the ride. Just a few miles from the monument, you'll reach the small village of Gila Hot Springs, where magma lies close to the surface and forms hot springs. Doc Campbell's Post is a small grocery store selling ice cream, snacks, gifts, and gas. The operation includes an RV campground, and you can use the showers, laundry, and hot springs pool for a nominal fee. If you have the time, there is a lot of history here. Doc built the post in 1963, before paved roads and electricity. He died in 1998 at the age of eighty-five.

You will climb to a high point on the spine of a mountain at Copperas Vista (elevation 7,400 feet). The viewpoint is also called Senator Clinton P. Anderson Overlook. The Gila River is 2,000 feet below on its way to Yuma, Arizona; and the Mogollon Mountains, on the western horizon, are the highest range in southwestern New Mexico. A long descent will take you into Sapillo Valley, a green creekside meadow of wildflowers, tall grasses, and hummingbirds. You can take a break at Grey Feathers Lodge, which includes a cafe, before retracing your route up and down again to the monument.

Nathan Shay runs Continental

Divide Tours and leads cycling trips on the Gila Inner Loop. He describes the climb—on what is by far his favorite road ride in the country—as "a virtual wall getting out of the river valley." He rides it for kicks almost daily. This is a mountainous road, winding with steep grades. You've got more than 1,500 feet of climbing in both directions, and of course, two thrilling descents.

Back at the Gila Cliff Dwellings National Monument, you can walk through the natural cliff-side caves and well-preserved Indian ruins. It is believed that the Mogollon people built these rock houses in the eroding volcanic rock in the late thirteenth century. The self-guided trail costs $3.00. The visitor center (a separate location about 1.5 miles away) houses interesting artifacts and exhibits, a bookstore, and a museum. You can also get information about the

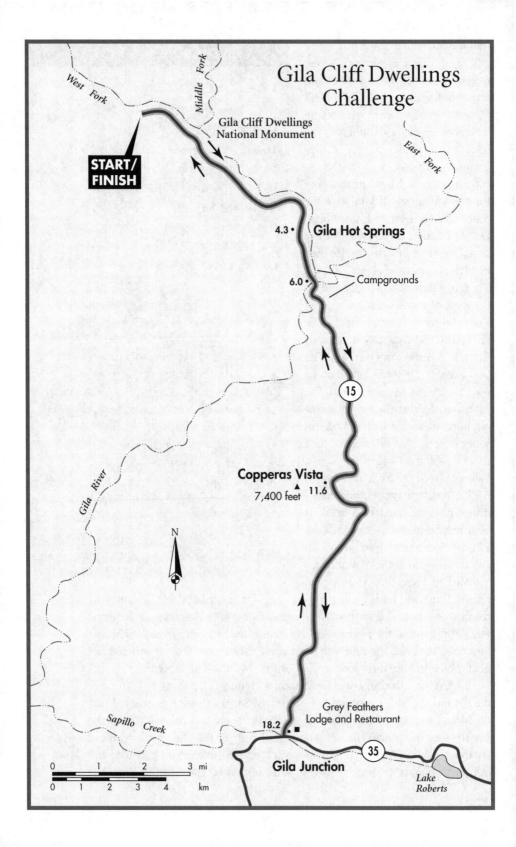

0.0 Leave the monument, heading back out the way you drove in. The road is flat with no shoulder. You will follow the West Fork of the Gila River and pass colorful sandstone cliffs.

0.2 Pass Upper Scorpion and Lower Scorpion campgrounds on the left.

0.8 Cross the West Fork of the Gila; pass several recreation sites with horse corrals.

1.5 T intersection with New Mexico Route 15; visitor center to the left. Turn right and enjoy the deciduous trees and shrubs of this canyon bottom.

4.3 Cross a county line, and climb a short hill to the village of Gila Hot Springs.

4.5 Stop in at Doc Campbell's Post on the left for ice cream and conversation.

4.6 Pass the RV park on the right.

4.7 The turnoff for the Wilderness Lodge on the left is followed by a short climb.

5.6 Pass the Forks Campground on the left and descend.

5.9 Grapevine, another forest service campground, on the left.

6.0 The steepest climbing begins here as you cross the Gila River.

6.5 Good views out to the right of the wilderness area and down to the river.

8.0 Catch your breath; the terrain levels off for a half mile.

10.0 Another break of about a half mile.

11.0 A short descent is followed by the last half mile of climbing, which is not quite as steep.

11.6 Reach Copperas Vista—the high point of the highway. A sign indicates the elevation of the overlook at 7,400 feet. Great views of the Gila Wilderness Area. It's mostly downhill from here through a dense ponderosa pine forest and along Copperas Creek.

18.2 Drop down to Gila Junction and Sapillo Creek; intersection with New Mexico Route 35; Grey Feathers Lodge to the left.

36.4 Back up and over Copperas Vista to return to the monument.

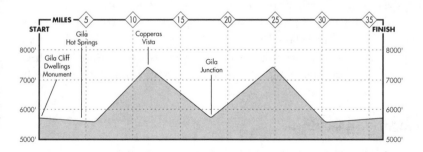

Gila Cliff Dwellings National Monument.

Gila Wilderness; both the cliff dwellings and the visitor center have trails that lead into the wilderness.

There are several free campgrounds to choose from near the cliff dwellings. Upper Scorpion and Lower Scorpion are just down the road and open year-round. You'll find flush toilets, drinking water, and picnic tables (in the winter, pit toilets and no water). South of Gila Hot Springs where the East Fork flows into the Gila River, there are two more campgrounds—Forks and Grapevine. Both are along the river, primitive with pit toilets and no water (also open year-round).

For a hike to a natural hot springs, park at the trailhead just north out of the large visitor center parking lot. The trail is marked MIDDLE FORK #157. Just a half mile of flat walking with two stream crossings will get you to several shallow pools called the Middle Fork Hot Springs. You'll see the steam rising on the east side of the river. The springs are about 130 degrees—yikes! Rocks have been organized to create a pool that allows the hot springs to mix with some of the cool river water. Ahhh!

LOCAL INFORMATION

◆ Gila National Forest, Wilderness District, HC 68, Box 50, Mimbres, NM 88049; (505) 536–2250.

♦ Silver City Grant County Chamber of Commerce (www.silvercity.org), 201 North Hudson, Silver City, NM 88061; (800) 548–9378.

EVENTS/ATTRACTIONS

♦ Gila Cliff Dwellings National Monument, HC 68, Box 100, Silver City, NM 88061; 505-536-9461 (summer hours for visitor center are 8:00 A.M. to 5:00 P.M. and for cliff dwellings, 8:00 A.M. to 6:00 P.M.; closed Christmas Day and New Year's Day).
♦ Doc Campbell's Post, HC 68, Box 80, Silver City, NM 88061; (505) 536–9551.

RESTAURANTS

♦ Grey Feathers Lodge, Junction NM 15 and 35, Silver City, NM 88061; (505) 536–3206.

ACCOMMODATIONS

♦ Wilderness Lodge, Route 11, Box 85, Silver City, NM 88061; (505) 536–9740 (riverside B&B in Gila Hot Springs).
♦ Grey Feathers Lodge, Junction New Mexico Route 15 and 35, Silver City, NM 88061; (505) 536–3206.

BIKE SHOPS

There are two bike shops in Silver City, 44 miles away.

REST ROOMS

♦ 0.0: Vault toilets at the monument.
♦ 4.5: Doc Campbell's Post.
♦ 18.2: Grey Feathers Lodge.

MAPS

♦ USGS 7.5-minute quads Copperas Peak, Gila Hot Springs, and Little Turkey Park.
♦ Delorme *New Mexico Atlas & Gazetteer,* map 45.

Bicycle Tour Companies

Bicycle tour companies come to New Mexico for the same reasons that we locals love cycling here—the scenic and cultural qualities and, of course, the weather. Madeleine Michels with Backroads feels that New Mexico "captures a rare mixture of natural beauty and cultural unique-ness not found in any other area of the country." Dick Gottsegen with Timberline Adventures says they've been leading tours in New Mexico for fifteen years, and the area has been "a long-standing part of their program because of the scenic quality, cultural and historic legacy, and great cycling opportunities."

Several bicycle tour companies offer trips in New Mexico, mostly in the northern part of the state. You can choose from weekend outings to week-long adventures. Most companies schedule tours between May and October, and prices range from $350 to $2,000. For the money, you get well-planned routes, knowledgeable staff, support vehicles, and outstanding food and lodging.

These companies are dedicated to making your trip an unforgettable experience, putting your needs and safety first. They can usually accom-modate cyclists of any ability, allowing individuals to go for high miles or jump on the van. Whether you are a visitor or a local, consider expe-riencing the Land of Enchantment with a bicycle touring company— sometimes it's nice to leave the logistical worries to someone else. Here are some good choices.

♦ Backroads (www.backroads.com), 801 Cedar Street, Berkeley, CA 94710-1800; (800) 462–2848 (biking adventures in Santa Fe and Taos).

♦ Bicycling Adventures (www.bicycleadventures.com), P.O. Box 11219, Olympia, WA 98508; (800) 443–6060 (trips include the High Road to Taos and the Enchanted Circle).

♦ Butterfield & Robinson (www.butterfield.com), 70 Bond Street, Toronto, Canada MSB 1X3; (800) 678–1147 (offers a bike trip from Santa Fe to Abiquiu that includes some hiking).

♦ Enchanted Lands Enterprise (www.enchantedlands.com), P.O. Box 1222, Los Alamos, NM 87544; (505) 661–8687 (our local company, offering a large variety of cycling trips in New Mexico).

♦ Timberline Adventures (www.timbertours.com), 7975 East Harvard, Suite #J, Denver, CO 80231; (800) 417–2453 (offers two tours in northern New Mexico; both highlight the High Road to Taos).

City of Rocks Cruise

L ocated in the Chihuahuan desert region of southwestern New Mexico, this ride is one of the most rural in the book. On this out-and-back, you will travel north on New Mexico Route 61 along the Mimbres River from City of Rocks State Park to the village of San Lorenzo, an old Spanish settlement. The river valley is significant in history because the Mimbres Indians, famous potters, lived here about a thousand years ago. Highlights include a visit to the "city" of bizarre volcanic boulders and a geothermal hot springs. This is a great weekend getaway—some sightseeing, some soaking, and some cycling with almost no traffic.

The Lower Mimbres Valley, between City of Rocks and San Lorenzo, is sparsely populated. You will pass a few settlements with family farms and ranches—Faywood, Sherman, and San Juan—and not all of the communities are marked with signs. Open fields and green pastures line the road, as well as orchards, heavy with apples in the fall. A few rough roads lead off into the brown hills. The desert vegetation includes prickly pear, yucca, and sage.

In this high desert region, the mountains rise up from the surrounding plains, allowing you to enjoy big views. Heading out from the state park, look to the east to see Round Mountain and the rhyolite dome, Taylor Mountain. Beyond and slightly south is the highest mountain in the area—Cooks Peak (elevation 8,488 feet). To the north-northeast is a tabletop mesa, as well as the prominent Mimbres Peak, composed entirely of volcanic rock, and the Whitehorse Mountains. More distant ranges like the Blacks are just hazy blue shapes on the horizon.

City of Rocks' bizarre volcanic boulders rising up from the floor of the Chihuahuan Desert.

The Mimbres Indians, a branch of the Mogollon culture, lived in villages up and down the banks of the river until the twelfth century. These famous potters were known for their distinctive designs. The Mimbres usually did black-on-white pottery of natural figures and geometric patterns. You can see examples of their exquisite work at Deming-Luna Mimbres Museum in Deming (505–546–2382) or Western New Mexico University in Silver City (505–538–6386).

Faywood Hot Springs, the site of a famous turn-of-the-twentieth-century hotel and spa, is located just 1.5 miles west of the state park. There is nothing like the effects of a good soak after a ride. This geothermal spa offers public and private outdoor tubs with a clothing-optional area, as well as campsites and several other lodging options including a tepee. Faywood Hot Springs is open from 10:00 A.M. to 10:00 P.M. every day of the year. If you are an overnight guest, you can use the public tubs all night. At the time of this writing, the facility was being expanded to include a new visitor center with a cafe, which will move the entrance road about 0.4 mile to the east. The visitor center will house a museum where you can learn more about the history of the resort and the surrounding area.

You will start by cycling out of the park along the 1.5-mile entrance road; once on New Mexico Route 61, you will follow the Mimbres River upstream, heading toward its origin between the Black Mountains and the Aldo Leopold Wilderness Area. For the next 20 miles, the road travels through what is called the Lower Mimbres Valley. There are no services along New Mexico Route 61, but you will pass a post office in Faywood.

Your destination, or turn-around point, is San Lorenzo. This small agricultural village marks the beginning of the Upper Mimbres Valley. Shortly after getting on New Mexico Route 35, you will reach La Tienda, a convenience store with gas, groceries, a post office, and a laundromat. The food choices include a Subway franchise and a grill.

THE BASICS

Start: City of Rocks State Park, between Deming and Silver City.

Length: 47.2 miles round-trip.

Terrain: Gently rolling with a slight upgrade toward San Lorenzo-about 700 feet elevation gain over 20 miles.

Traffic and hazards: No traffic, no shoulders, and no services. The road is in good shape, and there are several cattleguards.

Getting there: From Silver City, head east on U.S. Highway 180 for about 7 miles. At the traffic light at Bayard Road, New Mexico Route 152 veers off to the left. Continue on U.S. Highway 180. After about 20 miles, turn left on New Mexico Route 61. The 1.5-mile entrance road to City of Rocks State Park will be on the left after 3 miles. If you aren't camping at the park, leave your vehicle at the visitor center.

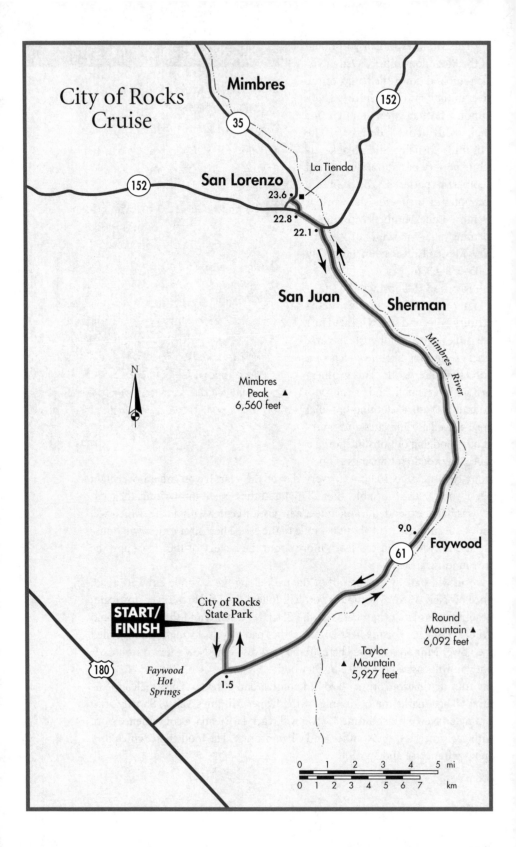

0.0 Begin cycling out of City of Rocks State Park along the 1.5-mile entrance road.

1.5 Turn left (east) on New Mexico Route 61.

7.0 Cross the county line from Luna County into Sierra County.

9.0 Pass the post office in Faywood on the left. Sign indicates the elevation at 5,075 feet.

22.1 Reach the junction with New Mexico Route 152 and turn left (west), gaining a wide shoulder.

22.8 Turn right to get on New Mexico Route 35; New Mexico Route 152 begins climbing toward Silver City.

23.3 Turn right again at an unmarked intersection to continue on New Mexico Route 35.

23.6 Reach La Tienda, a store with gas, groceries, and camping supplies. Grab a Subway sandwich before retracing your route back to the state park. The road just before the store's parking lot goes into the village of San Lorenzo.

47.2 Return to City of Rocks State Park.

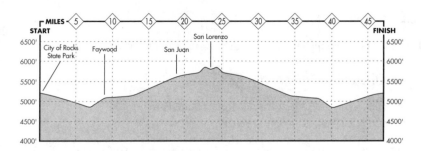

If you are interested in a longer tour, take a look at a state map and locate the 60-mile loop created by U.S. Highway 180, New Mexico Route 152, and New Mexico Route 61. (The ambitious cycle tourist could add this ride to the Gila Inner Loop Classic.) The Roadrunner Rally at City of Rocks State Park used this loop in 1998. This cycling event was held in connection with the dedication of the park's new visitor center, and avid cyclist Gov. Gary Johnson attended. The organizers, the Friends of City of Rocks, hope to make this an annual event (April). Contact the state park to find out the status of this ride.

LOCAL INFORMATION

♦ Deming–Luna County Chamber of Commerce, 800 East Pine, Deming, New Mexico Route 88031; (800) 848–4955.

♦ Silver City–Grant County Chamber of Commerce, 201 North Hudson Street, Silver City, NM 88061; (800) 548–9378.

EVENTS/ATTRACTIONS

♦ Faywood Hot Springs (www.faywood.com), HC 71, Box 1240, Faywood, NM 88034; (505) 539–9663.

RESTAURANTS

♦ La Tienda, 2674 Highway 35, San Lorenzo, NM 88041; (505) 536–3140 (Subway and a grill).
♦ At the time of this writing, a cafe was in the works at the new visitor center at Faywood Hot Springs. Also, rumor has it that someone bought the old Union Bar, just north of Faywood, and is putting in a bakery.

ACCOMMODATIONS

♦ City of Rocks State Park, P.O. 50, Faywood, NM 88034; (505) 536–2800 (day-use $4.00; campsites $7.00).
♦ Also, cabins and tent sites at Faywood Hot Springs, 1.5 miles west of the entrance to the state park.

BIKE SHOPS

The closest bike shops are in Silver City, about 30 miles away.

REST ROOMS

♦ Mile 0.0: Visitor center at City of Rocks State Park.
♦ Mile 23.6: La Tienda in San Lorenzo.

MAPS

♦ USGS 7.5-minute quads Taylor Mountain, Dwyer, Whitehorse Mountain, and San Lorenzo.
♦ Delorme *New Mexico Atlas & Gazetteer*, map 45.

34

Ski Apache Challenge

Ready for a hill challenge that climbs up the eastern slopes of the highest mountain in southern New Mexico—Sierra Blanca (elevation 12,003 feet)? This "white mountain," which the Mescalero Tribe believes to be the home of the Apache god Ussen, dominates the cyclist's view, especially when the summit is snowcapped, which can last into late spring or early summer. New Mexico Route 532, or Ski Run Road, travels from Alto 12 miles up to the base of Ski Apache and provides one of the most spectacular rides in the state. The real test of endurance comes about halfway to the ski basin with a series of narrow switchbacks crisscrossing the mountainside. Using those granny gears will be worth it when you reach the overlook at Windy Point.

This demanding out-and-back starts at the Smokey Bear Ranger Station on the north end of Ruidoso. You'll begin with gradual climbing to the small neighboring resort of Alto. When you turn off New Mexico Route 48 onto Ski Run Road, you'll be faced with a 3,000-foot gain over the next 12 miles. The first few gentle miles travel through private land dotted with cabins and trailers. The narrow road is in good shape, but there are no shoulders. Farther up, some drop-offs at the road's edge will take your breath away.

The road to Monjeau Lookout marks the beginning of Lincoln National Forest, which encompasses the White Mountain Wilderness. The White Mountains are a subrange of the Sacramentos, and the highest peak is Lookout Mountain (elevation 11,580 feet), part of the ski area. The 8,000-foot rise from the Chihuahuan Desert to the west up to the White Mountains is the greatest vertical relief in the state. The challenging hairpin turns begin about mile 8

THE BASICS

Start: Smokey Bear Ranger Station at the north end of the village of Ruidoso.

Length: 31.8 miles round-trip.

Terrain: A ski hill with a good warm-up, then pretty continuous climbing. The steepest part gains 2,000 feet in 6 miles. The first half of the descent involves extremely tight switchbacks.

Traffic and hazards: Steep, narrow road (without guardrails in some spots). Light recreational traffic and summer lightning storms.

Getting there: If you are coming into Ruidoso from the south (Alamogordo) off U.S. Highway 70, turn left at the first light onto Sudderth Drive (New Mexico Route 48). You'll pass the visitor center on the right after 1.5 miles and High Altitude, a bike shop, on the right after another mile. (You can start the ride from town, adding 4 miles. There are several public parking lots; follow signs at the next light, Eagle Drive.) To reach the ranger station, continue on Sudderth Drive for 0.6 mile and turn right at the traffic light onto Mechem Drive (still New Mexico Route 48). After 1.4 miles, you'll reach Smokey Bear Ranger Station on the left at Cedar Creek Road.

with the named Horseshoe Switchback. Almost every twist and turn along Ski Run Road has a name. For instance, Texas Bend is about as far as some drivers make it on a really snowy day before getting stuck. The road snakes up switchback after switchback for what seems like forever but equals about 6 miles.

You'll reach the high point of the ride before the ski area at an overlook called Windy Point. This vista at 10,000 feet makes it all worthwhile. Sierra Blanca towers behind you and the Sacramentos extend toward Cloudcroft. You can see the village of Ruidoso and some of its landmarks. The Capitan Mountains rise to the northeast, and the high arid plains are visible toward the eastern horizon. With the hard part over, the road follows the contour of the mountainside, then descends slightly to Ski Apache.

Winter brings skiers up this road. I can't imagine driving the treacherous switchbacks in bad weather. Ski Apache is one of the largest ski resorts in the Southwest, and the Mescalero Apache have owned and operated it for forty years. Most of their 460,000-acre reservation is south of Ruidoso and includes Sierra Blanca, a mountain they consider to be sacred. These enterprising people also run a casino and the luxury, lakeside resort, Inn of the Mountain Gods.

Oak Grove Campground (free) is on a ridgetop just off Ski Run Road at mile 9.2. There are thirty sites with tables and grills, plus vault toilets but no water. The campground closes with the first snow. (*Note:* The forest service may implement a fee for this area starting in 2002.) Another free camping area is located at the end of Cedar Creek Road (turn left at the Smokey Bear Ranger Station). After the road turns to gravel, there are wide spots to park and take advantage of what the forest service calls "dispersed camping."

I rode in November, which is the quiet off-season for Ruidoso and a nice opportunity to have the "main street" of this bustling resort getaway to your self. Some shops and restaurants even close for a few weeks. It was chilly up high, so I'd recommend visiting in the summer to take advantage of the cool temperatures and beautiful wildflowers, or better yet, in the fall to catch the brilliant colors of the maple, aspen, and oak.

LOCAL INFORMATION

♦ Ruidoso Valley Chamber of Commerce (www.ruidoso.net), 720 Sudderth Drive, Ruidoso, NM 88355; (800) 253–2255.
♦ Smokey Bear Ranger Station, 901 Mechem Drive, Ruidoso, NM 88345; (505) 257–4095.
♦ Mescalero Apache Tourism Office, P.O. Box 227, Mescalero, NM 83340; (505) 671–9191.

EVENTS/ATTRACTIONS

♦ Ski Apache (www.skiapache.com), NM 532, Ruidoso, NM 88345; (505) 336–4356.

RESTAURANTS

There are more than sixty restaurants in town. Here are two recommended by the folks at High Altitude—sure to please the cyclist's appetite. (*Note:* Many businesses are closed in November during the shoulder season.)
♦ Cafe Rio, 2547 Sudderth Drive, Ruidoso, NM 88345; (505) 257–7746 (unique—Greek, Cajun, Portuguese).
♦ Pub 48, 441 Mechem Drive, Ruidoso, NM 88345; (505) 257–9559 (the town brew pub featuring eight award-winning microbrews from Sierra Blanca Brewing).

ACCOMMODATIONS

♦ Ruidoso Central Reservations (www.ruidoso.net/reservations), P.O. Box 1864, Ruidoso, NM 88355; (888) 257–7577.
♦ Inn of the Mountain Gods, P.O. Box 269, Mescalero, NM 88340; (505) 257–5141 (turn on to Carrizo Canyon Road across from the Ruidoso visitor center).

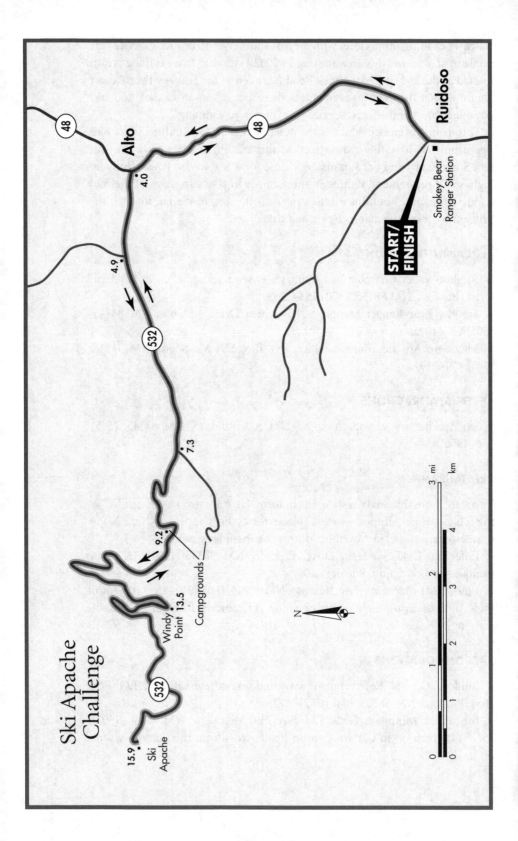

Ski Apache
Challenge

15.9 • Ski
Apache

Windy • 13.5
Point

Campgrounds

9.2 •

7.3 •

532

48

4.9 •

4.0 •
Alto

48

Ruidoso

START/
FINISH

■ Smokey Bear
Ranger Station

N

0   1   2   3 mi

0 1 2 3 4 km

0.0 Leave the parking lot at the ranger station and head north on New Mexico Route 48.

1.9 Gain a small shoulder as you begin climbing out of town toward Alto.

2.9 Reach the high point along New Mexico Route 48 and a sign indicating that Ruidoso's elevation is 6,900 feet, then descend.

4.0 Turn left on New Mexico Route 532, Ski Run Road; no shoulder for the next 12 miles. The climbing starts off gradually at this point as you follow Eagle Creek upstream. A gas station (Shell) was under construction on the corner at the time of this writing.

4.5 Look for the remains of a small ski area on the left that was open for a few years in the 1970s. The site, obviously too low for snow, is marked by stone pillars and you may see part of a lift.

4.9 The gravel road on the right leads to Skyline Picnic Area (trailheads for the White Mountain Wilderness) and Monjeau Lookout (a firetower with great views); continue straight.

7.3 Eagle Creek Road (left) leads to a campground run by the Mescalero Tribe. Leave Eagle Creek, and begin the steeper part of the climb.

7.7 Little Horseshoe Switchback, first of the named hairpin turns on this corkscrew of a road.

9.2 Oak Grove Campground on the right is operated by the forest service. Look up to see the road above—more switchbacks to come.

10.2 Gravel pullout at the northernmost switchback, Texas Bend.

13.3 Axle Bend, originally a sharper curve where trucks broke axles during the construction of the ski area.

13.5 Windy Point, overlook on the left with a large parking area (watch blind curve). This is the high point—at 10,000 feet—on Ski Run Road. From here, the riding mellows and you'll pass through a large stand of aspen.

15.0 Get your first glimpse of the ski area and descend.

15.9 Reach the base of Ski Apache; a sign indicates the elevation at 9,600 feet.

31.8 Enjoy the descent and return to the ranger station.

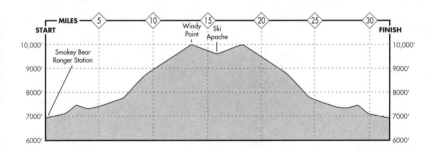

MS-150 Tour de Taos

The Rio Grand Division of the National Multiple Sclerosis Society hosts a two-day cycling event in August every year to raise money for research and local programs. The ride begins in Tijeras Canyon, just east of Albuquerque, and finishes in Taos with an overnight stop in Santa Fe. This challenging and scenic route includes the Turquoise Trail and High Road to Taos—a great way to see northern New Mexico. The ride is fully supported, with meals, sag wagons, and rest stops, and your registration fee includes everything. Participants are asked to raise a minimum of $200 to help in the fight against MS. Each year the organization hopes for 200 or more cyclists to raise a total of $100,000. For more information, contact the Rio Grande Division of the National MS Society of (505) 244–0625.

BIKE SHOPS

♦ High Altitude, 2316½ Sudderth Drive, Ruidoso, NM 88345; (505) 257–0120.

REST ROOMS

♦ Mile 0.0: Smokey Bear Ranger Station.
♦ Mile 4.0: Shell station on the left (not complete at the time of this writing).
♦ Mile 9.2: Oak Grove Campground (vault toilet).

MAPS

♦ USGS 7.5-minute quads Ruidoso, Angus, and Nogal Peak.
♦ Delorme *New Mexico Atlas & Gazetteer,* map 40.

Smokey Bear Country Cruise

E veryone knows of Smokey Bear, but most people have no idea about his birthplace, his burial site, or the story in between. This rural ride takes you through the town of Capitan, the home of Smokey Bear, where you may learn more than you wanted to know about this famous poster child for forest-fire prevention. The loop provides great rolling terrain in the juniper-pinon foothills between the Sacramento Mountains and Capitan Mountains, just north of Ruidoso. You'll get views of the high peaks in both ranges—Capitans going out and Sacramentos coming back. In addition to the state park dedicated to Smokey, you'll pass a historic old fort and a military cemetery.

I almost didn't find out about this great ride in southern New Mexico. I say "great" because it's a loop-hard to find in this state-and because of its rolling terrain, rural nature, and perfect weekend-warrior length. The book project was almost finished and I was on the phone with someone at High Altitude, the bike shop in Ruidoso. I had called about something else when the loop came up in conversation. It was pretty obvious on the map, but I hadn't seen it.

The ride follows a portion of the Billy the Kid Trail—about 35 miles of the 84-mile national scenic byway. The additional miles incorporate a loop to the south on U.S. Highways 380 and 70, including the towns of Ruidoso Downs, Hondo, and Lincoln. These roads are as rich with history as any area of the state and follow the trails of lawmen, outlaws, and warriors. For information on this scenic byway in its entirety, log on to www.byway.com and click on "For the Traveler," where you can search by keyword or state. The Billy the Kid Interpretive Center is located in Ruidoso Downs and has the byway painted on

Start: Smokey Bear Ranger Station on the north end of the village of Ruidoso.

Length: 41.5-mile loop.

Terrain: Rolling terrain mixed with several flat sections and some short, steep climbs.

Traffic and hazards: The road out to Fort Stanton is a cyclist's dream. A variety of shoulder and road conditions but almost no traffic. New Mexico Route 48 is probably the busiest road. Expect light truck traffic on New Mexico Route 48 and U.S. Highway 380.

Getting there: If you are coming into Ruidoso from the south (Alamogordo) off U.S. Highway 70, turn left at the first light onto Sudderth Drive (New Mexico Route 48). You'll pass the visitor center on the right after 1.5 miles and High Altitude, a bike shop, on the right after another mile. (You can start the ride from town, adding 4 miles. There are several public parking lots; follow signs at the next light, Eagle Drive.) To reach the ranger station, continue on Sudderth Drive for 0.6 mile and turn right at the traffic light onto Mechem Drive (still New Mexico Route 48). After 1.4 miles you'll reach Smokey Bear Ranger Station on the left at Cedar Creek Road.

the gallery floor complete with three-dimensional mountains. At Lincoln State Monument and National Landmark, you can learn more about famous Southwestern outlaws and the Lincoln County War, the last great shoot-out in the Old West. (*Note:* Lincoln is about 12 miles east from milepost 20.5.)

For this ride you'll begin just north of Ruidoso at the Smokey Bear Ranger Station, and once past the small resort community of Alto, you'll roll along through the countryside of the Rio Bonito Valley on a smooth stretch of pavement toward Fort Stanton. The Spencer Theater stands out in contrast to the rural landscape. This $20-million performing arts center, which opened in 1997, features world-class productions year-round—music, dance, and theater.

Back to the natural world. The view ahead is filled with the Capitan Mountains, unusual because they are one of few ranges that run east-west. While ponderosa pines cover some of the slopes and conifers grow on the ridgetops, most of the terrain is steep and rocky with large outcroppings like El Capitan, which rises to 10,083 feet. Dropping down off the mesa toward the Rio Bonito, you'll pass the Merchant Marine and Military Cemetery then Fort Stanton.

Along the river at the fort, you are almost halfway around the loop and at the lowest point of the ride. Although the terrain continues to roll up and down, you'll know you are climbing as you head back toward Alto. Your views now encompass the Sacramento Mountains, including the 12,003-foot Sierra Blanca, often snow-covered into early summer.

Fort Stanton, located on the banks of the Rio Bonito, was originally built in the 1850s as a temporary post to protect the settlers from the Apaches. Its presence encouraged settlement and acted as an economic center for the area. When Union forces came from Texas in 1861, the fort was almost completely destroyed, but after the reoccupation by Kit Carson, the military post was rebuilt. At one time it was manned by the Buffalo Soldiers of the Ninth Cavalry.

Public access is limited, but you can learn more about the history of Fort Stanton by visiting the roadside museum just before the post office. Since closing as a military post in the late 1890s, the location has served as a U.S. Marine Hospital, a tuberculosis sanitorium, a training school for people with mental disabilities, and a minimum security prison. Be sure to stop at the cemeteries dedicated to the American Merchant Marines. They may be among the few open, unguarded military cemeteries in the country.

U.S. Highway 380 takes you into Capitan, where they love their bear. You will cycle the main street through town on Smokey Bear Boulevard, where you can eat at Smokey Bear Restaurant, sleep at Smokey Bear Motel, and visit the Smokey Bear State Historical Park. It's not as touristy as it sounds. Capitan is a crossroads town that got its start in the 1880s serving nearby mining communities; then it lived on to serve local farmers and ranchers, as well as the tourists and outdoor enthusiasts visiting the area today. There are about 2,000 residents, including enough artisans to support an annual studio tour.

Smokey Bear State Historical Park, located in the center of town, has a visitor center that houses exhibits on forest-fire ecology and shows a film about Smokey's life. A half-mile interpretive nature trail leads to his gravesite. And so the story goes that in May of 1950, after a raging five-day fire that burned 17,000 acres throughout the Capitan area, firefighters found a five-month-old bear cub they named Hot Foot Teddy clinging to a burnt tree. After two months

In Capitan with the famous bear. (Photo by Rob Edwards.)

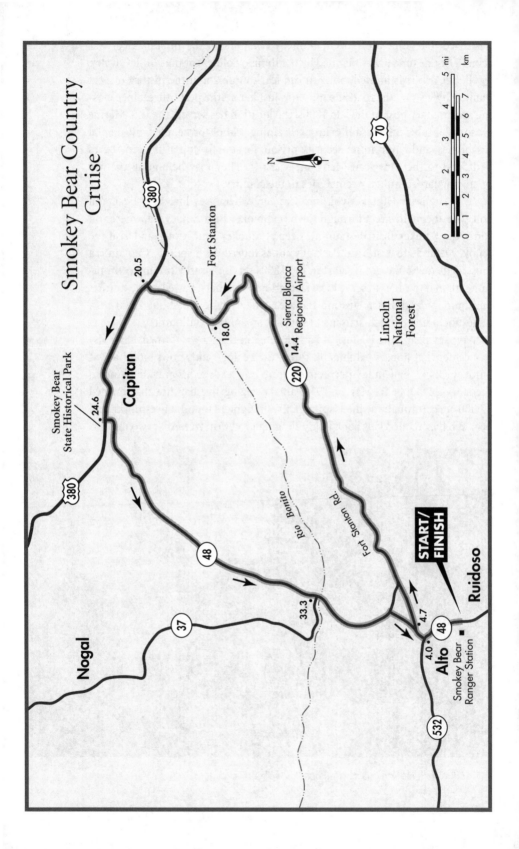

0.0 Leave the parking lot at the ranger station, and head north on New Mexico Route 48.

1.9 Gain a small shoulder as you begin climbing out of town toward Alto.

2.9 Reach the high point along New Mexico Route 48 and a sign indicating that Ruidoso's elevation is 6,900 feet, then descend.

4.0 Pass the turnoff for New Mexico Route 532, Ski Run Road, on the left; continue straight and lose the shoulder. A gas station (Shell) was under construction on the corner at the time of this writing.

4.7 Turn right on Fort Stanton Road; no shoulder or yellow line. Begin the descent into the valley. (Note: If you reach the Phillips 66 station on the left, you've gone about 0.1 mile too far.)

6.8 Reach a stop sign at a T intersection and turn right onto New Mexico Route 220 or Airport Road (no road sign). The large shoulder is bumpy with loose gravel; the pavement is very smooth. Gradual climbing for a mile.

8.0 Sign indicates you are cycling on part of the Billy the Kid National Scenic Byway.

9.5 As you pass Spencer Theatre on the right, note the interesting architecture.

11.4 Lose shoulder.

14.4 Pass Sierra Blanca Regional Airport.

16.2 Reach a stop sign and T intersection where a sign indicates that Fort Stanton Museum is to the left. The road right is gravel; turn left.

17.4 Worth a stop—the Merchant Marine and Military Cemetery—on the right.

18.0 Reach Fort Stanton; the museum is on the left. Lowest elevation along the ride.

18.3 Cross the Rio Bonito.

19.5 Horse trailer parking area on the right; vault toilet.

20.5 Reach U.S. Highway 380 (stop sign at T intersection); historic Lincoln is to the right. Turn left; not much shoulder.

21.3 Smokey Bear Vista—an information board points out various peaks in the Capitan Mountains.

(continued)

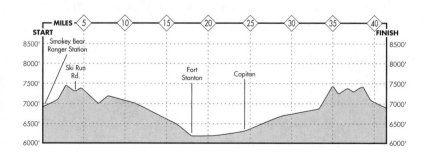

24.1 Reach Capitan; sign indicates elevation at 6,350 feet.

24.2 Stop to read the historic marker about the area.

24.5 Farmers Country Market and Lincoln Country Mercantile on the right.

24.6 Reach your turn onto New Mexico Route 48 on the left, but spend some time in Capitan before you finish the loop. The state park is just ahead on the right. Once on New Mexico Route 48, there is a small shoulder. Enjoy flat riding for a few miles before climbing back toward Alto.

28.7 Another Smokey Bear Vista (benches).

33.3 Cross the Rio Bonito again, and reach the junction with New Mexico Route 37 on the right (leads to Bonito Lake). Continue straight and begin a 2-mile, steep climb.

35.0 Reach a high point and descend.

35.7 Junction with New Mexico Route 220 on the left; continue straight.

36.7 Pass Sun Valley Road and the Phillips 66 on the right.

36.8 Pass Fort Stanton Road (the beginning of the loop) on the left.

41.5 Continue on New Mexico Route 48 back to the Smokey Bear Ranger Station.

of care and an unsuccessful attempt to be returned to the wild, he was flown to the National Zoo in Washington, D.C., where he became Smokey Bear.

You know the motto: "Only YOU can prevent forest fires." For twenty-six years, Smokey was part of a campaign to increase national awareness about forest fires. He had his own zip code, and his picture appeared on a postage stamp. The state park dedicated to this famous bear was completed in 1976, the year Smokey died, and he was flown home to be buried.

LOCAL INFORMATION

♦ Capitan Chamber of Commerce, P.O. Box 441, Capitan, NM 88316; (505) 354–2273.

♦ Smokey Bear Ranger Station, 901 Mechem Drive, Ruidoso, NM 88345; (505) 257–4095.

♦ Ruidoso Valley Chamber of Commerce (www.ruidoso.net), 720 Sudderth Drive, Ruidoso, NM 88355; (800) 253–2255.

EVENTS/ATTRACTIONS

♦ Fort Stanton, P.O. Box 1, Fort Stanton, NM 88323; (505) 336–7711 (museum open 10:00 A.M. to 4:00 P.M. Thursday through Monday).

◆ Smokey Bear State Historic Park, 118 Smokey Bear Boulevard, Capitan, NM 88316; (505) 354–2748 (9:00 A.M. to 5:00 P.M. daily; closed Thanksgiving, Christmas, and New Year's Day).

RESTAURANTS

◆ Smokey Bear Restaurant, 310 Smokey Bear Boulevard, Capitan, NM 88316; (505) 354–2257 (open daily).

ACCOMMODATIONS

◆ Smokey Bear Motel, 316 Smokey Bear Boulevard, Capitan, NM 88316; (505) 354–2253 (reasonable rates).
◆ Buffalo Girls B&B, 311 Smokey Bear Boulevard, Capitan, NM 88316; (505) 354–2858 (option includes camping out in a covered wagon).

BIKE SHOPS

◆ High Altitude, 2316½ Sudderth Drive, Ruidoso, NM 88345; (505) 257–0120.

REST ROOMS

◆ Mile 0.0: Smokey Bear Ranger Station.
◆ Mile 4.0: Shell station on the left (not complete at the time of this writing).
◆ Mile 19.5: Vault toilet at horse trailer parking.
◆ Mile 24.5: Capitan—roadside businesses or the state park.
◆ Mile 36.7: Phillips 66 station.

MAPS

◆ USGS 7.5-minute quads Ruidoso, Angus, Capitan, Fort Stanton, and Nogal.
◆ Delorme *New Mexico Atlas & Gazetteer*, map 40.

36

Cloudcroft to Ruidoso Cruise

R
ide from bike shop to bike shop for more than 40 miles along a scenic back road that follows the crest of the Sacramento Mountains in south-central New Mexico. High Altitude has a bike shop in Cloudcroft and in Ruidoso, and the forested New Mexico Route 244 stretches between the two resort villages, passing through Lincoln National Forest and the Mescalero Apache Reservation. While these two mountain towns, located in the highest range in the southern half of the state, are well known to tourists as year-round playgrounds, the ride itself travels through a beautiful unpopulated area.

To ride from High Altitude in Cloudcroft to its sister store in Ruidoso, you'll follow U.S. Highway 82, New Mexico Route 244, U.S. Highway 70, and New Mexico Route 48, in that order, with the majority of the ride on New Mexico Route 244. You'll enjoy miles of dense pine forest, mountain valleys, and cattle grazing as you travel through national forest and Indian reservation land. There are very few communities or businesses between Cloudcroft and Ruidoso following this route—only a country store at Silver Springs RV Campground.

The ride follows the crest of the Sacramento Mountains, one of the largest mountain chains in the state. Only the Sangre de Cristos (Santa Fe to Taos) are higher. Part of the scenery includes occasional views of Sierra Blanca (elevation 12,003 feet), with its treeless top, and for a good part of the year, a snow-covered summit. Just north of Ruidoso, the "white mountain" holds snow longer than surrounding peaks, sometimes into early summer.

The first five miles will have you climbing, steeply at times, as you pass several forest service campgrounds outside of Cloudcroft. The woodlands include pine, spruce, fir, and aspen; and this section is great for viewing the fall foliage. Silver Springs Canyon provides a nice descent and some level riding through an open valley; and the Mescalero Apache Reservation, the biggest portion of the ride, is mostly unpopulated, hilly terrain lined with ponderosa pine. The reservation lies between two large portions of Lincoln National Forest that surround Cloudcroft and Ruidoso. You'll have more traffic along U.S. Highway 70 but incredible views of Sierra Blanca near Apache Summit and a 10-mile descent into Ruidoso.

While Ruidoso (population 8,000) is much larger than Cloudcroft (population 750), both resort towns rely heavily on year-round tourism, each acting as a mountaintop oasis for people living in desert cities like Alamogordo and Roswell. It's not a surprise that Texans frequent both areas. They come for the cool temperatures in the summer and the skiing in the winter, in addition to the hiking, biking, camping, fishing, golfing, dining, and shopping. Both villages have a Western-style main street lined with gift

shops, galleries, restaurants, and historic buildings—Cloudcroft, the block of businesses on Burro Avenue, and Ruidoso, the mile-long midtown.

And both villages have a bike shop. High Altitude operates a bike shop in Cloudcroft and Ruidoso. A shuttle service is not something they advertise, but the owners always try to help out visiting cyclists however they can. The fee would be reasonable and you could ride this route in either direction. An out-and-back of about 85 miles is, of course, an option, as well as basing in one town and spending the night in the other before you return. Cloudcroft and

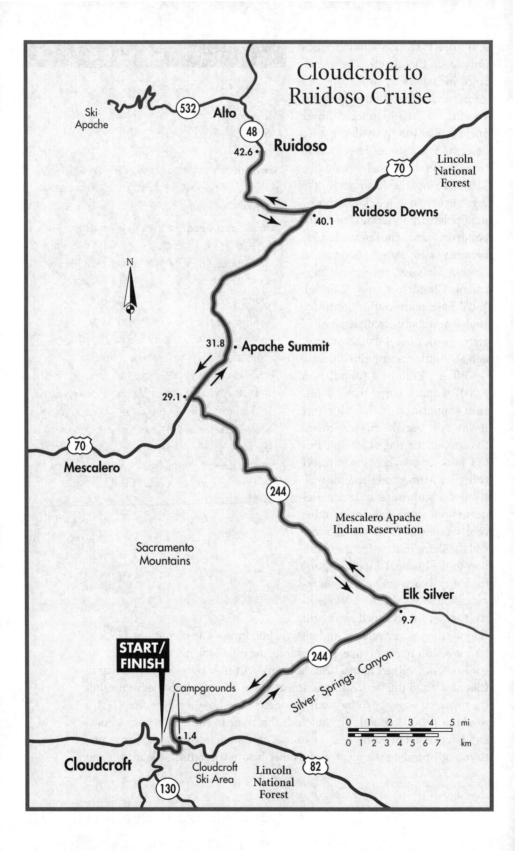

Cloudcroft to Ruidoso Cruise

Ski Apache

532 Alto

48 Ruidoso

42.6

70 Lincoln National Forest

40.1 Ruidoso Downs

N

31.8 Apache Summit

29.1

70 Mescalero

244

Mescalero Apache Indian Reservation

Sacramento Mountains

Elk Silver

9.7

START/FINISH

244

Silver Springs Canyon

Campgrounds

1.4

Cloudcroft

Cloudcroft Ski Area

Lincoln National Forest

82

130

0 1 2 3 4 5 mi

0 1 2 3 4 5 6 7 km

0.0 Leave the bike shop in Cloudcroft, heading east on Burro Avenue. After 1 block, turn right on Swallow Place.

0.2 Reach the T intersection with U.S. Highway 82 and turn left, heading east out of town.

0.4 Pass Zenith Park on the right; sheltered picnic tables.

0.5 Pass the log cabin on the right that houses the chamber of commerce.

1.4 Turn left on New Mexico Route 244 and begin climbing. You'll have a 1- to 3-foot shoulder along this rural road for the next 6.5 miles. The quality of the shoulder varies; some sections are chewed up.

1.9 Pines Campground on the left; a forty-four-site forest service facility with pit toilets, picnic tables, and water. Good choice if camping in the area.

3.2 Forest service recreation areas on the right and high point of the ride. Begin your descent through Silver Springs Canyon.

5.6 The terrain flattens out as you enter an open valley.

7.2 Leave the national forest. In a half mile, enter the Mescalero Apache Reservation and lose the shoulder.

9.7 Silver Springs RV Campground—be sure to stop in the country store for home-made goodies (April through October). For the next 15 miles, expect rolling terrain where you'll gain and lose a couple hundred feet several times.

24.0 Begin descending to U.S. Highway 70.

29.1 At the stop sign turn right on the four-lane U.S. Highway 70 (Mescalero to the left). Enjoy a wide shoulder and smooth road surface as you climb toward Apache Summit.

31.8 Apache Summit (elevation 7,600 feet); descend!

33.0 Historic marker on the right provides information about Sierra Blanca; continue your descent.

34.8 Road on the left leads to the Inn of the Mountain Gods; a back way into Ruidoso that will bring you out at the traffic light at the visitor center (mile 41.6). U.S. Highway 70 narrows to two lanes with little shoulder.

(continued)

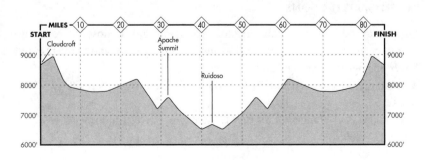

38.8 Enter Lincoln County and gain a wide shoulder. Begin passing billboards, motels, and RV parks.

40.1 Turn left at the first traffic light, which is Sudderth Drive (New Mexico Route 48). There is a bike lane through town.

41.6 Visitor center on the right at the traffic light for Carrizo Canyon Road. There is a park along the river behind the building.

42.6 Reach High Altitude in Ruidoso on the right.

Ruidoso offer a wide variety of B&Bs, rental cabins, and campgrounds.

The Mescalero Apache are remembered as fierce warriors because they fought the Spanish and Anglo settlement of their homeland. Today, they are one of the most prosperous tribes in the nation. In addition to owning and operating Ski Apache, they run a casino and the luxury, lakeside resort, Inn of the Mountain Gods. The Mescaleros also do well with timber and cattle and sell fishing and hunting licenses.

The reservation was established in 1872, and the headquarters is in Mescalero, about 5 miles from mile 29.1 on this ride. The tribe's name comes from their extensive use of the mescal (agave) plant. Every year around the Fourth of July, the Mescaleros celebrate with a four-day festival; many of the events, which include colorful dances, powwows, and a rodeo, are open to the public.

LOCAL INFORMATION

♦ Cloudcroft Chamber of Commerce (www.cloudcroft.net), P.O. Box 1290, Cloudcroft, NM 88317; (505) 682–2733.

♦ Ruidoso Valley Chamber of Commerce (www.ruidoso.net), 720 Sudderth Drive, Ruidoso, NM 88355; (800) 253–2255.

♦ Mescalero Apache Tourism Office, P.O. Box 227, Mescalero, NM 83340; (505) 671–4494.

EVENTS/ATTRACTIONS

Other than the resort communities of Cloudcroft and Ruidoso, there are no events or attractions along this ride—just a country store and trout pond at Silver Springs RV Campground.

♦ Sacramento Ranger District, P.O. Box 288, Cloudcroft, NM 88317; (505) 682–2551.

♦ Smokey Bear Ranger Station, 901 Mechem Drive, Ruidoso, NM 88345; (505) 257–4095.

Relaxing on Burro Alley in Cloudcroft.

RESTAURANTS

Here are recommendations from the folks at High Altitude—sure to please the cyclist's appetite:

♦ Far Side Food & Health, 91 Little Glorieta, Cloudcroft, NM 88317; (505) 682–5000 (great for lunch).

♦ Western Bar & Cafe, 304 Burro Avenue, Cloudcroft, NM 88317; (505) 682–2445 (Mexican and American fare).

♦ Dave's Cafe & Pine Stump Mall, 300 Burro Avenue, Cloudcroft, NM 88317; (505) 682–2127.

♦ Cafe Rio, 2547 Sudderth Drive, Ruidoso, NM 88345; (505) 257–7746 (unique—Greek, Cajun, Portuguese).

♦ Pub 48, 441 Mechem Drive, Ruidoso, NM 88345; (505) 257–9559 (the town brew pub featuring eight award-winning microbrews from Sierra Blanca Brewing).

ACCOMMODATIONS

♦ Silver Springs RV Campground, P.O. Box 965, Cloudcroft, NM 88317; (505) 682–1148 (on-route).

♦ Ruidoso Central Reservations (www.ruidoso.net/reservations), P.O. Box 1864, Ruidoso, NM 88355; (888) 257–7577.

♦ For Cloudcroft, contact the chamber of commerce, or go to their Web site and click on "Lodging."

BIKE SHOPS

♦ High Altitude, 310 Burro Avenue, Cloudcroft, NM 88317; (505) 682–1229.

♦ High Altitude, 2316½ Sudderth Drive, Ruidoso, NM 88345; (505) 257–0120.

REST ROOMS

♦ Mile 0.0: Public rest rooms on Burro Avenue in Cloudcroft, across from the bike shop and a half block to the right.

♦ Mile 41.6: Visitor center in Ruidoso on the right.

♦ Public rest rooms are scarce on this ride. You'll find a couple forest service facilities in the first few miles, and gas stations and fast food places a few miles before the finish.

MAPS

♦ USGS 7.5-minute quads Cloudcroft, Firman Canyon, Elk-Silver, Apache Summit, and Ruidoso.

♦ Delorme *New Mexico Atlas & Gazetteer,* maps 40 and 48.

Sunspot Scenic Byway Cruise

The ride up to the National Solar Observatory along the Sunspot Scenic Byway is a great workout without being as steep and grueling as some of the state's ski area roads. Along the way you can stop at overlooks with views of the Tularosa Basin, including White Sands National Monument. You'll be riding the crest of the Sacramento Mountains through Lincoln National Forest; and at the terminus of the byway, you can follow a self-guided trail and learn more about the observatory and its telescopes.

Locally known as the Sunspot Highway, the road up to the observatory begins just south of Cloudcroft, a small mountain retreat popular with Texans and people living in southern New Mexico. The climbing is gradual with a good shoulder, and the high point isn't at the end of the road but rather about halfway up near Alamo Peak, so you'll have some up and down in both directions.

The Sacramento Mountains are composed mostly of limestone and the road winds through a thick forest of Douglas fir, ponderosa pine, blue spruce, gamble oak, and other trees. The ride is awesome in the fall when the maple and aspen splash color on the hillsides. No matter what time of year, you'll enjoy the scent of pine. You can see Sierra Blanca (12,003 feet) outside Ruidoso from a few spots on the way down. It's the highest point in the Sacramentos, and Ski Apache is located on the east slopes.

Along the way, you'll pass a "snow play" area, hiking and mountain biking trailheads, and several scenic overlooks. You may see cross ties and sections of an old railroad bed. A small logging railroad accessed this part of the

Start: Overlook parking on the Sunspot Scenic Byway just south of Cloudcroft.

Length: 26.6 miles round-trip.

Terrain: A hill climb with a good shoulder and gradual grade; some up and down in both directions.

Traffic and hazards: The road surface is in good condition and the traffic is light.

Getting there: From Alamogordo head east on U.S. Highway 82 for about 16 miles to Cloudcroft. Turn right on New Mexico Route 130 just before you reach the village proper. If you pass the ranger station and Mountain Top Grocery and Bakery on the right, you just missed the turn. Travel 1.7 miles and turn right on New Mexico Route 6563, the Sunspot Scenic Byway. After about a mile there is a good parking lot on the right at an overlook.

Sacramentos before good roads were built, and the scenic byway follows some of the old rail route.

Cloudcroft, a village of 750, attracts visitors with its cool summer temperatures (low seventies) and its mild winters (southernmost downhill ski area in the country). The town is surrounded by national forest with great hiking and mountain biking trails, including the infamous singletrack Rim Trail. The town motto is "9,000 feet above stress level."

Be sure to spend some time before or after your ride on Burro Avenue. On this Western-style boardwalk, you'll find a variety of shops, as well as the restaurants listed here and the local bike shop, High Altitude. Turn left on Curlew Place just across the street from the Mountain Top Grocery and Bakery, another spot worthy of a visit. Just a block off U.S. Highway 82, you'll intersect Burro Avenue. The bike shop is just to the right.

Cloudcroft has dozens of motels, hotels, B&Bs, and cabin rentals. The accommodations listed here give you a couple choices in different price ranges. For camping, contact the Sacramento Ranger District. Deerhead Campground is on the right along New Mexico Route 130 about a half mile before you turn onto the Sunspot Highway; and the turnoff for Sleepygrass Campground is on the left. These two forest service campgrounds are open from mid-May through mid-October and cost $8.00. Showers are available for $3.00 at Silver Overflow Campground on New Mexico Route 244, about 4 miles away.

The National Solar Observatory, located on Sacramento Peak, is a scientific research center for the study of the sun, as well as other stars in the galaxy. The sky conditions here are ideal for solar research. The facility consists of several large telescopes including the world's largest coronagraph, a powerful tool for looking at the sun's corona. The museum in the visitor center costs $2.00, the self-guided trail is free, and guided tours are offered on Saturdays at 2:00 P.M. in the summer. Bring along some quarters for the viewing scope so you can

White Sands from the Sunspot Scenic Byway.

get a close-up look at the Tularosa Basin, White Sands, and the San Andres Mountains to the west.

Note: Just before the observatory, Forest Road 537 heads off to the left to the small community of Timberon. At the time of this writing, half of the highway project to pave this road was complete—about 8 miles. Work on the second half is scheduled to start in the spring of 2002 and be completed the following winter. Check with the folks at High Altitude to find out about this new ride.

LOCAL INFORMATION

♦ Chamber of Commerce (www.cloudcroft.net), P.O. Box 1290, Cloudcroft, NM 88317; (505) 682–2733.

♦ Sacramento Ranger District, P.O. Box 288, Cloudcroft, NM 88317; (505) 682–2551.

EVENTS/ATTRACTIONS

♦ National Solar Observatory (www.sunspot.noao.edu), Sacramento Peak, Sunspot, NM 88349; (505) 434–7000 (visitor center open daily 10:00 A.M. to 6:00 P.M. from March through October).

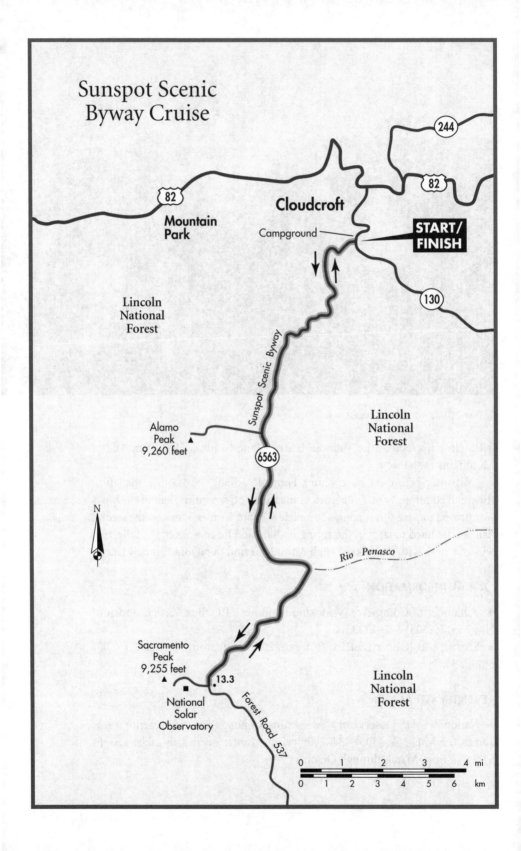

Sunspot Scenic
Byway Cruise

244

82

Cloudcroft

82

**Mountain
Park**

Campground

**START/
FINISH**

130

Lincoln
National
Forest

Sunspot Scenic Byway

Alamo
Peak
9,260 feet ▲

6563

Lincoln
National
Forest

N

Rio Penasco

Sacramento
Peak
9,255 feet ▲
■   .13.3

National
Solar
Observatory

Forest Road 537

Lincoln
National
Forest

| 0 | | 1 | | 2 | | 3 | | 4 mi |
| 0 | 1 | 2 | 3 | 4 | 5 | 6 km |

0.0 Leave the overlook, and turn right to head up the Sunspot Scenic Byway. Enjoy a smooth road surface and good shoulder for the entire ride.

1.5 On the left Triple M Snow Play, a snow tubing area with a lift. The area also offers snowmobile tours.

2.5 Nelson Canyon Vista Trail on the right; a quarter-mile self-guided trail to an overlook.

3.0 One of several access points for the Rim Trail on the right. The infamous mountain bike singletrack parallels a majority of the byway.

4.3 Upper Karr; good view from here of Sierra Blanca on the descent.

5.5 Paved road (0.5 mile) to the right leads to an overlook at Alamo Peak.

7.1 A sign marks Atkinson Canyon.

8.9 Begin another climb.

10.7 Paved parking lot on the right for Cathey Vista Trail; another quarter-mile trail to a vista (picnic tables).

11.3 Begin a 9 percent downgrade. Yeehaw!

12.5 Road on the left leads to Apache Point Observatory, a new neighbor to the National Solar Observatory.

12.9 Enter through the main gate of the National Solar Observatory.

13.0 Turn left on Visitor Center Drive.

13.3 Reach the parking lot for the observatory; water, rest rooms, and picnic tables. You can purchase juice and sports drinks in the visitor center.

26.6 Return to the parking lot at the overlook.

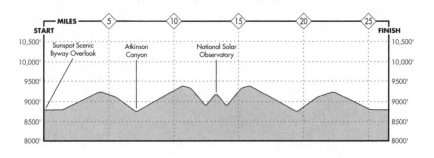

RESTAURANTS

♦ Far Side Food & Health, 91 Little Glorieta, Cloudcroft, NM 88317; (505) 682–5000 (great for lunch).

♦ Western Bar & Cafe, 304 Burro Avenue, Cloudcroft, NM 88317; (505) 682–2445 (Mexican and American fare).

♦ Dave's Cafe & Pine Stump Mall, 300 Burro Avenue, Cloudcroft, NM 88317; (505) 682–2127.

ACCOMMODATIONS

♦ The Lodge at Cloudcroft (www.thelodgeresort.com), #1 Corona Place, Cloudcroft, NM 87317; (800) 395–6343 (historic lodge and resort).
♦ Spruce Cabins (www.sprucecabins.com), 100 Lynx Avenue, Cloudcroft, NM 88317; (505) 682–2381 ($36–$70).
♦ Cloudcroft Mountain Park Hostel, 1049 Highway 82, Mountain Park, NM 88325; (505) 682–0555 (about $17).

BIKE SHOPS

♦ High Altitude, 310 Burro Avenue, Cloudcroft, NM 88317; (505) 682–1229.

REST ROOMS

♦ Mile 13.3: National Solar Observatory.
♦ This part of the national forest is considered a "dispersed area," and there are no rest room facilities until you reach the visitor center at the top.

MAPS

♦ USGS 7.5-minute quads Cloudcroft, High Rolls, and Sacramento Peak.
♦ Delorme *New Mexico Atlas & Gazetteer,* map 48.

Taylor Ranch Ramble

I have cyclist Chisom Wilson and the bike shop Outdoor Adventures in Alamogordo to thank for this city perimeter loop- it's a great spin. Chisom and I rode on a beautiful November day, leaving from the Motel 6 (mile 4.1) where I was staying overnight. The loop incorporates several of the local cyclists' favorite roads, including Taylor Ranch Road to the south of town and the new bypass, Tularosa Relief Route, to the west. You'll encounter city street riding, quiet residential areas, and rural countryside. Views include the Tularosa Basin, White Sands, the Sacramento Mountains, and the 12,003-foot Sierra Blanca.

This ride makes a long, skinny loop around the city of Alamogordo, which lies in the shadow of the Sacramento Mountains and just 15 miles east of White Sands National Monument. Here the arid desert meets the pine-covered mountains. You can get in 30 miles of riding around town without much more than a little elevation gain here and there, but if you leave town in any direction other than toward the basin, expect some steep climbing.

The loop starts on Tenth Street, one of main business strips in town; within a mile of leaving the bike shop, you'll be cycling on an undeveloped section of Scenic Drive along the west-facing escarpment of the Sacramento Mountains. Enjoy views of Tabletop, Alamo Canyon, and Long Ridge (towers on top). The markers along the right side of the road are used by the many walkers who use this mile-long stretch for exercise.

After passing through a residential section of town and the Desert Lakes Golf Course, you'll be heading south into the countryside, the least traveled

Start: Outdoor Adventures in downtown Alamogordo.

Length: 30.9-mile loop.

Terrain: A spin on relatively flat terrain; all climbs have a very gradual grade. Most of the elevation gain is on U.S. Highway 82 and Scenic Drive.

Traffic and hazards: Light traffic on rural roads (no shoulders). U.S. Highway 54 and the Tularosa Relief Route have large shoulders. Watch parked cars in residential sections, especially along Scenic Drive.

Getting there: From White Sands Boulevard (U.S. Highway 70/82/54), which runs through Alamogordo, turn east toward the mountains on Tenth Street. The Alamogordo Zoo is on the northwest corner of this intersection. Travel about 2 miles on Tenth Street, and locate Outdoor Adventures on the right. The cross street is Madison Avenue. There is ample on-street parking near the bike shop; try Madison on the east side of the shop.

part of this loop, on bumpy Old El Paso Highway and Taylor Ranch Road. U.S. Highway 54 brings you back into the city limits and onto the new Tularosa Relief Route—no traffic lights or stop signs for 5.5 miles. This highway was built just west of U.S. Highway 70/54 to relieve the traffic flow through town and provides you with a large shoulder and views north of Sierra Blanca, the highest peak in southern New Mexico.

As you climb east of town, you'll gain some elevation—just enough to see the sparkle of White Sands National Monument in the Tularosa Basin to the west, if it's a clear day. Scenic Drive runs alongside the hillside at the edge of the Sacramentos, just above the city, and passes the Alamogordo Campus of New Mexico State University, the new Gerald Champion Regional Medical Center, and the ride's big attraction, the International Space Center.

Alamogordo, located in the Tularosa Valley at an elevation of 4,300 feet, was founded in the late 1890s as a planned railroad town with wide streets lined with cottonwoods—hence, the name, Alamogordo, or "Big Cottonwood." This small desert town expanded with the establishment of the Holloman Air Force Base during World War II. The base originally trained B-17 bomber crews and has been home to many commands and military missions. Today it is the largest employer in the county, a big influence on Alamogordo's economy.

The main attraction on-route is the International Space Center. This impressive facility includes a museum, IMAX theater, planetarium, space hall of fame, and more. For a small admission fee, you can learn about the history of space explorations, and even try some "space food." The Space Center is open daily from 9:00 A.M. to 5:00 P.M. in the summer. Turn left at mile 28.7!

While you are visiting Alamogordo, Oliver Lee Memorial State Park makes a great base for the bicyclist. Located in Dog Canyon, about 12 miles south of town, the state park offers campsites for $7.00 with showers and flush toilets. Dog Canyon is relatively lush because springs flow year-round, and a hiking trail leads up onto the ridges, climbing 3,500 feet in 4.5 miles. The ride out to Dog Canyon is another local favorite. Check with the folks at Outdoor Adventures about this route (and others).

LOCAL INFORMATION

◆ Alamogordo Chamber of Commerce (www.alamogordo.com), 1301 North White Sands Boulevard, Alamogordo, NM 88310; (800) 826–0294.

EVENTS/ATTRACTIONS

◆ International Space Center (www.spacefame.org), P.O. Box 533, Alamogordo, NM 88311-0533; (877) 333–6589 (open daily 9:00 A.M. to 5:00 P.M.).

RESTAURANTS

◆ Compass Rose Brew Pub, 2203 East First Street, Alamogordo, NM 88310; (505) 434–9633 (not an actual brew pub but good beer and decent food).
◆ *Note:* Call Outdoor Adventures for other dining suggestions.

ACCOMMODATIONS

◆ Chain motels clustered on the south end of town off U.S. Highway 70/54 (White Sands Boulevard).
◆ Oliver Lee Memorial State Park, 409 Dog Canyon, Alamogordo, NM 88310; (505) 437–8284.

BIKE SHOPS

◆ Outdoor Adventures (www.zianet.com/outdooradventures), 1516 East Tenth Street, Alamogordo, NM 88310; (505) 434–1920.

REST ROOMS

◆ Mile 0.0: Outdoor Adventures.
◆ Mile 5.2: Desert Lakes Golf Course.
◆ Mile 25.0: Chevron on the right.

MAPS

◆ USGS 7.5-minute quads Alamogordo North and Alamogordo South.
◆ Delorme *New Mexico Atlas & Gazetteer,* map 48.

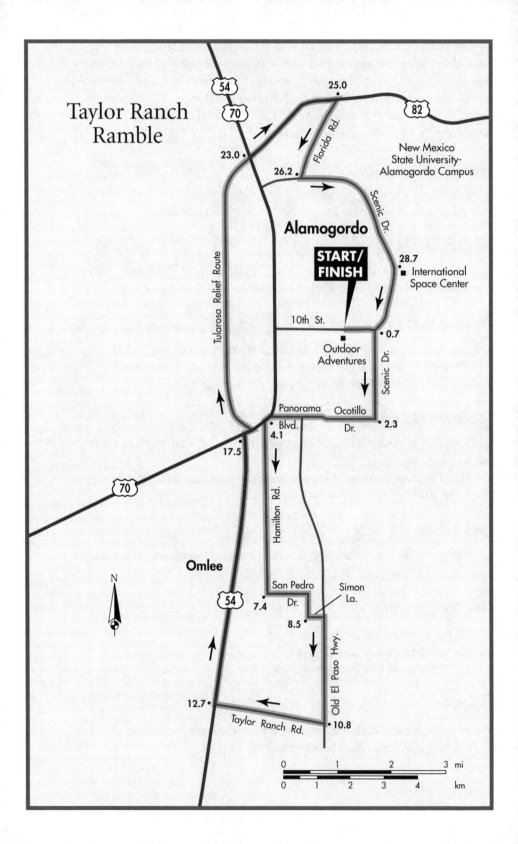

Taylor Ranch
Ramble

54
70

25.0

82

New Mexico
State University-
Alamogordo Campus

23.0

26.2

Florida Rd.

Scenic Dr.

Alamogordo

START/
FINISH

28.7
International
Space Center

Tularosa Relief Route

10th St.

0.7

Outdoor
Adventures

Scenic Dr.

Panorama

Ocotillo

Blvd.
4.1

Dr.

2.3

17.5

70

Hamilton Rd.

Omlee

54

San Pedro

Simon
La.

7.4

Dr.

N

8.5

Old El Paso Hwy.

12.7

10.8

Taylor Ranch Rd.

0   1   2   3   mi
0   1   2   3   4   km

0.0 Leave the bike shop heading east (right) on Tenth Street. Continue straight as you go through the traffic light at College Avenue.

0.7 Reach the stop sign at Scenic Drive and turn right.

1.2 Reach the stop sign at First Street and continue straight. (*Note:* The Compass Rose Brew Pub is just down First Street a block or so to the right.) The next mile on Scenic Drive is not developed; slight climb.

2.3 Scenic Drive ends; turn right on Ocotillo Drive. Cycle through a residential section of town; no shoulder and slight descent. Several stop signs will slow you down.

3.7 Octotillo Drive becomes Panorama Boulevard after you cross Florida Avenue.

4.1 Pass the Motel 6, then turn left on Hamilton Road (no shoulder).

5.2 You'll encounter several stop signs as you pass through Desert Lakes Golf Course.

7.4 Take a left on San Pedro Drive.

8.5 Take another left on Simon Lane, which curves right and becomes Old El Paso Highway.

10.8 Old El Paso turns to dirt; head right on Taylor Ranch Road.

12.7 Cross the railroad tracks, and turn right on U.S. Highway 54; busy highway but large, smooth shoulder.

15.8 Cycle back into the city limits of Alamogordo.

17.5 Reach the junction with U.S. Highway 70. Turn right to get on the Tularosa Relief Route, which will take you under U.S. Highway 70.

20.0 One of several access points along the bypass to downtown. Here, Tenth Street leads back to the bike shop.

23.0 Tularosa Relief Route ends. Continue straight at the traffic light, crossing U.S. Highway 70, and begin cycling on U.S. Highway 82, which leads to Cloudcroft. Gentle upgrade, and you will still have a shoulder here.

25.0 Flashing light and Chevron station on the right-hand corner. Take a right on Florida Road (shoulder); no sign. Good views of White Sands.

(continued)

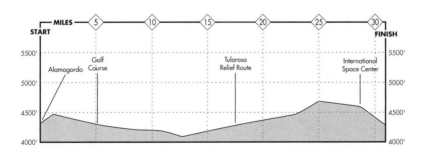

26.2 At the stop sign, turn left on Scenic Drive (no shoulder). The Deutsche Schule, a school for German children whose parents are stationed at Holloman Air Force Base, is located on the southwest corner.

28.0 Pass the Gerald Champion Regional Medical Center on the right, the new state-of-the-art facility and joint venture with Holloman Air Force Base.

28.6 Pass New Mexico State University at Alamogordo on the left. Gain a shoulder (actually a parking lane) as you enter another residential section of town.

28.7 The International Space Center sits on the hill to the left.

30.2 Reach the stop sign at Tenth Street and turn right, heading back toward the bike shop.

30.7 Continue straight through the traffic light at College Avenue.

30.9 Return to your vehicle at Outdoor Adventures on the left.

White Sands Moonlight Ramble

*C*ycle through the largest gypsum dune field in the world under the brilliant light of a full moon. Several times a year you can ride on Dunes Drive in White Sands National Monument for several hours after sunset when all vehicles have left the park. A full moon reflected on the glistening white sand provides a unique and magical biking experience. The 230 square miles of sand dunes that make up the monument are located in the Tularosa Basin, the northern part of the Chihuahuan Desert. The basin is surrounded by mountains, the San Andres to the west and the Sacramentos to the east, and you will be able to see Sierra Blanca (12,003 feet) outside Ruidoso to the northeast. White Sands is probably one of the state's strangest and most impressive sights.

White Sands National Monument has been scheduling moonlight bicycle rides since about 1994. When a full moon falls on or near a weekend in the spring and fall, usually May and September, the park reopens to the participants for three hours after dark. This is a popular event, and cycling clubs often attend from Albuquerque, Las Cruces, and El Paso.

The first 170 people to register get to ride. Check the monument's Web site ("events calendar"), and call ahead for reservations (cost $5.00). Helmets are required, as well as some sort of light. You can bring a headlamp or even tape a flashlight to your bike. If you miss the moonlight rides, you can cycle on Dunes Drive until about 10:00 P.M. in the summer and until an hour after sunset in the winter.

Start: The visitor center at White Sands National Monument, about 15 miles west of Alamogordo.

Length: 14.3 miles round-trip.

Terrain: Flat, easy terrain, although there can be strong winds and sand storms.

Traffic and hazards: No traffic on the moonlight ride; otherwise, traffic is light (no shoulder). About 5 miles on a hard-packed surface with loose sand that can be handled by most road bikes. Hot in summer, but mornings and evenings are great.

Getting there: From Alamogordo, head west on U.S. Highway 70 for about 15 miles. White Sands National Monument will be on the right. The park is about 50 miles east of Las Cruces.

At White Sands National Monument, the yucca blooms between late May and early June.

This out-and-back starts along U.S. Highway 70 at the visitor center, a good place to learn about the formation and history of the dunes, as well as the flora, fauna, and geology of the area. As you head toward the nature center, there are wayside exhibits along the road, as well as several marked trails. On the Interdune Boardwalk (0.3 mile), you can leave your bike at the parking lot and see it the whole time while you follow the wooden walkway. The cryptobiotic crust of the interdune provides a nutrient-rich soil that allows a variety of plants to grow. Desert wildflowers are blooming by late April, and yucca from late May to early June.

The dunes are closely spaced and larger (up to 50 feet) as you head deeper into the Heart of the Sands. The Alkali Flat Trail (4.6 miles), the longest trail in the park, gives you the chance to hike in an unvegetated area

Cycle through the largest gypsum dune in the world at White Sands National Monument.

and explore the endless white sand dunes. You can lock your bike at the nature center, which is about a mile from the trailhead. While hiking, photography, and identifying animal tracks are popular activities, sand sledding seemed to be the biggest hit when I was there.

Sleeping under the stars in the dunes is not to be missed. The moonlight creates an eerie landscape, and first light turns the dunes pink and gold. It would be hard to pick the best time to experience White Sands—sunrise, sunset, or a full moon. You might be able to catch them all. The monument doesn't have a campground, but there are a few backcountry sites available on a first-come, first-served basis for $3.00 per person. You must register at the visitor center during business hours (8:00 A.M. to 7:00 P.M. in the summer) on the day you intend to camp. These primitive sites have no water or toilet and involve about a mile hike in.

The average elevation is about 4,000 feet, and Dunes Drive is flat as a pancake. The prevailing southwest winds present the biggest challenge. Winds are especially strong from February through May. Summer temperatures can exceed 100 degrees, making the night rides more inviting. There are vault toilets and sheltered picnic tables at the end of the road, but water is only available at the visitor center at the start. (*Note:* Because the monument is completely surrounded by the White Sands Missile Range, the park and U.S.

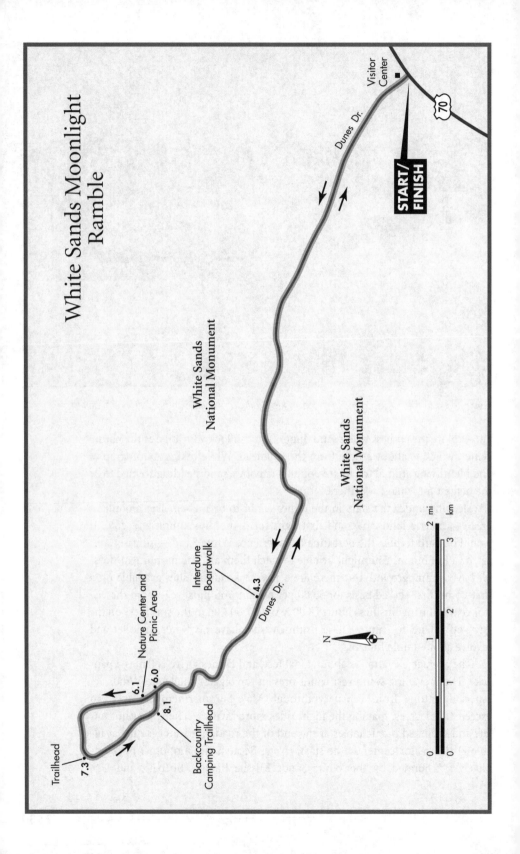

White Sands Moonlight Ramble

White Sands National Monument

White Sands National Monument

White Sands National Monument

Visitor Center

Dunes Dr.

START/FINISH

70

Interdune Boardwalk

Dunes Dr.

4.3

Nature Center and Picnic Area

6.1

6.0

Trailhead

7.3

Backcountry Camping Trailhead

8.1

N

0   1   2 mi

0   1   2   3 km

0.0 Leave the parking lot at the visitor center and turn right onto Dunes Drive. Ride past the entrance station. There is no shoulder.

4.3 Interdune Boardwalk on the right. This is an elevated wooden walkway through an interdune area. You could leave your bike at the start where you'd be able to see it while you stroll along the trail.

4.6 Pavement ends. Ride on a hard-packed surface for the next 5 miles, which is not too bad on a road bike.

6.0 Reach the point where the road splits and the short loop begins, the Heart of the Sands. Go to the right.

6.1 Pass a picnic area and the nature center on the right.

7.3 The parking lot for Alkali Trail, the longest marked trail in the park. To hike here you should lock your bike back at the nature center.

7.9 Ride through another picnic area where there are sheltered tables and grills.

8.1 The parking lot for the backcountry campsites on the right.

8.3 Reach the end of the loop and retrace your route on Dunes Drive.

9.7 Pavement begins...ahhhh!

14.3 Return to the visitor center at U.S. Highway 70.

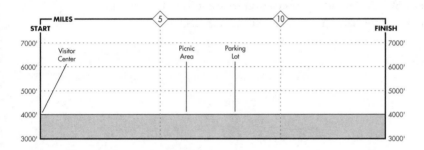

Highway 70 are occasionally closed for safety reasons during missile testing. Closures occur once or twice a week and usually last about an hour or two.)

LOCAL INFORMATION

♦ Alamogordo Chamber of Commerce (www.alamogordo.com), 1301 North White Sands Boulevard, Alamogordo, NM 88310; (800) 826–0294.

EVENTS/ATTRACTIONS

♦ White Sands National Monument (www.nps.gov/whsa), P.O. Box 1086, Holloman AFB, NM 88330; (505) 479–6124 (open year-round except Christmas; $3.00 per person).

RESTAURANTS

The gift shop at the visitor center sells sandwiches, sodas, and snacks.

ACCOMMODATIONS

There are no accommodations at the monument except the backcountry campsites. A good option is the state park south of Alamogordo.
♦ Oliver Lee Memorial State Park, 409 Dog Canyon, Alamogordo, NM 88310; (505) 437–8284 (has showers).

BIKE SHOPS

There are two bike shops in Alamogordo, about 15 miles away.

REST ROOMS

♦ Mile 0.0: Visitor center.
♦ Mile 6.1: Nature center (vault toilets).
♦ There are also vault toilets between miles 6.1 and 8.1 at the two picnic areas, the Alkali Flat Trail, and the backcountry camping trailhead.

MAPS

♦ USGS 7.5-minute quads Garton Lake and Heart of the Sands.
♦ Delorme *New Mexico Atlas & Gazetteer,* map 47.

Mesilla Valley Cruise

I *found this loop on the New Mexico Touring Society's Web site,*
and the Mesilla Valley sounded inviting. Once in Las Cruces, the
folks at Outdoor Adventures added some details and a few good options
for getting in and out of the city. For most of the 60 flat miles, you will
pedal through rural farmland irrigated by the Rio Grande. To the east,
the jagged Organ Mountains rise to 9,000 feet. Ride highlights include
a shaded tunnel of pecan trees, a historic plaza, ruins of a nineteenth-
century fort, and a state park along the Rio Grande.

The Mesilla Valley was inviting, indeed. The Rio Grande, which you will
cross four times, flows through the middle of the valley and is used for irrigation. Because of the river and good weather, this part of south-central New
Mexico has become a large agricultural center. Fertile farmland yields many
crops, including some of the state's famous green chiles. Throughout the ride,
you will be surrounded by agricultural land—cotton, onions, alfalfa. I also saw
watermelon and pumpkins. And then there are the pecans!

Las Cruces was originally called La Placitas de las Cruces, "the place of the
crosses." White crosses once marked the burial sites of travelers on El Camino
Real who were killed by Apaches in 1830. Three modern crosses are located at
Solano Drive and Main Street (near mile 56.3). Today, the population of Las
Cruces is 75,000-plus, making it the second-largest city in New Mexico. It is the
crossroads of several major highways, the commercial hub for the south-central part of the state, and home to New Mexico State University (Go Aggies!).

This cruise begins at the Pan Am Plaza, where you will find Milagro's Coffee
Y Espresso, a popular meeting spot for cyclists on weekend rides. There is also
a Dairy Queen and a Bennigans in the shopping center. New Mexico State

Checking out the pecan trees on the Mesilla Valley Cruise.

University's Pan Am Center is across the street—home to Aggies basketball, concerts, and other special events. Look to the east to see the hump of Tortugas (tortoise) Mountain, or "A" Mountain for the Aggies symbol on the hillside.

A section of this ride goes through a tunnel of pecan trees, which provides several miles of shade and is spectacular in the spring when the orchard is full of blossoms. As I stood between the manicured rows, I wondered about the pecan harvest ... do workers shake the trees and collect the nuts off the ground? Back home on the Internet, I found out that the shaking and collection is, of course, mechanical.

Stahmanns, one of the largest pecan growers in the world, planted their first trees here in 1932. Today the stats read "4,000 acres, 180,000 trees, and 8–10 million pounds of pecans per year." The country store along New Mexico Route 28 is worth a stop. The amazing variety of homemade pecan goodies include log rolls, pralines, brittle, popcorn, cakes, cookies, and pies.

You will pass through several small communities, the oldest of which is Dona Ana (1839). The loop doesn't go through La Mesilla, but

you can turn right at mile 22.1 to visit the shops, galleries, and restaurants on the narrow streets around this historic old plaza, once a stop for the Butterfield Stagecoach. The restaurant La Posta comes highly recommended, and San Albino Church, originally built in 1851and replaced in 1906, is one of the oldest missions in the valley.

Just off-route at the north end of the valley, you will find Fort Selden State Monument and Leasburg Dam State Park. The army post, built in April 1865 to protect settlers and travelers, is now a state monument and provides a look

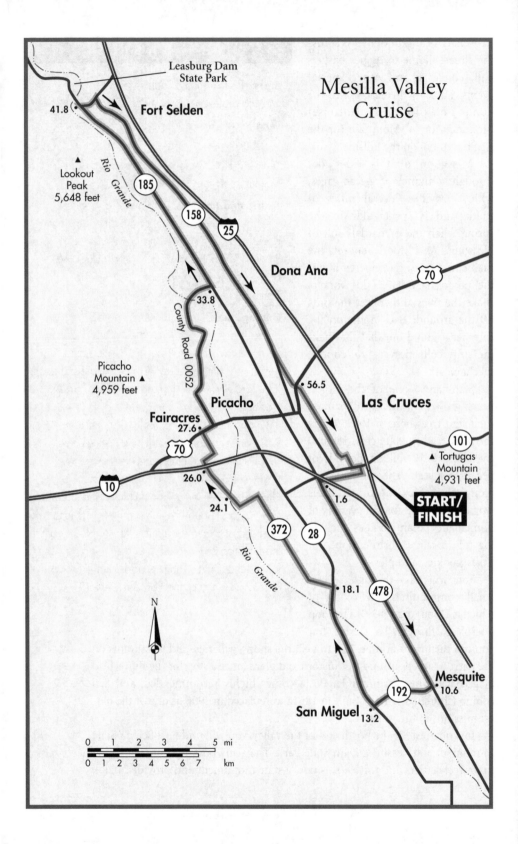

Mesilla Valley Cruise

Leasburg Dam State Park

Fort Selden

41.8

Rio Grande

Lookout Peak 5,648 feet

185

158

25

Dona Ana

70

33.8

County Road 0052

Picacho Mountain ▲ 4,959 feet

Picacho

56.5

Las Cruces

Fairacres
27.6

70

101

▲ Tortugas Mountain 4,931 feet

10

26.0

24.1

1.6

START/ FINISH

372

28

Rio Grande

18.1

478

N

192

Mesquite
10.6

San Miguel
13.2

0 1 2 3 4 5 mi

0 1 2 3 4 5 6 7 km

0.0 From the parking lot at the Pan Am Plaza, go straight through the light at Triviz Drive toward the front of the Pan Am Center. The road will curve to the left (east) and then immediately to the right (south) to circle around the side of the building. The dirt lot for stadium parking will be on your left. Note the round mountain to the east with the big "A" for Aggies.

0.4 At the southeast corner of the Pan Am Center, turn right on Stewart Street. You'll pass through several stop signs in the next mile as you cycle through part of the university.

1.6 Reach a traffic light at a T intersection and turn left on Union Avenue, then go under I–10.

2.0 Traffic light at Main Street (New Mexico Route 478); turn left and go straight through several more lights as you head south out of town. You will have a wide shoulder on this busy road all the way to Mesquite. There are several roadside stands selling chiles and pecans.

10.6 Reach the village of Mesquite. A community park on the left has picnic tables. Services include a mercantile and a bakery (also on the left).

10.8 Turn right on New Mexico Route 192, and cross over the railroad tracks.

12.0 Cross the Rio Grande for the first time.

13.2 At the T intersection, New Mexico Route 192 ends at the community of San Miguel. Turn right onto New Mexico Route 28 (no shoulder).

13.5 Pass the San Miguel Catholic Church on the left.

14.5 Gain a small shoulder as you ride through a huge pecan orchard. A shaded tunnel is created by the canopy closing in overhead.

16.5 Stahmanns Country Store on the left. The sign is inviting—PECANS, ICE CREAM, GIFTS.

17.3 Leave the pecan tunnel and cross the Rio Grande.

18.1 Turn left on Snow Road (New Mexico Route 372). There is no shoulder on this quiet road.

(continued)

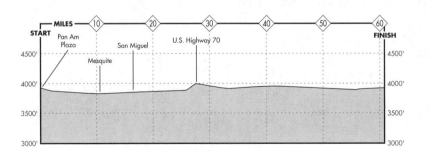

22.1 A sign indicates LA MESILLA, although the historic plaza is located a few blocks east.

23.1 At the stop sign and T intersection, turn left on Calle Del Norte. The old plaza is to the right.

24.1 Cross the Rio Grande.

26.0 Travel under I–10.

26.5 At the stop sign and T intersection, turn left (North Aries Drive).

27.6 Turn right at the T intersection at U.S. Highway 70 (Picacho Avenue). You'll have a shoulder on the short stretch of this busy road, and there are several convenience stores.

28.0 Just before the Fina convenience store, turn left on Shalem Colony Trail (no shoulder). (*Note:* To shorten the loop and head back to the university, continue straight on U.S. Highway 70.)

32.8 Cross the Rio Grande for the last time.

33.8 Reach New Mexico Route 185 at a T intersection and turn left. The large shoulder doesn't last long, but the new blacktop is very smooth.

41.8 Turn right on New Mexico Route 157 (Fort Selden Road) and turn right again immediately to follow the road south that parallels an irrigation ditch. (To reach Fort Selden and Leasburg Dam State Park, continue straight on New Mexico Route 157.)

50.9 Just before the historic marker about Dona Ana, turn left on New Mexico Route 320 (Thorpe Road).

51.6 A Citgo station on the left—the first of several convenience stores as you near town.

51.9 Turn right on El Camino Real.

52.5 Go straight through two stop signs to remain on El Camino Real.

55.9 A sign indicates the elevation at 3,900 feet.

56.3 At the stop sign, turn right on Spitz Street.

56.5 Cross Main Street and immediately turn right on Mesquite Street.

57.4 Cross Picacho Avenue; the shorter loop comes in here.

58.9 At the traffic light for Idaho Avenue, turn left and go through two traffic lights.

59.2 Turn right on Solano Drive.

59.6 Pass Solano Plaza on the left at Missouri Avenue; Papa Johns and Outdoor Adventures.

60.4 Reach University Avenue and turn left.

60.9 Traffic light at Triviz Drive; Pan Am Plaza on the left and Pan Am Center on the right.

Riding beside cotton fields in the Mesilla Valley.

at nineteenth-century frontier military life. Fort Selden includes a museum, self-guided trail, and well-preserved adobe ruins of the fort. Nearby Leasburg Dam State Park offers picnicking and camping (with showers) along the Rio Grande. The dam, one of the oldest diversion dams in the state, was constructed in 1908, and the system irrigates farmland in the Mesilla Valley.

You can shorten this loop by returning to town at mile 28 for a total of 35.5 miles. Instead of turning left onto Shalem Colony Trail, continue straight on U.S. Highway 70, where you'll have a good shoulder for several miles. You will pass a park along the Rio Grande with rest rooms and picnic tables; and after 1.5 miles, you will reach the intersection with New Mexico Route 292, the beginning of a series of traffic lights and a strip with motels and restaurants. At mile 3.7, cross Main Street; and at mile 4.0, reach the intersection with Mesquite Street (mile 57.4 on the longer loop). Turn right and follow the remaining directions to return to the Pan Am Plaza.

Note: The Mesilla Valley Bicycle Coalition is the cycling advocacy group for southern New Mexico, and members include university students and faculty, retirees, folks from local bike clubs, commuters, and racers. The mission of the organization is to make the area "an ideal place for bicycling." Bravo! Check out their Web site at www.hipnt.com/mvbc.

LOCAL INFORMATION

♦ Greater Las Cruces Chamber of Commerce (www.lascruces.org), P.O. Drawer 519, Las Cruces, NM 88004; (505) 524–1968.

EVENTS/ATTRACTIONS

♦ Stahmanns Country Store, P.O. Box 130, San Miguel, NM 88058-0130; (505) 526–8974.
♦ Fort Selden State Monument, 1280 Fort Selden Road, Radium Springs, NM 88054; (505) 526–8911 (8:30 A.M. to 5:00 P.M. daily; cost $2.00).

RESTAURANTS

♦ Milagro's Coffee Y Espresso, 1733 East University, Las Cruces, NM 88001; (505) 532–1042.

ACCOMMODATIONS

♦ Leasburg Dam State Park, P.O. Box 6, Radium Springs, NM 88054; (505) 524–4068.

BIKE SHOPS

♦ Outdoor Adventures, 1424 Missouri Avenue, Las Cruces, NM 88001; (505) 521–1922.
♦ Ride On Sports, 525 Telshor Boulevard, Las Cruces, NM 88011; (505) 521–1686.

REST ROOMS

♦ Mile 0.0: Milagro's Coffee Y Espresso.
♦ Mile 10.6: Mesquite Mercantile.
♦ Mile 16.3: Stahmanns Country Store.
♦ Mile 27.6: Several convenience stores on U.S. Highway 70.
♦ Mile 41.8: Fort Selden State Monument and Leasburg Dam State Park (off-route).
♦ Mile 51.6: Citgo station—first of several convenience stores as you come back into town.

MAPS

♦ USGS 7.5-minute quads Las Cruces, San Miguel, Black Mesa, Leasburg, and Dona Ana.
♦ Delorme *New Mexico Atlas & Gazetteer,* maps 46, 47, 54, and 55.

About the Author

Nicole Blouin, a transplant from the Southeast, is back in sunny New Mexico after trying to live several other places. She is an avid cyclist, as well as a freelance writer and editor. This is her fifth guidebook. Her articles have also appeared in local newspapers and publications such as *Wildside Magazine*. She lives in Santa Fe where she keeps up an active schedule of road biking.